# Higher Education Research and Science Studies

**Series Editor**

Deutsches Zentrum für Hochschul- und Wissenschaftsforschung GmbH,
Hannover, Niedersachsen, Germany

In der Reihe „Higher Education Research and Science Studies" (HERSS) werden Monografien und referierte Sammelbände in deutscher oder englischer Sprache im Themenspektrum der Hochschul- und Wissenschaftsforschung veröffentlicht. Sie trägt mit der Fokussierung auf interdisziplinäre und international anschlussfähige Forschung insbesondere zur innovativen Entwicklung dieses Forschungsfeldes in der Schnittmenge von Hochschul- und Wissenschaftsforschung bei. Herausgegeben wird die Reihe HERSS vom Deutschen Zentrum für Hochschul- und Wissenschaftsforschung (DZHW), einem nationalen und internationalen Kompetenzzentrum für die Hochschul- und Wissenschaftsforschung. Das DZHW betreibt erkenntnis- und problemorientierte Forschung zu aktuellen und langfristigen Entwicklungen auf allen Ebenen des Hochschul- und Wissenschaftssystems.

More information about this series at http://www.springer.com/gp/series/16454

Jana Berg · Michael Grüttner ·
Bernhard Streitwieser
Editors

# Refugees in Higher Education

Questioning the Notion of Integration

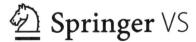

*Editors*
Jana Berg
DZHW, Hannover, Germany

Michael Grüttner
DZHW, Hannover, Germany

Bernhard Streitwieser
Department of Educational Leadership
George Washington University
Washington, DC, WA, USA

ISSN 2662-5709　　　　　　　ISSN 2662-5717　(electronic)
Higher Education Research and Science Studies
ISBN 978-3-658-33337-9　　　ISBN 978-3-658-33338-6　(eBook)
https://doi.org/10.1007/978-3-658-33338-6

© The Editor(s) (if applicable) and The Author(s), under exclusive license to Springer Fachmedien Wiesbaden GmbH, part of Springer Nature 2021
This work is subject to copyright. All rights are solely and exclusively licensed by the Publisher, whether the whole or part of the material is concerned, specifically the rights of translation, reprinting, reuse of illustrations, recitation, broadcasting, reproduction on microfilms or in any other physical way, and transmission or information storage and retrieval, electronic adaptation, computer software, or by similar or dissimilar methodology now known or hereafter developed.
The use of general descriptive names, registered names, trademarks, service marks, etc. in this publication does not imply, even in the absence of a specific statement, that such names are exempt from the relevant protective laws and regulations and therefore free for general use.
The publisher, the authors and the editors are safe to assume that the advice and information in this book are believed to be true and accurate at the date of publication. Neither the publisher nor the authors or the editors give a warranty, expressed or implied, with respect to the material contained herein or for any errors or omissions that may have been made. The publisher remains neutral with regard to jurisdictional claims in published maps and institutional affiliations.

Responsible Editor: Stefanie Eggert
This Springer VS imprint is published by the registered company Springer Fachmedien Wiesbaden GmbH part of Springer Nature.
The registered company address is: Abraham-Lincoln-Str. 46, 65189 Wiesbaden, Germany

# Contents

**Editorial Section**

**Introduction: Refugees in Higher Education—Questioning the Notion of Integration** .......................................... 3
Jana Berg, Michael Grüttner, and Bernhard Streitwieser

**Higher Education and Study Preparation from the Perspective of Refugee Students in Germany** .................................... 19
Nail Kara, Abedallah Abuhawa, and Pizzo

**Empirical Research**

**Online Education, Offline Integration? Supporting Refugees' Social Integration by Online Education** ............................ 29
Belma Halkic and Patricia Arnold

**Refugee Students in German Higher Education: How Perceptions of *Time* and *Language* Impact on Academic Experiences** ............. 55
Anika Müller-Karabil and Claudia Harsch

**From Refugee Programmes to a Benefit for All: The Extension of University Study Preparation Programmes to Other Target Groups in Germany** .............................................. 77
Steffen Beigang

**Refugee and Third-Generation Migrant Students in Comparison: Class Position and Integration Discourse** .......................... 99
Emre Arslan

"But I Am (not) from…": A Qualitative Analysis of Intragroup
Self-Differentiation Processes Among International Degree
Seeking Students in Germany .................................... 127
Jesús Pineda

Facilitating Access of Syrian Refugees to Higher Education
in Turkey as an Instrument for Integration ........................ 147
Armağan Erdoğan and M. Murat Erdoğan

**Desk Research**

Admissions Policy and Practice Regarding Refugee Students
in U.S. Higher Education: What is Known? ........................ 173
Bryce Loo

The Politics of Restricted Meritocracy: Refugees in Higher
Education in Germany ............................................ 193
Christin Younso and Hannes Schammann

Beyond "Integration"—Why There is More at Stake ................. 205
Katrin Sontag

# Editorial Section

# Introduction: Refugees in Higher Education—Questioning the Notion of Integration

Jana Berg, Michael Grüttner, and Bernhard Streitwieser

## 1 Dynamics Of Integration—Introducing the Symposium

After 2015, when many qualified people from Syria and other crises regions migrated to Germany, higher education institutions (HEIs) expanded their capacities for study preparation of refugees, language and subject related pre-study courses, mentoring or tandem programs among others. The German federal Government as well as the German Länder began programs to fund these activities. One of these programs, and certainly the largest of them, is the Integra program, which was funded by over €100 million by the Federal Ministry of Education and Research and carried out by the German Academic Exchange Service (DAAD) (Fourier et al. 2020).

As higher education for refugees has been marginalized in educational research for a long time (Dryden-Peterson 2012), there has been a dearth of empirical studies and the development of theoretical knowledge to meaningfully drive these support programs. Only in very recent years, accompanied by public interest, has

---

J. Berg (✉) · M. Grüttner
Deutsches Zentrum für Hochschul-und Wissenschaftsforschung (DZHW), Bildungsverläufe und Beschäftigung, Hannover, Germany
E-Mail: berg@dzhw.eu

M. Grüttner
E-Mail: gruettner@dzhw.eu

B. Streitwieser
George Washington University, Graduate School of Education and Human Development, Washington D.C., USA
E-Mail: streitwieser@gwu.edu

© The Author(s), under exclusive license to Springer Fachmedien Wiesbaden GmbH, part of Springer Nature 2021
J. Berg et al. (eds.), *Refugees in Higher Education*, Higher Education Research and Science Studies, https://doi.org/10.1007/978-3-658-33338-6_1

the topic developed into a dynamic research field. Yet international scholarship has more often dealt with the national contexts of the United Kingdom, Australia and the United States of America, rather than the German higher education sector. Therefore, researchers from the German Centre for Higher Education Research and Science Studies (DZHW) and the Berlin Refugee Research Group organized the symposium, *"Higher Education equals Integration? Integration dynamics and competencies in the German university landscape using the example of refugees,"* which was funded by the Volkswagen Foundation and brought together researchers from different disciplinary fields to discuss the current state of research on refugee students and possible future directions. The general focus of the meeting was on developing a common understanding of pathways into universities, integration processes at universities, and associated competencies.

This symposium provided an opportunity for a lively exchange and discussion among scientists on the goals and means of integration within higher education from different disciplinary, methodological and theoretical perspectives. Beyond that, while integration is still too often understood in an imbalanced and narrow way, we aimed to collaboratively question the notion of integration. As Kogan and Kalter (2020) recently argued, "a comprehensive understanding of integration requires conceptualizing it as a dynamic feedback process of interactions," that involves the interplay of opportunity structures of host societies as well as of individual resources and preferences. Therefore, we discussed integration and competencies as two-sided, co-constructed phenomena that involve both refugee students and higher education institutions.

The following research questions characterised the outline of the symposium: What do the individual integration pathways of refugee students look like? What practices do they adopt and what competencies do they develop to help them succeed in their studies? Do higher education institutions have the organisational competencies to shape refugee students' educational pathways properly and to support their educational success? What has been learned so far by studying support programs for refugees at universities and preparatory colleges that may also help other student groups such as international students or first-generation students?

During the three-day meeting, researchers from higher education, international education, migration and refugee studies, practitioners and refugee students engaged in a robust exchange of ideas around access to higher education, possibilities for successful integration, and the role played by organizational and institutional contexts. While the general focus of the meeting was on Germany, international comparisons were also included. To reflect the different perspectives that were represented at the symposium, the editorial section of this edited volume also includes the contributions of three refugee students. These students, in tandem with three other students of refugee background, organised a panel to discuss their experience of access and integration in higher education. We would like to thank all of our participants and in particular our keynote speakers, Sue Webb (Monash University) and Annette Korntheuer (Katholische Universität Eichstätt-Ingolstadt). We are grateful to have had the opportunity to organise this symposium with Maria Anne Schmidt (HTW Berlin), Lukas Brück (Bosch Foundation), Susanne Ress (University of Bamberg), Stefanie Schröder, Daniel Matthes, Petra Noelle and Monika Jungbauer-Gans (all DZHW), and with the support of the Volkswagen Foundation. Last but not least, we would like to thank the six refugee students that shared their experiences in their own panel.

Admittedly, despite our best efforts, our modest time together did not allow us to fully address all of the questions noted above. Nevertheless, some points were further developed. The symposium laid the foundation for further cooperation along these lines and gave rise to new impulses that will accelerate a quickly growing, dynamic, and socially relevant field of research. The result of these efforts is the present volume, which gathers contributions from participants of the symposium that focus on both sides, the individuals and the institutions, to further shape our understanding of integration into higher education in a broad and multifaceted manner that comprises access, participation and belonging.

Below we describe the current state-of-research on refugee student integration into higher education, and then conclude with brief summaries of each chapter and final remarks.

## 2  State of Research

Repeatedly, researchers have emphasized the various benefits that higher education holds for refugee students (Saiti and Chletsos 2020). They include obtaining locally recognized cultural capital, better access to the labour market and better job-positions in the receiving country (Lenette 2016; Marcu 2018; Grüttner et al. 2018; Streitwieser and Brück 2018). Higher education fosters agency and thus the ability to participate in the host society (Grüttner et al. 2018). Further, studying can allow refugee students to build or increase their social network and is a factor in increasing their psychological health and wellbeing (Lenette et al. 2019; Grüttner 2019). Thus, higher education can be seen as a motor of social integration (Ager and Strang 2008). At the same time, a number of benefits from providing refugees with higher education opportunities have been identified on the social and institutional level. One of them is the chance to recruit motivated students with high academic aspirations (Brücker et al. 2016; Stevenson and Willott 2007). Additionally, refugees can help to pluralise the student body, creating an environment that allows more intercultural and diverse experiences at home campuses (Abamosa et al. 2019; Unger-Ullmann 2017). The experiences with a new target group have been described as a chance to re-evaluate structures and communication-strategies to engage with students (Streitwieser et al. 2018a; Sontag 2018). Finally, some authors note that higher education can provide refugees' with the opportunity to support their families in their home country (Harris and Marlowe 2011) and further on the training to rebuild their countries of origin (Karipek 2017; Unangst 2019; Avery and Said 2017) and build opportunities for future diplomatic relations (Ergin et al. 2019).

A variety of studies have looked into the various challenges preventing or obstructing refugees' access to and success in higher education. Some of those challenges seem to occur throughout different national and institutional contexts. International studies have repeatedly pointed out the importance of language proficiency (Park 2019; Shakya et al. 2010), the recognition of credentials (Morrice 2013; Schammann and Younso 2016; Loo 2016) and previously obtained competences (Morrice 2013; Kanno and Varghese 2010) and access to comprehensive and comprehensible information about higher education and higher education institutions as well as approachable and well-suited support and counselling (Earnest et al. 2010; Morrice 2013; Shakya et al. 2010; Baker et al. 2017; Molla 2019; Cin and Doğan 2020). Lambrechts (2020) focuses on the intersections between these different types of barriers developing a concept of "super-disadvantaged". While some of the challenges for refugee students are similar to those that are usually faced by international students (Morris-Lange 2017; Berg et al. 2018b), others result from the circumstances of forced migration. Among them are potentially lacking documents and psychological distress (Berg 2018a; Erdoğan and Erdoğan 2018). Berg (2020) has reconstructed how German HEI-members and refugee students refer to implicit ideal higher education transition and study situations and further how the situation of refugee students differs from those ideals, finding that institutional norms are built around certain expectations and ideals. Desciptions of the diversion from those ideals reflect Baker und Irwins' (2019) findings that institutional norms can themselves become an obstruction for refugee students. Among the numerous challenges for refugee students, Baker et al. (2019) describe a potential demoralisation based on the feeling of wasted time during lengthy processes of recognition and social as well as academic inclusion. In other words, taking the necessary steps and overcoming boundaries in order to participate in higher education can take so long that the feeling of lost times becomes a challenge in itself.

Some academic papers have discussed refugee students in the context of the internationalisation of higher education. The work in this area has partly been conceptual, such as Streitwieser's differentiation of international student mobility that is either based on migration "for Enlightenment, for Opportunity and for Survival" (Streitwieser 2019) or Ergin et al.s' (2019) approach to frame engagement with refugee students in higher education as "forced internationalization driven by a humanitarian rationale" (2019, p. 10; Streitwieser et al. 2019). Empirical studies have looked into Canadian media discourses on international and refugee students, finding that refugee students are often mentioned in the context of need and support (Anderson 2019), and organisational discourses on refugee students in Germany, finding that support for refugee students is framed as diversity management, internationalisation and HEI's social responsibility (Berg in print a).

Along with the public and academic interest, support for refugee students increased in recent years. One focus of research on higher education for refugees has been to investigate the numerous measures taken to support the academic and social integration of refugee students. A growing number of studies has introduced and evaluated the development of support programmes for refugee students either at individual institutions (Bacher et al. 2019; Bajwa et al. 2017, 2018, 2019; Park 2019; Streitwieser et al. 2018a), in refugee camps (Brown et al. 2017; Dahya and Dryden-Peterson 2017; Bellino and Hure 2018; Yesufu and Alajlani 2019) or on a national level (Marcu 2018; Abamosa et al. 2019; Tzoraki 2019; Streitwieser et al. 2020).

In Germany, support services for refugee students were broadly introduced after the refugee influx in 2015 and 2016 (Unangst and Streitwieser 2018; Schröder et al. 2019; Grüttner et al. 2018; Streitwieser et al. 2018b; Berg 2018a; Beigang et al. 2018; Beigang and Blumenthal 2016). At first, those measures mostly focussed on study preparation and were usually specifically targeted at refugee students. Among the typical developments of support structures has been to open refugee-specific offers for all international students and to add support for enrolled students as well as services to help refugees in entering the German labour market (Berg in print b).

Among the measures to provide higher education opportunities for refugee students is the extension of online-learning-programmes, providing a decentral opportunity for flexible learners to obtain knowledge and prepare for education programmes (Crea and Sparnon 2017; Muñoz et al. 2018; Brunton et al. 2017). However, many of the previously established challenges for refugees in obtaining higher education also apply to online education. To give some examples, online learners need certain time-management-skills, to speak the language and to have quiet learning spaces and stable internet connections available. In combination with difficulties in addressing the very diverse target group of online education, those challenges were reflected in low completion rates (Brunton et al. 2017; Halkic and Arnold 2019; Reinhardt et al. 2018; Zlatkin-Troitschanskaia et al. 2018). One challenge for such programs is ensuring the social integration of participants (Farrell et al. 2020).

To conclude, higher education for refugees has emerged into a growing and dynamic research field during recent years (Ramsay and Baker 2019; Unangst and Crea 2020). This edited volume aims to shed light on a number of various aspects of this broader field and extend our current conceptual and empirical knowledge.

## 3 Introducing the Research Papers

This book is divided into two sections. Section I is built around six empirical research studies that investigated a range of factors related to the higher education aspirations of students of refugee background, while Section II details three robust desk research studies that focused on broader societal questions around policy, programming, meritocracy and current paradigms driving societal perceptions of migration, refugees, and the role of higher education.

In the first article in section I, Belma Halkic and Patricia Arnold discuss the impact of online education support measures as a vehicle for social integration in Germany, by providing an analysis of curricula by the Berlin-based startup, Kiron Open Higher Education. Kiron has been offering online education to refugee and migrant populations since 2015. Halkic and Arnold's survey of 203 participants and a small selection of qualitative interviews suggests that students prefer in-person, one-on-one offline social interaction and picking and choosing what best suits their needs, rather than following a prescribed online curriculum. While students of refugee background value how Kiron's platform helps them to establish contacts with other newcomers in the host setting, those contacts remain confined primarily to the Kiron community and do not stand the test of time. Making friends with locals remains elusive due to persistent linguistic and cultural barriers.

The second article, by Anika Müller-Karabil and Claudia Harsch, investigates how new refugee student studying for the first time at German universities experience its academic culture and language. They focus particularly on the notion of time as a construct for understanding integration, and the impact of language proficiency on students' perceptions of academic pressure and its relation to completion of or attrition from their intended studies. Müller-Karabil and Harsch's findings indicate that the language barrier is the single most important challenge facing students of refugee background who are new to the rigors of studying at a German university. This pressure exerts itself in myriad ways, from the additional time they need to learn, to engaging in socialization, to participating in leisure activities that are critical for their well-being. To their credit, these difficulties turn out to be relatively short lived and within three semesters many have already managed to find balance in their workload and social life such as to be able to adequately cope with the demands of their new learning environment.

In the third article, Stefen Beigang analyzes the transferability of educational support programs for refugees at German higher education institutions to broader segments of the student population. Using the framework of utilitarian, functional, legitimation- and power-based mechanisms that enable or hinder institutional change, Beigang's interview-based study with administrators at three selected universities sheds light on the notion of transfer, which is also a robust area of research within Comparative Education scholarship. Although he does not find the experience of programming for refugee student to be directly transferable to programming for international students per se, he uncovers instructive and valuable lessons. Beigang urges higher education institutions and DAAD support mechanisms to more proactively enact additional, fundamental reforms that are needed to support the currently existing slate of higher educational institutional programming.

The fourth article, by Emre Arslan, utilizes in-depth autobiographic narrative interviews with students at two German universities to comparatively explore the experiences of newly arrived refugee students with those of third-generation migrant students. Taking a social equality perspective that is based on relational class position analysis, Arslan finds through fascinating biographical and experiential testimonials that children of migrant families perceive considerably more intransigent socially embedded obstacles to social advancement and university study than do newly arrived refugees from educational backgrounds unencumbered by these homegrown impediments. Contrary to previous research on educational integration, Arslan's investigation reveals that newly arrived refugee students are thereby more comfortable adjusting to and progressing within the German university system than are migrant students who were born in Germany and educated within its very school system.

The fifth article, by Jesús Pineda, addresses intragroup self-differentiation among international students with a qualitative content analysis of testimonials from a larger longitudinal mixed-methods study he has been conducting. Pineda's article is especially helpful to differentiate the varied discourses around guest workers, highly skilled migrants, international students, and refugees within German society and how these labels impact their identities and experiences. Pineda's initial analysis of a selection of 2423 comments from larger study investigating sociological and psychological determinants of academic success or drop-out of international students in Germany, illustrates ways that international students negotiate between statistical, legal categorizations on the one hand and their own complex biographical trajectories and motivations on the other. His analysis of intragroup tensions, ambivalence, and diversity among international students in Germany makes evident the need for institutions to promote integration as a way to develop a more sensitized, shared understanding of the perceptions of both international students and their domestic counterparts. In this way, Pineda argues, institutions will avoid reproducing stigmatizing labels and exacerbate existing intergroup conflict. The preliminary results of this broader research also suggest that perceived distinctions between groups may not in fact accurately reflect the real diversity evident in some of Germany's higher education institutions today.

The final article in Section I, by Armağan Erdoğan and M. Murat Erdoğan, addresses perhaps the most visible refugee catastrophe of the past decade: the plight of the Syrian diaspora. With an analysis of Turkey's role since 2014 as host to the largest concentration of refugees in the world and data from their funded "Elite Dialogue" study, Erdogan and Erdogan discuss the profiles, needs, and expectations of Syrian students attempting to adapt to Turkish universities and society. Their analysis of 747 student surveys (75% male, 40% in STEM fields) found that while Turkey can be commended for providing significant opportunities for integration, a long list of challenges remains to be addressed. A more comprehensive integration strategy must be developed, along with more inclusive and transparent communication to facilitate integration between refugees and Turkish citizens. The authors posit that while Syrian refugees are likely to remain in Turkey with civil war in Syria seeing no end, it can only be through greater support for language training, mentoring, financial and employment assistance, and gender balance that integration in Turkish society will succeed. To facilitate success, they argue, Syrian students in Turkey must accept their role as an educated elite among their displaced counterparts and serve as mediators to bridge their community with Turkish society at large.

In Section II of the book, which profiles three desk study research projects, the first article by Bryce Loo focuses on the United States. Loo's contribution provides a broad ranging conceptual analysis of U.S. policy toward refugees, the complex bureaucratic web they must navigate to securing eventual citizenship, and recent efforts by the tertiary sector to facilitate access. Loo's analysis focuses specifically on two systemic and seemingly intransigent barriers: academic qualifications for admission and financing. He argues that these and other less visible barriers will require extensive work by both students and policy makers in the years ahead if educational integration is to succeed. Loo concludes his analysis by offering a list of suggested incentives for U.S. higher education to change course and directly address these barriers. Confirming previous research, he advocates that inclusion of refugees in society must not merely provide refugees with access but also the empowerment so crucial to success.

The second article in the section, by Christin Younso and Hannes Schammann, addresses numerous crucial barriers that were initially identified in their 2016 study, *Studium nach der Flucht*, and continue to confound refugee students seeking access into higher education. Their updated analysis is based on new desk research and participant observations conducted over the past three years that show how meritocratic and restrictive logics converge in higher education and refugee politics. They argue that the complex interplay of asylum and higher education laws continue to pose challenges that further reinforce a politics of restricted meritocratic opportunities for refugee students. Higher education institutions continue to place the burden on students to master daunting legal and other challenges that prevent them from completing their academic studies, while failing to develop innovative mechanisms that can address the increasingly diverse student population. Younso and Schammann conclude by suggesting that higher education institutions that established programming to foster refugee student social inclusion and cohesion must embrace this spirit more energetically as a guiding moral principle.

The final article in the book is by Katrin Sonntag, who provides an appropriate conclusion to this volume addressing students of refugee background and their higher education aspirations by bringing us back to the core challenge we face: understanding and unpacking the critical notion of integration which lies at the heart of the Germany's heightened migration experience since 2015–2016. Sonntag argues that while the notion of integration remains a vexingly fuzzy and controversial concept, the academy must not lose sight of its focus on broader structural issues that will need to be addressed, including access, cost, and internationalization. She points out how current framings of integration remain problematic and narrowly focused on who should integrate, while considerations of the broader benefits of diversity and the unique contribution brought by newcomers are not being sufficiently accounted for. Sontag advocates that going forward scholars will need to engage in a more thorough analysis of education systems and the organizations within them and rethink issues related to access, economization, internationality, organizational learning, and diversity. Most forcefully, she urges universities to exhibit greater flexibly in a world impacted by globalization and to seize the opportunity to rethink that paradigms that have so far determined the perceptions of migration, refugees, and the capability of higher education to move us beyond methodological nationalism, Western-centrism, and classism.

## 4 Some Implications for Further Research and Development

The contributions of this volume clearly show that a more pronounced attention to studies comparing refugees and asylum seekers to other categories of migrants with regard to their chances for access, successful participation and belonging in higher education would be a fruitful direction for further research. Doing so can bring the differences as well as the overlaps between groups of migrants to the fore and strengthen our understanding of the significant diversity we find in the higher education sector.

Some of the studies presented here have adopted established theoretical concepts within their respective disciplines and show how studies of refugees and higher education can benefit from these approaches. This strategy prevents refugee research from developing its concepts completely detached from established approaches of integration and migration studies and social sciences as a whole.

By looking at the enabling behaviour and the capacities and motivations for organisational change of higher education institutions, this volume reveals a perspective on further possible developments within the German higher education sector. Integration processes are embedded in institutional contexts and both individual biographies and higher education institutions are intertwined with one another as well as with an assemblage of various national institutional frameworks. These frameworks have to fit together if higher education for refugees is to develop its full potential for integration.

## References

Abamosa, J. Y., Hilt, L. T., & Westrheim, K. (2019). Social inclusion of refugees into higher education in Norway: A critical analysis of Norwegian higher education and integration policies. *Policy Futures in Education 7*(186), 147821031987832. doi: https://doi.org/10.1177/1478210319878327.

Ager, A., & Strang, A. (2008). Understanding Integration. A Conceptual Framework. *Journal of Refugee Studies, 21(2)*, 166–191.

Anderson, T. (2019). News Media Representations of International and Refugee Postsecondary Students. *The Journal of Higher Education 45*(4), 1–26. doi: https://doi.org/10.1080/00221546.2019.1587977.

Avery, H. & Said, S. (2017). Higher Education For Refugees: The Case Of Syria. *Policy & Practice: A Developmental Education Review* (24), 104–125.

Bacher, J., Fiorioli, E., Moosbrugger, R., Nnebedum, C., Prandner, D., & Shovakar, N. (2019). Integration of refugees at universities: Austria's more initiative. *Higher Education 41*(6), 379. doi: https://doi.org/10.1007/s10734-019-00449-6.

Bajwa, J., Abai, M., Couto, S., Kidd, S., Dibavar, A., & McKenzie, K. (2019). Psychological capital and life satisfaction of refugees in Canada: Evidence from a community-based educational support program. *Journal of community psychology 47*(3), 504–516. doi: https://doi.org/10.1002/jcop.22134.

Bajwa, J. K., Abai, M., Kidd, S., Couto, S., Akbari-Dibavar, A., & McKenzie, K. (2018). Examining the Intersection of Race, Gender, Class, and Age on Post-Secondary Education and Career Trajectories of Refugees. *Refuge 34*(2), 113–123.

Bajwa, J. K., Couto, S., Kidd, S., Markoulakis, R., Abai, M., & McKenzie, K. (2017). Refugees, Higher Education, and Informational Barriers. *Refuge 33*(2), 56–65. doi: https://doi.org/10.7202/1043063ar.

Baker, S., Ramsay, G., Irwin, E., & Miles, L. (2017). 'Hot', 'Cold' and 'Warm' supports: Towards theorising where refugee students go for assistance at university. In: *Teaching in Higher Education 37*(1), 1–16. Retrieved from: https://doi.org/https://doi.org/10.1080/13562517.2017.1332028.

Baker, S., & Irwin, E. (2019). Disrupting the dominance of 'linear pathways': how institutional assumptions create 'stuck places' for refugee students' transitions into higher education. *Research Papers in Education 12*(1), 1–21. doi: https://doi.org/10.1080/02671522.2019.1633561.

Baker, S., Irwin, E., & Freeman, H. (2019). Wasted, manipulated and compressed time: adult refugee students' experiences of transitioning into Australian higher education. *Journal of Further and Higher Education 7*(1), 1–14. doi: https://doi.org/10.1080/0309877X.2019.1586849.

Beigang, S. & Blumenthal, J. v. (2016). Institutionelle Anpassungsfähigkeit von Hochschulen. Erste Ergebnisse einer Umfrage unter allen deutschen Hochschulen bezüglich der Integration von Geflüchteten in ein Studium. Berliner Institut für empirische Integrations- und Migrationsforschung. Berlin.

Beigang, S., Blumenthal, J. v., & Lambert, L. (2018). Studium für Geflüchtete. Aufgaben für Hochschulen und Politik. (eds.) v. bicc Bonn International Center for Conversion. Institut für Migrationsfroschung und Interkulturelle Studien (Policy Brief, 08b).

Bellino, M. J., & Hure, M. (2018). Pursuing Higher Education in Exile: A pilot partnership in Kakuma Refugee Camp. *Childhood Education 94*(5), 46–51. doi: https://doi.org/10.1080/00094056.2018.1516472.

Berg, J. (in print a). Expectations, experiences and anticipated outcomes of supporting refugee students in Germany. A systems theoretical analysis of organisational semantics. Accepted manuscript in print.

Berg, J. (in print b). Support for prospective refugee students in Germany: Quo vadis? Accepted manuscript in print.

Berg, J. (2018). A New Aspect of Internationalisation? Specific Challenges and Support Structures for Refugees on Their Way to German Higher Education. In A. Curaj, L. Deca & R. Pricopie (Ed.), European Higher Education Area: The Impact of Past and Future Policies, (pp. 219–235), Bd. 84., Cham: Springer International Publishing.

Berg, J. (2020). Which person is presumed to fit the institution? How refugee students' and practitioners' discursive representations of successful applicants and students highlight transition barriers to German higher education. In A. Curaj, L. Deca & R. Pricopie (Ed.), The Future of Higher Education - Bologna Process Researchers' Conference 2020 (online first). Heidelberg: Springer.

Berg, J.; Grüttner, M., Schröder, S., (2018). Zwischen Befähigung und Stigmatisierung? Die Situation von Geflüchteten beim Hochschulzugang und im Studium. Ein internationaler Forschungsüberblick. *Zeitschrift für Flüchtlingsforschung* 2(1), 57–90.

Brown, S., Saint, M., & Russel, C. (2017). Education in an extreme environment: A university in a refugee camp. In: Sunny Korea (Ed.), GHTC 2017, IEEE Global Humanitarian Technology Conference. DoubleTree by Hilton San Jose, California, USA, October 19–22, 2017 : 2017 conference proceedings. Piscataway, NJ: IEEE.

Brücker, H., Rother, N., & Schupp, J. (Ed.) (2016). IAB-BAMF-SOEP-Befragung von Geflüchteten. Überblick und erste Ergebnisse. Berlin: DIW Berlin Deutsches Institut für Wirtschaftsforschung (DIW Berlin, 116). Retrieved from: https://hdl.handle.net/10419/149124.

Brunton, J., Brown, M., Costello, E., Farrell, O., & Mahon, C. (2017). Giving Flexible Learners a Head Start on Higher Education: Designing and Implementing a Pre-induction Socialisation MOOC. In C. D. Kloos, P. Jermann, M. Pérez-Sanagustín, D. T. Seaton & S. White (Ed.), Digital Education: Out to the World and Back to the Campus, (pp. 10–19), Bd. 10254. Cham: Springer International Publishing (Lecture Notes in Computer Science)

Cin, F. M. & Doğan, N. (2020). Navigating university spaces as refugees: Syrian students' pathways of access to and through higher education in Turkey. *International Journal of Inclusive Education* 27(2), 1–15. doi: https://doi.org/10.1080/13603116.2019.1707309

Crea, T. M.; Sparnon, N. (2017). Democratizing education at the margins: faculty and practitioner perspectives on delivering online tertiary education for refugees. *Int J Educ Technol High Educ* 14(1), 3. doi: https://doi.org/10.1186/s41239-017-0081-y.

Dahya, N., & Dryden-Peterson, S. (2017). Tracing pathways to higher education for refugees: the role of virtual support networks and mobile phones for women in refugee camps. *Comparative Education* 53(2), 284–301. doi: https://doi.org/10.1080/03050068.2016.1259877.

Dryden-Peterson, S. (2012). The politics of higher education for refugees in a global movement for primary education. *Refuge: Canada's Journal on Refugees* 27(2): 10–18.

Earnest, J., Joyce, A., Mori, G. d., & Silvagni, G. (2010). Are Universities Responding to the Needs of Students from Refugee Backgrounds? *Australian Journal of Education* 54(2), 155–174. doi: https://doi.org/10.1177/000494411005400204.

Erdoğan, A., & Erdoğan, M. M. (2018). Access, Qualifications and Social Dimension of Syrian Refugee Students in Turkish Higher Education. In: Adrian Curaj, Ligia Deca und Remus Pricopie (Ed.): European Higher Education Area: The Impact of Past and Future Policies, (pp. 259–276), Bd. 12., Cham: Springer International Publishing.

Ergin, H., de Witt, H., & Leask, B. (2019). Forced Internationalisation of Higher Education: An Emerging Phenomenon. *IHE* (97), 7–9. doi: https://doi.org/10.6017/ihe.2019.97.10938.

Farrell, O., Brunton, J., Costello, E., Delaney, L., Brown, M., & Foley, C. (2020). 'This is two different worlds, you have the asylum world and you have the study world': an exploration of refugee participation in online Irish higher education. *Research in Learning Technology* 28. doi: https://doi.org/10.25304/rlt.v28.2368.

Fourier, K., Estevez Prado, P., & Grüttner, M. (2020). Integration von Flüchtlingen an deutschen Hochschulen - Erkenntnisse aus den Hochschulprogrammen für Flüchtlinge: Information 3. Einstieg ins Fachstudium und Studienbegleitung. Bonn: DAAD, Abgerufen am 15. Mai 2020 von https://www.daad.de/de/infos-services-fuer-hochschulen/expertise-zu-themen-laendern-regionen/fluechtlinge-an-hochschulen/downloads/

Grüttner, M. (2019). Belonging as a Resource of Resilience: Psychological Wellbeing of International and Refugee Students in Study Preparation at German Higher Education Institutions. In: *Student Success 10*(3). doi: https://doi.org/https://doi.org/10.5204/ssj.v10.i3.1275.

Grüttner, M., Schröder, S., Berg, J., & Otto, C. (2018). Refugees on Their Way to German Higher Education: A Capabilities and Engagements Perspective on Aspirations, Challenges and Support. *Global Education Review 5*(4),

Halkic, B., Arnold, P. (2019). Refugees and online education: student perspectives on need and support in the context of (online) higher education. *Learning, Media and Technology 44*(3), 1–20. doi: https://doi.org/10.1080/17439884.2019.1640739.

Harris, V., Marlowe, J. (2011). Hard yards and high hopes: The Educational challenges of African refugee University students in Australia. *International Journal of Teaching and Learning in Higher Education, 23 (2)*, 186–196.

Kanno, Y., & Varghese, M.M. (2010). Immigrant and Refugee ESL Students' Challenges to Accessing Four-Year College Education. *Journal of Language, Identity & Education, 9 (5)*, 310-328.

Karipek, Y. Z. (2017). Asylum-Seekers Experience and Acculturation: A Study of Syrian University Students in Turkey. *Turkish Journal of Middle Eastern Studies*, 105–133.

Kogan, I., & Kalter, F. (2020). An empirical-analytical approach to the study of recent refugee migrants in Germany. Soziale Welt 71(1-2), 3-23. doi https://doi.org/10.5771/0038-6073-2020-1-2-3.

Lambrechts, A. A. (2020). The super-disadvantaged in higher education: barriers to access for refugee background students in England. *Higher Education*. doi:https://doi.org/10.1007/s10734-020-00515-4

Lenette, C. (2016). University students from refugee backgrounds: why should we care? In: *Higher Education Research & Development 35*(6), 1–5. doi: https://doi.org/10.1080/07294360.2016.1190524.

Lenette, C., Baker, S., & Hirsch, A. (2019). Systemic Policy Barriers to Meaningful Participation of Students from Refugee and Asylum Seeking Backgrounds in Australian Higher Education. In J. L. McBrien (Ed.), Educational Policies and Practices of English-Speaking Refugee Resettlement Countries: Brill | Sense.

Loo, B. (2016). Recognizing Refugee Qualifications. Practical Tips for Credential Assessment. World Education Services. Retrieved February 09, 2018 from https://knowledge.wes.org/wes-research-report-recognizing-refugee-credentials.html

Marcu, S. (2018). Refugee Students in Spain: The Role of Universities as Sustainable Actors in Institutional Integration. *Sustainability 10*(6), 1–21. doi: https://doi.org/10.3390/su10062082.

Molla, T. (2019). Educational aspirations and experiences of refugee-background African youth in Australia: a case study. *International Journal of Inclusive Education 8*(3), 1–19. doi:https://doi.org/10.1080/13603116.2019.1588924.

Morrice, L. (2013). Refugees in higher education. Boundaries of belonging and recognition, stigma and exclusion. *International Journal of Lifelong Education 32*(5), 652–668. doi: https://doi.org/10.1080/02601370.2012.761288.

Morris-Lange, S. (2017). Allein durch den Hochschuldschungel. Hürden zum Studienerfolg für internationale Studierende und Studierende mit Migrationshintergrund. Studie des SVR-Forschungsbereichs 2017–2. (Hrsg.), Forschungsbereich beim Sachverständigenrat deutscher Stiftungen für Integration und Migration (SVR) GmbH, Sachverständigenrat deutscher Stiftungen für Integration und Migration. Berlin.

Muñoz, J. C., Colucci, E., & Smidt, H. (2018). Free digital learning for inclusion of migrants and refugees in europe: A qualitative analysis of three types of learning purposes. *International Review of Research in Open and Distance Learning 19(2)*, 1–21. doi: https://doi.org/10.19173/irrodl.v19i2.3382.

Park, E. S. (2019). Refugee-Background Students' Experience with College English Requirements: The Case of North Korean Students in South Korea. *Journal of Language, Identity & Education* 21, 1–14. doi: https://doi.org/10.1080/15348458.2019.1650278.

Ramsay, G., & Baker, S. (2019). Higher Education and Students from Refugee Backgrounds: A Meta-Scoping Study. *Refugee Survey Quarterly* 38 (1), 55–82. doi: https://doi.org/10.1093/rsq/hdy018.

Reinhardt, F., Zlatkin-Troitschanskaia, O., Deribo, T., Happ, R., & Nell-Müller, S. (2018). Integrating refugees into higher education – the impact of a new online education program for policies and practices. *Policy Reviews in Higher Education 2*(2), 198–226. doi: https://doi.org/10.1080/23322969.2018.1483738.

Saiti, A., & Chletsos, M. (2020). Opportunities and Barriers in Higher Education for Young Refugees in Greece. *Higher Education Policy 24*(2), 104–215. doi: https://doi.org/10.1057/s41307-020-00180-3.

Schammann, H., & Younso, C. (2016). Studium nach der Flucht? Angebote deutscher Hochschulen für Studieninteressierte mit Fluchterfahrung. Hildesheim, Hildesheim: Universitätsverlag Hildesheim.

Schröder, S., Grüttner, M., & Berg, J. (2019). Study Preparation for Refugees in German 'Studienkollegs'. Interpretative Patterns of Access, Life-wide (Language) Learning and Performance. *Widening Participation and Lifelong Learning 21*(2), 67–85.

Shakya, Y. B., Guruge, S., Hynie, M., Akbari, A., Malik, M., Htoo, S., Khogali, A., Mona, S. A., Murtaza, R., & Alley, S. (2012). Aspirations for Higher Education among Newcomer Refugee Youth in Toronto: Expectations, Challenges, and Strategies. *Refuge: Canada's Journal on Refugees 27*(2), 65–78. https://doi.org/https://doi.org/10.25071/1920-7336.34723

Sontag, K. (2018). Highly skilled asylum seekers: case studies of refugee students at a swiss university. *Migration Letters 15*(4), 533–544.

Stevenson, J. & Willott, J. (2007). The aspiration and access to higher education of teenage refugees in the UK. *Compare: A Journal of Comparative and International Education 37*(5), 671–687. doi: https://doi.org/10.1080/03057920701582624.

Streitwieser, B., Duffy Jaeger, K., Roche, J. (2020). Included yet Excluded: The Higher Education Paradox for Resettled Refugees in the USA. *Higher Education Policy 33*(2), 203–221. doi: https://doi.org/10.1057/s41307-020-00183-0

Streitwieser, B., Loo, B., Ohorodnik, M., & Jeong, J. (2019). Access for refugees into higher education: A review of interventions in North America and Europe. *Journal of Studies in International Education 23*(4), 473-496.

Streitwieser, B., Schmidt, A., Gläsener, K., Brück, L. (2018a). Not a Crisis But a Coping Challenge: How Berlin Universities Responded to the Refugee Influx. In K. Arar, K. Haj-Yehida, D. Ross & Y. Kondakci (Ed.), *Refugees and Global Challenges in Higher Education*. Frankfurt: Peter-Lang (Equity in Higher Education Theory, Policy, and Praxis).

Streitwieser, Bernhard (2019): International Education for Enlightenment, for Opportunity and for Survival: Where Students, Migrants and Refugees Diverge. *Journal of Comparative and Higher Education* (11), 3–8. doi: https://doi.org/10.6017/ihe.2019.97.10939.

Streitwieser, B., Brück, L. (2018. Competing Motivations in Germany's Higher Education Response to the "Refugee Crisis". *Refuge 34*(2), 38–51.

Streitwieser, B., Schmidt, M. A., Gläsener, K. M., & Brück, L. (2018b): Needs, Barriers, and Support Systems for Refugee Students in Germany. *Global Education Review 5*(4), 136–157.

Tzoraki, O. (2019). A Descriptive Study of the Schooling and Higher Education Reforms in Response to the Refugees' Influx into Greece. *Social Sciences 8*(3), S. 72. doi: https://doi.org/10.3390/socsci8030072.

Unangst, L., & Crea, T. M. (2020). Higher Education for Refugees: A Need for Intersectional Research. *Comparative Education Review 64*(2), 228-248, doi: https://doi.org/10.1086/708190

Unangst, L.; Streitwieser, B. (2018): Inclusive practices in response to the German refugee influx: support structures and rationales described by university administrators. In A. Curaj, L. Deca & R. Pricopie (Ed.), European Higher Education Area: The Impact of Past and Future Policies, ( pp. 287–300), Cham: Springer International Publishing.

Unangst, L. (2019). Refugees in the German higher education system: implications and recommendations for policy change. *Policy Reviews in Higher Education 3*(2), 144–166. doi: https://doi.org/10.1080/23322969.2019.1643254.

Unger-Ullmann, D. (2017): Sprachorientierte Maßnahmen für AsylwerberInnen im universitären Kontext. *Magazin Erwachsenenbildung.at 11*(31). Retrieved from https://www.pedocs.de/volltexte/2017/14623/pdf/Erwachsenenbildung_31_2017_Unger_Ullmann_Sprachorientierte_Massnahmen_fuer_AsyslbewerberInnen.pdf.

Yesufu, L., & Alajlani, S. (2019). Measuring Social Innovation for Education and Resource Development in Refugee Camps: A Conceptual Study. *International Journal of Higher Education 8*(4), 208-220. doi: https://doi.org/10.5430/ijhe.v8n4p208.

Zlatkin-Troitschanskaia, O., Happ, R., Nell-Müller, S., Deribo, T., Reinhardt, F., Toepper, M. (2018). Successful Integration of Refugee Students in Higher Education: Insights from Entry Diagnostics in an Online Study Program. *Global Education Review 5*(4), 158–181.

# Higher Education and Study Preparation from the Perspective of Refugee Students in Germany

## Nail Kara, Abedallah Abuhawa, and Pizzo

**Editorial note**
When we drafted the schedule for the symposium, the organising team shared the sentiment that refugee students should participate in shaping the academic discourse on refugee students. Thus, one of the symposium's panels was reserved for refugee students. All decisions on content and format of this panel were made by the students themselves. In preparation, a call for participation was send out followed by a preliminary meeting which was prepared and supported by Maria Anne Schmidt and Lukas Brück. This meeting was used by a group of refugee students from different cities to meet up and prepare their panel. The six panel-organisers presented their perspectives on and experiences with recognition processes, mobility and housing, integration projects, studying with children, study preparation courses and language requirements.

In this section, three of the panel-organisers and presenters give an overview of this panel. Their contributions have only been edited for clarity and are otherwise printed as they have been sent to us. First, Pizzo describes the preparations and topics that were presented at the symposium, and briefly refers to issues of housing and mobility. Then, N. Kara gives an insight to the difficulties for non-recognised refugees in obtaining higher education with a focus on language requirements. Finally, Abedallah Abuhawa talks about challenges for refugee students and the importance of participatory support projects.

---

N. Kara (✉) · A. Abuhawa · Pizzo
Hannover, Germany
E-Mail: berg@dzhw.eu

© The Author(s), under exclusive license to Springer Fachmedien Wiesbaden GmbH, part of Springer Nature 2021
J. Berg et al. (eds.), *Refugees in Higher Education*, Higher Education Research and Science Studies, https://doi.org/10.1007/978-3-658-33338-6_2

## 1 Pizzo: Vorbereitung für das Symposium

**Pizzo**

Am 23.06.2019 um 14.00 Uhr bis 17.00 Uhr in Berlin fand ein Vorbereitungstermin für das Symposium statt. Nach der Ankunft am Berliner Hauptbahnhof sind wir zusammen zur Hochschule für Technik und Wirtschaft (HTW) Berlin gefahren, und dort saßen wir in einem Raum, als erstes haben wir uns kennengelernt. Wir waren sechs Geflüchtete und zwei Veranstalter (Maria Anne Schmidt und Lukas Brueck).

Nach dem Kennenlernen sind wir ins Thema (Studium gleich Integration) eingestiegen und Maria Anne Schmidt hat uns gefragt was wir gerne beim Symposium sprechen wollen, wir haben dann einer nach dem anderen unsere Ideen vorgestellt. Als zweites haben wir das Panel organisiert, indem wir die Themen diskutiert haben und geeinigt was wir gerne sagen wollen und wer für was zuständig ist, dazu auch wie die Reihenfolge bei der Präsentation sein soll. Wir haben danach die Themen unter fünf Gruppen geteilt und zwar:

1. Anerkennung & Aufenthalt
2. Mobilität & Wohnung
3. Integrations-Projekte & Mit Kind Studieren
4. Vorbereitungsstudium
5. Sprache

Jeder von uns sechs hat ein Thema bekommen und sollte es präsentieren, die beiden Veranstalter haben uns bei dem Timing und Organisationsstruktur geholfen. So sah die Vorbereitung für das Symposium aus.

**Symposium**

Am 11.07.2019 um 9.30–11.00 Uhr in dem Schloss Herrenhausen Hannover hatten wir unser Panel am Symposium, und wir haben das Hauptthema (Studium = Integration?) ins Detail diskutiert.

Meine Präsentation befasste sich mit Wohnungssuche und Umzugsschwierigkeiten, diese sind unter der zweite Gruppe (2. Mobilität & Wohnung).

**Wohnungssuche**

Hier habe ich erläutert wie schwer es für die Geflüchteten ist, eine Wohnung zu finden, da sie Ausländer sind und einige Deutsche kein Vertrauen in sie haben. Das ist ein grosses Problem für Flüchtlinge, denn sie haben wenige Chancen eine Wohnung zu finden.

**Umzugsschwierigkeiten**
In diesem Teil habe ich klar erklärt wie das System für Ausländerbehörder kompliziert ist. Wenn ein Flüchtling keine Aufenthaltserlaubnis hat, ist es ihm aufgrund eines Studiumplatzes unmöglich, von einem Bundesland in einen anderen zu ziehen. Dies widerspricht dem Hauptthema (Studium = Integration?).

**Lösungsvorschlag für den ersten Punkt**
Es wäre schön wenn die Geflüchteten, die bereits am Studienkolleg oder Studiumvorbereitungsprogramme sind, wenn sie einen Zimmer im Wohngemeinschaft (WG) an der Universität bekommt oder wo anders.

**Lösungsvorschlag für den zweiten Punkt**
Es wäre hilfreich wenn die Geflüchteten, die einen Studiumplatz bekommen haben, dorthin ziehen könnten, wo sich dieser Studiumplatz befindet. Damit sie besser studieren und sich an der Universität integrieren können.

## 2  N. Kara

In the beginning of my words, I want to state that I will mainly be talking about the differences regarding the educational options when a person's application to asylum is rejected.

I want to talk specifically about the language and application to higher education which I have encountered myself due to the rejection decision.

First of all, learning the German language to get into an educational institution, to study Bachelor's or Master's in Germany is highly required. Without the satisfied German language skills, the options are very much limited. So, one should learn the language before applying to any universities. The acknowledged refugees on this matter are supported and handled by JobCenter. But the rejected ones get a different treatment. Unless the not acknowledged refugee is from one of the 5 unsafe countries (Eritrea, Iraq, Iran, Syria and Somalia), he or she may not attend the integration courses; this is the official response from BAMF. Although in some districts the situation is handled differently, namely in favor of the refugees, but it is only thanks to the good incentive from the respective social agents. And we already know they are very rare. If the "not acknowledged" refugee finds a job, works for enough time so that they can prove they no longer need the social aid from Sozialamt, only then they can apply to be transferred to another city other than stated on their "green Ausweiss". Consequently, the only thing they can do is to attend if there is ever a course held by some volunteers' initiatives. Then again due to the lack of quality and quantities, such courses are far from being a response to the need.

Let's say I learn the language despite these challenges, without neither a guidance nor moral or financial support from the officials, the problems don't end there. I (am) was actually just in that step where I (will) apply to a Hochschule for a new Bachelor's or Master's program. A recognized refugee has already many difficulties during the application process such as collection of the required documents, providing the non-digital original versions of the documents etc. The transfer process from a city to another due to the educational purposes itself is also not very easy to do. The not recognized refugee have even more difficulties because of the restrictions on their residence permit.

As it seems very clearly, the biggest difference between recognized and not recognized refugees is the restrictive factors on residence permit which makes it almost impossible to move. And what draws the line between two of them is the decision mechanism of BAMF. So, to better understand the educational matters of a refugee, BAMF effect should be considered seriously. As you may already know, according to ProAsyl's report,[1] almost a third of the rejection decisions of BAMF were then changed by the court in favor of the refugee side. This tells us the unfortunate fact that; a refugee may easily but falsely be deprived of rights and educational opportunities that could enable him/her to integrate to the society.

At the end of my words, I want to offer my contribution to the matter for the sake of finding a solution to this strong problem. In a lot of the cases, the attitude of the respective agents whether it be Foreigners Office or officials in Sozialamt or the social workers in Rathaus are the most decisive factors. Because by law, they are given the right to last say, in this case, whether the refugee can or cannot leave restricted area. This is the power given by the government. But these agents are unfortunately very shy to use this authority to decide in favor of refugees and they usually tend to not take any "risks" by allowing what may seem extraordinary. But they should know this right to take language courses and pursue further educational purposes are nothing extra but should only be considered the basic rights.

I spend almost 6 months in the camps, where no proper language courses are offered. During that time, my asylum application was rejected, and I had to deal with the appeal process. And then I was transferred to a small town and a social worker was assigned to take care of the usual procedures. I asked to visit a proper

---

[1] https://www.ecre.org/pro-asyl-makes-recommendations-for-improving-decision-making-and-asylum-procedures/

language course, but my request was rejected. So, if I were to simply take this "no" as an answer, I would have spent these 15 months (since I left the camps and assigned to a municipality) at the house, haven't make a progress and still be waiting for the court decision, which is yet to come and may not come in a year more (it has been 30 months and still no decision from the court has arrived). Because this is the only option the system leaves to you.

So I think a potential solution to the problem should include well-informed and encouraged social agents and officials who would not see providing the permissions needed for integration as "risks" and wouldn't opt to deny any relevant requests.

## 3  Abedallah Abuhawa

In der Studienorientierung und beim Studieneinstieg stehen Geflüchtete vor spezifischen Barrieren, die ihnen gegenüber anderen Studieninteressierten und Studierenden Wettbewerbsnachteile verschaffen und die es durch lebenswelt- und kompetenzorientierte Unterstützungsmaßnahmen auszugleichen gilt. Damit sie die Gesellschaft mitgestalten können, muss Raum für gesellschaftliche Teilhabe und Mitbestimmung geschaffen werden. Abedallah Abuhawa erläutert im folgenden Beitrag aus der Perspektive eines Studieneinsteigers und Teilnehmers des Vorbereitungsstudiums der Arbeitsstelle Migration an der HAW Hamburg, wie ein erfolgreicher Studieneinstieg und eine Integration in die Gesellschaft gelingen kann.

### 3.1  Erfolgreicher Studiensteig durch Studienvorbereitung

Bei Angeboten zur Vorbereitung von internationalen Studieninteressierten mit Fluchthintergrund auf ein Studium sollten Hochschulen den Fokus nicht allein auf sprachliche Unterstützungsmaßnahmen legen. Es macht einen riesigen Unterschied, in welcher Lebenssituation man sich befindet und deshalb benötigt diese Gruppe vielfältige Unterstützung und Begleitung, um ein Studium erfolgreich zu beginnen und abzuschließen. Geflüchtete Studieninteressierte und Studierende gehören zwar zur Gruppe der internationalen Studierenden, doch ihre Lebenswelt und die damit einhergehenden Einflussfaktoren auf das Studium unterscheiden sich grundlegend.

Geflüchtete sind aufgrund unterschiedlichster Herausforderungen in einer konstanten Drucksituation. Sie müssen sich nicht nur innerhalb kürzester Zeit das erforderliche Deutsch-C1-Sprachniveau erarbeiten und im Studium fortlaufend den sprachbedingten Wettbewerbsnachteil ausgleichen. Aufgrund der Flucht mussten sie ihren Wissenserwerb meist für längere Zeit unterbrechen und entsprechend kann auf benötigtes Fachwissen als Voraussetzung für ein erfolgreiches Studium oft nur lückenhaft zurückgegriffen werden, was zu Herausforderungen im Studienalltag führt. Die problembelastete Lebenssituation geflüchteter Studieninteressierter und Studierender ist geprägt durch Faktoren wie:

- den Asylstatus und die damit verknüpfte Frage einer Zukunftsperspektive in Deutschland,
- die eigene psychische Verfasstheit sowie die Ansprüche an das eigene Leistungsvermögen beim Quereinstieg in das fremde Bildungssystem,
- die häufig herausfordernde, individuell sehr unterschiedliche, familiäre Lebenssituation,
- das gefühlt meist nicht ausreichende soziale Netzwerk,
- die räumliche Segregation des Wohnortes durch die dezentrale Wohnlage oder
- der häufig fehlende Raum zum konzentrierten Arbeiten.

Die Hochschulen sollten diese Lebenssituation anerkennen und mit ihren Maßnahmen mehrdimensional ansetzen, um Studieninteressierte und Studierende mit Fluchthintergrund zu stärken und zu unterstützen. Maßgeblich geht es darum, ihnen Orientierung zu geben und sie dabei zu unterstützen, die eigenen Ziele zu klären und Schritt für Schritt zu verfolgen.

Es geht hier nicht nur um die Vermittlung von Fakten und Wissen, sondern darum, persönliche Wegbegleiter zu installieren, die diese besonderen Erschwernisse nachvollziehen und verstehen können, die Motivation und Kraft geben. Das hilft Studieninteressierten und Studierenden mit Fluchterfahrung, das eigene Selbstvertrauen wieder zu finden und den Mut zu haben, das eigene Leben nach der Flucht zu gestalten. Es ist schwierig, in einem neuen Land mit einem vollkommen anderen System anzukommen, eigene Ziele zu definieren und diese zu erreichen.

Für geflüchtete und auch andere internationale Studieninteressierte ist es oft nicht ausreichend, Beschreibungen verschiedener Studiengänge im Internet zu lesen und sich theoretisch zu informieren, weil sich die Bildungssysteme sehr unterscheiden. Um die Entscheidung für den richtigen Studiengang zu treffen, ist es hilfreich, das Studieren praktisch auszuprobieren.

Das Vorbereitungssemester für Geflüchtete „Kompetenz Kompakt" an der Hochschule für Angewandte Wissenschaften Hamburg bietet diese Möglichkeit in allen Bachelor-Studiengängen. Geflüchtete Studieninteressierte können dort reguläre Lehrveranstaltungen besuchen, Prüfungsleistungen erwerben, die nach erfolgreicher Bewerbung für den Regelstudienplatz anerkannt werden. Mit der steigenden Zahl geflüchteter Studieninteressierter sowie Studieneinsteigerinnen und -einsteiger hat die HAW Hamburg eine migrationsbedingte Hochschulentwicklung eingeleitet und ihre Immatrikulationsordnungsordnung im Mai 2017geändert, um dieses aus meiner Sicht vorbildliche Konzept des gestreckten Studieneinstiegs für geflüchtete Studierende zu ermöglichen.

Es ist wichtig, die Unterstützungsangebote für geflüchtete Studieninteressierte und Studierende immer von den Teilnehmenden aus zu denken. Ein Politiker hat mir einmal gesagt: „Es gibt genügend Unterstützungsangebote für geflüchteten Studieninteressierte und Studierende und das ist einheimischen Studierenden gegenüber unfair." Ich habe geantwortet: „Ja, es gibt viele Unterstützungsangebote, aber die Frage ist: Wie sind diese Angebote gestaltet? Es ist überhaupt nicht unfair. Geflüchtete haben auf dem Weg zum Studieneinstieg aufgrund ihrer Lebenslage einen Wettbewerbsnachteil im Vergleich zu anderen Studierenden, der durch diese Angebote ausgeglichen werden soll. Gleichbehandlung und Gerechtigkeit sind zwei unterschiedliche Dinge und in diesem Fall wäre Gleichbehandlung nach derzeitigem Standard für geflüchtete Studieninteressierte schlicht ungerecht, weil sie durch ihre besondere Lebenslage im deutschen Bildungssystem erhebliche Benachteiligungen erfahren."

Durch das Vorbereitungssemester konnte ich wieder an mich glauben. Vor meinem Studium gab es viele freundliche Menschen um mich herum, die mir geholfen haben, mich aber auch ständig an meinen Flüchtlingsstatus und die Schwierigkeiten erinnerten. Dass ich als Geflüchteter ständig Hilfe brauche, dass ich schwach und kraftlos bin und den Weg in die Gesellschaft allein nicht finden werde. Das Vorbereitungsstudium der Arbeitsstelle Migration an der HAW Hamburg hat mich darin unterstützt, wieder auf eigenen Beinen zu stehen und wieder Subjekt zu sein.

## 3.2 Teil der Gesellschaft durch Teilhabe

Es sollte einen Raum dafür geben, dass Geflüchtete selbst sich beteiligen, ihre Kompetenzen entfalten, weiterentwickeln und an andere weitergeben können. Aus meiner persönlichen Erfahrung kann ich sagen, dass eine Balance zwischen Beratung, Unterstützung einerseits und Selbstbestimmung andererseits sehr wichtig für einen erfolgreichen Studieneinstieg und die Integration in die Gesellschaft ist. Die Arbeitsstelle Migration hat mit dem Vorbereitungsstudium an der HAW Hamburg und der Gründung der eigenen studentischen Initiative „Bunte Hände" Räume geschaffen, die diese Balance ermöglichen. Wir, als Studierende, schaffen für neue Studieninteressierte und Studierende eine familiäre Atmosphäre – ein WIR-Gefühl. Wir glauben aneinander und wir vertrauen einander. Wir unterstützen uns gegenseitig. Diese Grundhaltung ist entscheidend, um den Weg ins Studium zu schaffen und die vielen Herausforderungen im Studienalltag erfolgreich zu bewältigen.

Unsere Initiative „Bunte Hände" wurde ausgehend von geflüchteten Studierenden, die zuvor erfolgreich das Vorbereitungsstudium „Kompetenz Kompakt" absolviert haben, gegründet. Mittlerweile engagieren sich über 60 geflüchtete, internationale und deutsche Studierende in unterschiedlichsten Projekten und auch politisch für mehr Vielfalt. Ziel ist es, Studierende bis zum erfolgreichen Studienabschluss zu unterstützen und für alle mit Spaß und gegenseitiger Neugierde neue Begegnungsmöglichkeiten zu schaffen. Mit unseren Erfahrungen und Kompetenzen können wir die nächsten Generationen von Studieninteressierten und Studierenden mit und ohne Fluchthintergrund unterstützen.

Durch die Teilhabe, die das Engagement für „Bunte Hände" ermöglicht, sind wir nicht nur Gast, dem geholfen wird. Jeder Mensch sollte sein Handeln bestimmen dürfen – wir sollten uns gegenseitig auf Augenhöhe begegnen und diese Gesellschaft gemeinsam gestalten. Es ist an der Zeit, dass nicht länger nur über Geflüchtete gesprochen wird, ohne dass ein einziger Geflüchteter mitspricht. Geflüchtete sollten aktiv und gleichberechtigt integriert werden. Das wird nicht nur die Integrationsangebote selbst bereichern, da Geflüchtete wertvolle Erfahrungen und Kompetenzen beitragen. Dieser Ansatz macht zudem Geflüchtete zum Subjekt, drückt Wertschätzung aus und ebnet gesellschaftliche und politische Teilhabe als unerlässlichen Bestandteil erfolgreicher Integration.

# Empirical Research

# Online Education, Offline Integration? Supporting Refugees' Social Integration by Online Education

Belma Halkic and Patricia Arnold

## 1 Introduction

To increase equity in higher education, many initiatives have been developed that use digital approaches to facilitate refugees' access to higher education. Online education offers seem to be flexible in time and place and can therefore make study programs "portable" even on a protracted trajectory of flight, with many different locations (e.g. Colucci et al. 2017; Crea 2016; Crea and Sparnon 2017; Dryden-Peterson et al. 2017; GIZ 2016; Moser-Mercer 2014; UNESCO 2018). In general, access to higher education is very limited for refugees and they face a multitude of challenges when trying to take up higher education in their host countries (e.g. Berg et al. 2018; Dryden-Peterson 2016; Fincham 2017; UNESCO 2018; DAAD 2017; Grüttner et al. 2018; Lambert et al. 2018; Streitwieser et al. 2017).

Up to now little is known about the effects of "[l]everaging technology to support [higher] education for refugees" (UNESCO 2018, title). Many of the digital approaches are still in pilot phases and lack comprehensive evaluation (UNESCO 2018; GIZ 2016). Even less is known about the effects of support measures for refugees who use the online educational offers. General research on online education showed that support measures are necessary in order to make an online education offer successful in terms of student retention in study programs and

---

B. Halkic (✉) · P. Arnold
Department of Applied Social Sciences, Hochschule München University of Applied Sciences, Munich, Germany
E-Mail: belma.halkic@hm.edu

P. Arnold
E-Mail: patricia.arnold@hm.edu

© The Author(s), under exclusive license to Springer Fachmedien Wiesbaden GmbH, part of Springer Nature 2021
J. Berg et al. (eds.), *Refugees in Higher Education*, Higher Education Research and Science Studies, https://doi.org/10.1007/978-3-658-33338-6_3

learning outcomes (Arnold et al. 2018; Baxter 2012; Bauer and Knauf 2018; Salmon 2011). This forms the backdrop of the research project SUCCESS ("Study Success and Study Opportunities for Refugees"), funded by the German Ministry of Education and Research in 2017 to 2020, in which we investigated the effects of support measures within the online educational offer of Kiron Open Higher Education (Kiron). Kiron as a social enterprise is one of the initiatives that try to provide digital solutions for the challenge of limited access to higher education for refugees. Kiron's online education offer consists of a MOOC-based modularized curriculum and accompanying support measures such as a Buddy Program, Counselling, or Career Mentoring.

For this paper, we focus on Kiron students' social integration and the effects support measures have on it.[1] Our research questions for this paper are: How do refugee students at Kiron experience social integration in Germany and how do support measures within the Kiron offer impact on their social integration? We analyze students' experiences along three different stages of their educational pathway: upon arrival in Germany, as Kiron students, and as students at German universities. As our research field is mainly uncharted territory, we draw on work from various fields. For this study specifically, we reviewed research results on study success and dropout in general, on social integration of refugees and international students in the German higher education context, and on support for social integration in online higher education.

We organize our paper as follows: First, we share the results of our literature review in the above fields (Sect. 2). In Section 3, we describe our research context and design. Section 4 presents findings both from our quantitative and qualitative data. In the following section, we discuss findings as related to our research questions. Section 6 entails conclusions and suggestions for further research.

## 2 Literature Review

We present findings from previous research in three fields relevant to our research questions, Sect. 2.1 and 2.3 summarize research results concerning higher education research in general without a special focus on refugee students or international students. Section 2.2 focuses on what we know about the social situation of refugee students or international students in general in Germany.

---

[1] The students included in this study form a subgroup—referred to as the "SUCCESS cohort" (N = 1375) within the text—of the entire student population registered at Kiron Open Higher Education. Students of the SUCCESS cohort had signed up on the Kiron platform between May and September 2017.

## 2.1 Study Success and Dropout

Social integration at university has been highlighted as an indicator for study success early on by many seminal study dropout researchers in the American tradition of higher education (Spady 1970; Tinto 1975; Bean and Metzner 1985). According to Spady a lack of social integration into the higher education system (cf. Spady 1970) is a key factor for dropout. Student consensus with institutional norms of the university, support from friends, intellectual development and performance influence the degree of social integration, which itself affects student satisfaction and commitment to the respective university (Spady 1970). According to Tinto (1975), social integration means students' "integration into the social system" (Tinto 1975, p. 107) of the higher education institution. It manifests in a successful realization of "informal peer group associations, semi-formal extracurricular activities, and [in] interaction with faculty and administrative personnel" (Tinto 1975, p. 107). These interactions furthermore influence students' institutional and goal commitment during their study course. With a focus on non-traditional students Bean and Metzner (1985) considered influences from outside the university more relevant. They define "non-traditional students" as older, part-time students who are not living on campus. For this specific group, they identify aspects within students' life situation as influential on dropout, such as parallel employment or family obligations, next to academic performance and individual student characteristics.

Studies use different theoretical approaches (for an overview cf. Neugebauer et al. 2019) but nowadays mostly several perspectives are integrated and study drop out is understood as a mismatch of personal characteristics students bring into the study situation, their resulting engagement when studying, and the institutional requirements and framing conditions on the other hand (cf. e.g. Berthold et al. 2015; Kuh et al. 2006; Mergner et al. 2015). More recent research on study drop out in Germany identifies several factors that increase the risk for dropout; among them lower socio-economic status, a history of migrationand an alternative way of obtaining university entrance qualifications. As regards social integration, these studies also find that students who have difficulties in relating to faculty or peers are at higher risk of dropping out (Heublein et al. 2017). Not surprisingly, students' financial difficulties add to this risk (Isphording and Wozny 2018). Employment next to studying, however, does not increase risk as such, as long as it does not use up a huge proportion of students' time budget or is in a sector not connected to the study field (Heublein et al. 2017).

## 2.2 Refugee and International Students in Germany

Within the international research context on refugees' in higher education, mainly qualitative studies have been published so far (Berg et al. 2018). Missing social networks are highlighted as a factor relevant to refugees' access to information (Naidoo 2015; Morrice 2013). Refugee students face a lack of information regarding higher education and often "receive[] unreliable, unhelpful, or inaccurate guidance" (Bajwa 2017, p. 59) at the official level. Not least because of that, it is common among refugees to gather information from social networks (Bajwa 2017). Guidance for local orientation is essential, but should first be provided physically before continuing virtually (Plasterer 2010). Besides functional support, there is a great need for more emotional support, which could be realized through peer-to-peer mentoring (ibid.).Considering that most refugees did not study German before entering the country already points towards a critical aspect for their integration process. Missing language skills turn out to be one of the key barriers for access to higher education (Unangst and Streitwieser 2018). Refugee students in study preparation programs at German universities report about social isolation after arriving in Germany, which is related to language barriers and challenges with everyday interactions (Grüttner et al. 2018). This can lead to additional emotional stress as part of refugees' overall difficult life situation. Furthermore, experiences of discrimination affect refugee students' social integration. Participating in support measures, however, does not seem enough to reduce isolation if students are not at the same time enabled to join study groups and connect to students of the host country. Refugees have a great interest in connecting with German students but recruiting the latter for Buddy Programs for example proved difficult (ibid.). As regards social support, there seems to be a preference for informal support (Baker et al. 2018). People who can provide such "warm support" do not officially belong to the university apparatus, but are trustworthy individuals who are familiar with the higher education system (ibid).

Recent reports on the situation of international students[2] in German higher education show that social integration is a great issue (cf. Apolinarski and Brandt 2018). Around one third (31%) of international students state to have big or very big difficulties concerning contact with locals as well as with German students (28%) while only 13% claim the same regarding contact with university teachers (Apolinarski and Brandt 2018). In addition to that, 34% report big or very big

---

[2]International students are defined as "students who have no German citizenship and who gained their higher education entrance qualification outside of Germany" (Apolinarski and Brandt 2018, p. 5).

difficulties with communicating in German (ibid.). Language barriers occur with technical language as well as with the daily use of German (Morris-Lange 2017). As a consequence, international students tend to have more contacts with people from the same country of origin and other international students than with German students (DAAD 2014). At university, every sixth international student claims to have no friends among domestic students at all (Morris-Lange 2017.). In addition to that, individual efforts to make contacts are often limited by other obligations such as university and language studies as well as part time jobs. Collaborating with domestic students as part of study groups does not necessarily help international students to make friends, as they, for example, feel forced to cope with stereotypes or to prove not to be the weakest member of the group (ibid.).

## 2.3 Support of Social Integration in Online Higher Education Environments

Online education in higher education in the tradition of distance learning is connected with the risk of social isolation. From the beginning of online education offers the need for support measures for online learners has been pointed out on various levels to reduce social isolation, foster social integration and learning outcomes (cf. Arnold et al. 2002; Haythornthwaite 1998; Paloff and Pratt 1999; Preece 2002; Putz and Arnold 2001). Several studies show that community building in online education settings is possible, given a good fit of educational design, online and offline support measures and instructional technologies (for an overview cf. Pilcher 2017). The seminal work of Gilly Salmon (2011) differentiates online support measures both on a social and technological level and in five different phases during online courses. In each of the five phases, support for social integration features strongly, with a varying degree of direct relation to course content.

A general key element in creating a sense of belonging in online education is a focus on online interactions among students as well as with tutors and lecturers. The facilitation of online interaction furthermore influences students' motivation and student identity (Baxter 2013). Another crucial element is timely feedback (Bauer and Knauf 2018) and a space for informal communication (Beins 2016). However, all of these findings apply to the design of online education offers in higher education in the framework of online courses with around 30 participants. In contrast, in Massive Open Online Courses (MOOCs), with large numbers of participants, creating a learning community is usually not part of the overall educational design. These course offers focus more on flexible, individual learning opportunities, and usually about only 5–15% of the participants complete a MOOC entirely (Breslow et al. 2013; Jordan 2015).

These findings concern online higher education offers in general; there is less known about social integration, support measures or online community building for refugees or international students. A recent study about online education offers used by Syrian youth reveals that there is too little interaction and not enough consideration of the special living circumstances, for example, of refugees living in low-resourced environments like camps (Fincham 2017). Other studies, however, show that social networks and especially the use of mobile phones can help female refugees in camps build up virtual networks that ease their way to higher education (Dahya and Dryden-Peterson 2017).

## 3 Research Context and Design

### 3.1 Research Context

Our study is part of the joint research project SUCCESS in which three German universities have conducted independent research (e.g. Halkic and Arnold 2017, 2019, 2019a; Reinhardt et al. 2018; Zlatkin-Troitschanskaia et al. 2018) and collaborated with Kiron who provides access to the research field. Kiron is a social enterprise, founded in late 2015, with the vision of enabling refugees to access higher education in host countries by an online education offer. As of December 2019, more than 6000 refugees from various countries have registered at Kiron (www.kiron.ngo).

Kiron is offering an online curriculum, which is based on existing MOOCs, and other online courses, put together into modularized curricula in five different study tracks. Kiron students can use the offer free of charge. Ideally, they will accumulate up to 60 credit points by completing MOOCs and other online courses and then transfer to a partner university,[3] with their credits recognized in Europe by the European Credit Transfer and Accumulation System (ECTS). Most partner universities are based in Germany but some are also located in other host

---

[3] A university with which Kiron has formally agreed a partnership (either signed a Memorandum of Understanding and/or a Learning Agreement) towards supporting refugees' access to higher education.

| Support Measure | Description |
| --- | --- |
| Kiron Navigator | Online orientation tool on Kiron website |
| Study/ Orientation Weekend | Thematic offline get-together at Kiron offices |
| Newsletter | General e-mail newsletter |
| Online Mentoring | Individualized mentoring with volunteer |
| Career Mentoring | Single offline offers in cooperation with corporates |
| Buddy Program | One-on-one on-/offline partnership between Kiron students and university students |
| Counselling | Professional psychological online counselling (external provider) |
| Online Tutorials | Study accompanying tutorials for single MOOCs |
| Help Desk | Online support from Kiron |
| Student Forum | Part of the Kiron study platform |
| Study Groups | feature in Student Forum for students to communicate |
| Transfer Guidance | One-on-one counselling related to university application |
| Online Tutorials | Study accompanying tutorials for single MOOCs |

**Fig. 1** Support measures offered at Kiron, as of: February 2017

countries. Partner universities agree to recognize credit gained in Kiron's educational offer towards specific degree programs. Nevertheless, recognition has to be decided upon individually by the responsible examination board of the university.

The Kiron curriculum is accompanied by various support measures as well as online and offline language courses. The Kiron support measures consist of different on- and offline offers with different regional scopes. At the beginning of the project SUCCESS, the Kiron support measures in Germany comprised thirteen different measures (cf. Fig. 1), which we included in our analysis.

## 3.2 Research Design & Methods

Due to the explorative character of our study, we have not tested a particular theory. Our theoretical foundation draws from work by Mergner et al. 2015 at the German Centre for Higher Education Research and Science Studies (DZHW). Within their suggested model, study success is "resulting from a successful matching between students and study conditions" (Mergner et al. 2015, transl. by authors). Depending on how well internal (individual) and external (institutional) factors match, students will be either successful in their studies or dropout from university (ibid.). Furthermore, in the line of Heublein et al. (2017), who extended Tinto's (1975) approach, we took *academic*, *social* and *institutional* integration as key indicators of this matching. As mentioned earlier, in this paper the focus is on *social* integration, and we investigate how well support at Kiron matches with the actual needs that students have in terms of social integration.

Our results are based on data from a quantitative online survey on student support ("support survey") and qualitative semi-structured interviews with present and former Kiron students. The students included in our study form a subgroup—referred to as the "SUCCESS cohort" (N = 1375)—of the entire student population at Kiron who had signed up on the Kiron platform between May and September 2017. Qualitative interviews were conducted with a selected sample of students from the SUCCESS cohort.

As Kiron aims to support refugees' access to universities, investigating social integration into the Kiron environment itself was not considered a priority. Instead, the potential of the offer to contribute to refugee students' social integration related to higher education was paramount. The analysis of social integration focused on Kiron students' interpersonal relations as part of their experiences at Kiron. Building on results of the literature review, another emphasis was put on students' life situation in Germany.

### 3.2.1 Online Survey and Semi-structured Interviews

Questions within our support survey (n = 203, response rate = 14,8%) adapt questionnaires by the German Academic Exchange Service (DAAD) (DAAD 2014) and by the German National Association for Student Affairs (Apolinarski and Poskowsky 2013) to our context. The survey contained questions about student satisfaction with support at Kiron, their overall evaluation on the helpfulness of support at Kiron, difficulties students are facing in life and at Kiron as well as the kind of support they personally consider important. As regards social integration, students were asked, 1) to what extent the support services[4] were helpful for making social contacts with a) other students, b) academics from their field of studies, c) professionals from their field and d) local people, 2) to what extent they have faced difficulties regarding a) contact with other students, b) communication in the local language, c) contact with local people and 3) how important they personally consider support for a) making contact with local people and b) participating in cultural and free time activities. Quantitative data was mainly analyzed using descriptive statistics and was supposed to give an overview of the student population and provide orientation for qualitative investigations.

---

[4] Kiron terms their support measures as "Support Services".

In-depth semi-structured interviews covered two stages of students' pathway: 1) Experiences with Kiron including a broad analysis of experiences with support measures and 2) experiences within their life situations since arrival in the country. For interviewees who were already studying at a university at the time of the interview, an additional section on their 3) experiences at the respective university was added. Part 1 included students' motivation to sign up at Kiron in consideration of the individual educational background, experiences with online learning and the parallel use of other online education resources as well as previous experiences with online learning. As regards support measures, motivation, satisfaction and helpfulness for a) social integration, b) access to university, and c) for life were assessed. Part 2 focused on social integration within the host society, the job situation, the influence of students' legal status, difficulties students face in life and missing support. Part 3 explored experiences with university studies, interaction with other students and teachers on campus as well as the use of and need for support measures at university. The interviews were conducted online using Skype calls and students could choose English or German as interview language.

After transcription, the interviews were analyzed with the structural content analysis approach developed by Schreier (2012). Schreier's Qualitative Content Analysis (QCA) is a systematic, flexible and data-reducing analysis method (cf. Schreier 2012). Categories were formed both deductively drawing from theoretical concepts and inductively resulting from interviews (cf. ibid., 60) by systematically reducing data material to main and sub-categories.

### 3.2.2 Participants

Table 1 gives an overview of the interviewee sample by gender, country of origin, age, highest education, whether students used support measures at Kiron and how many years they have spent in Germany at the time of the interview. Initially, cases within the sample were contrasted by used support measures, courses (no/started/completed), gender, age, origin. Due to insufficient reachability of the SUCCESS cohort, the sample does not entirely cover the intended diversity.

## 4 Research Results

### 4.1 The Broader Picture

As part of the support survey students of the SUCCESS cohort were asked to assess the level of difficulties they are facing regarding different aspects of life. 42% (n = 60) of students stated to have some to great difficulties related to

**Table 1** Interview participants

| Interview | 1 | 2 | 3 | 4 | 5 | 6 | 7 | 8 | 9 | 10 | 11 | 12 | 13 | 14 | 15 |
|---|---|---|---|---|---|---|---|---|---|---|---|---|---|---|---|
| Gender | m | m | m | m | m | m | f | m | m | m | m | m | m | f | m |
| Origin[a] | S | S | A | S | Eth[b] | S | S | N | S | S[c] | S | S | S | S | M[d] |
| Age | 27 | 27 | 23 | 35 | 23 | 42 | 26 | 31 | N.A | 24 | 27 | 36 | 28 | 30 | N.A[e] |
| Education[f] | BA | BA | HS | N.A | IHE | MA | HS | BA | IHE | BA IHE | BA | BA | IHE | BA | IHE |
| Support | ✓ | ✓ | ✓ | ✓ | ✓ | ✓ | ✓ | ✓ | ✓ | ✓ | ✓ | ✓ | ✓ | x | ✓ |
| Years in Germany | 3 | 5 | 3 | 3 | 3 | 5 | 3 | 4 | 3 | 5 | 3 | 3 | 4 | 4 | 4 |

[a]S = Syria, A = Afghanistan, Eth. = Ethiopia, N = Nigeria, M = Mali
[b]Born in Somalia
[c]Lived in Iraq and Egypt before coming to Germany
[d]Grew up in Nigeria
[e]N.A. = no answer
[f]BA = Bachelor Degree, MA = Master Degree, HS = High School Diploma, IHE = Interrupted Higher Education

making contact with local people, 43% (n = 60) with the local language and 39% (n = 59) have difficulties related to contact with other students. However, there are other aspects of students' life situation which provide difficulties for more students such as finding a job (56%, n = 59), cost of living (55%, n = 60) and admission to university (52%, n = 60). In addition to that 72% (n = 61) of students consider language courses as very important support in life. This is followed by 61% (n = 61) who find opportunities to meeting university students very important and 52% (n = 61) who consider support for making contacts with academics from their study area as very important. Furthermore, half of the students (50%, n = 60) consider support for making contact with local people as very important.

*Helpfulness of Support*

Furthermore, students were asked to assess the helpfulness of the Kiron support services for making more contacts with professionals from their field, with academics from their study area, with local people and with other students. Figure 2 shows results for students in Germany. More than half of the students evaluate the Kiron support measures as quite to very helpful for making social contacts. Less than 20% perceive support measures as not helpful at all for making contacts with any of the different social groups. 13% think so as regards other students while 18% find support not helpful at all for making contacts with academics from their field.

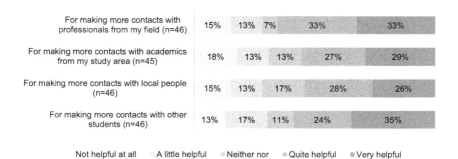

**Fig. 2** Student evaluation of support measures

Source: Support Survey, filter: Students in Germany, n=60, field date: 1.06.2018–15.07.2018 Question: "To what extent were the support services helpful to you?" Answer: "For making more …".

## 4.2 In-depth Analysis

### 4.2.1 Social Integration in the Host Society

*Students' Needs*
Making social contacts is often connected to specific desires, which can result from the general situation of being a refugee in a new country. Students who experienced war and social deprivation express the wish to start a new life and to forget the past. Meeting new people is a crucial part of this process: "We always need contact with people and we always need to be active in order to forget." (I1) In addition to that, access to university can become a place of hope regarding social integration as this student points out: "The only thing on my mind is how to go into the university, further my study, because I believe in the university I will find right friends. That's the reason why making friends on the street is not actually part of me." (I8) While there seems to be different rationalities behind the goal of making social contacts, there is also a need to simply make friends to have someone to talk and "be like a normal person" (I8). Whether students successfully make contacts with locals or not can have positive or negative consequences for their well-being and motivation. Even if students reached their highly desired goal of university admission, and get a safe residence status, they still may be unhappy as they suffer from low social integration into the host society.

*Contacts with Locals*
After students arrive in Germany, the first contacts they make except the authorities are with local volunteers. Often these volunteers are pensioners from the neighborhood willing to help refugees integrate. In some cases, bonds with these initial helpers may remain but mostly they occur only punctually for special occasions like Christmas. Students who receive help gratefully talk about the positive experiences they made with these helpful locals. Whether they receive help from people is a common criterion for the overall assessment of their social situation. When talking about the usually elderly helpers, students problematize their age and mention the need for contacts with peers which in contrast seem to be rare.

*What Limits Social Integration?*

There are various reasons why social contacts remain few and sporadic. Although students wish for more interaction with peers, they also criticize that German peers smoke and drink when they go out and they feel forced to do so, too, if they want to make friends. These experiences make them feel as if they "don't have a lot of mutual things or ideas with the young people here" (I2). Other perceptions about the local culture are that Germans work a lot and thus have no time for leisure activities compared to people in Syria. When students reflect upon their new place of residence in comparison to their former hometowns, they prefer their old neighborhoods where they experienced close contact among neighbors and where "you can walk on the street and talk to anyone" (I11) as people are "not afraid and without prejudice" (ibid.). Most of the interviewed Kiron students find it difficult to make contacts or even friends with local people in Germany. Although students claim to be "very open, it is unfortunately not that many contacts" (I10) they have. Thus, locals are perceived as "closed [and] distanced" (I10) and seem to be "building fences" (I10). Some have the feeling that people are afraid of them due to negative stereotypes which students trace back to media discourse around refugees, terrorism and Islam:

> I1: "We know a lot about Germany and about German, but the German people don't know a lot about us. Most of the times they ask questions that for us are something like crazy. They ask us if we had cars in Syria or once there was one guy who asked me if we had bananas in Syria. […] I don't know if there is any way to explain about us, about our lifestyle in Syria. For me, I had a good life. I care for Muslim but it's not radical Muslim or something like this. We don't have anything forbidden, not everything is forbidden. I have members in my family, they drink, they have girlfriends, we have a normal life. But there are these stereotype ideas that we beat [women] and we marry more than one time and stuff like this."

Nevertheless, some interviewees also emphasize that there is good and bad people in every society and that once they "got through" (I3) to someone and overcame the initial barriers "it's really amazing" (I3).

Language barriers are another reason why students, even after years in the country, only have few and sporadic contacts. While for other aspects in life an intermediate level of German may be enough, this may not be enough to become friends with someone. Furthermore, health issues can limit both academic and social integration. One interviewee had to quit everything because his mental health issues became stronger and he had to stay in hospital. Another aspect, which makes social integration difficult and requires a lot of adaptability, is frequent changes of residence as can be decided by the authorities. For interviewees who live alone in Germany, making friends and getting emotional support from locals seems to be even more important than for others. Their families often live far away in other countries and the only communication channel is via video calls.

### 4.2.2 Social Integration through Support

*Use of Kiron Support*
The Kiron educational model consists of online curricula based on MOOCs and different accompanying support measures of which some are offline, online or a mix of both formats. Like the majority of Kiron students within the SUCCESS cohort (cf. Halkic and Arnold 2019), the interviewed students only studied a few single courses from Kiron's online curriculum. Yet, interviewees were more active regarding the use of support measures. Most of the interviewed students had joined offline events at the Kiron offices in Berlin or Munich or participated in the Online Mentoring. Fewer had experiences with online support offers such as Online Tutorials or the Study Forum. Interviewees widely used the Kiron support complementary to other sources of support by other providers such as universities. Furthermore, they used single support measures independent of the educational offer, but in line with their individual needs and possibilities.

Social integration seems to play a key role for students' choice of support since they prefer support that enables social interaction, personal guidance/counselling & language learning (e.g. Online Mentoring, Study/ Orientation Weekends, Transfer Guidance). Especially Online Mentoring is a very popular support measure among the interviewed students because of the individualized one-on-one support, which is rarely provided outside of Kiron.

*Kiron Students & Staff*
Meeting other refugees as part of Kiron support measures is considered valuable as students often suffer from "a lack of information" (I10, transl.), especially right after arrival in the host country. Thus, talking to people who are in a similar situation enables students to exchange experiences made in the host country as well as useful information about the integration process. Students state that they used Study/Orientation Weekends to meet people and interact while the actual theme of these events was less important. Besides meeting other refugees, students consider getting in touch with Kiron staff as making contacts with locals. Therefore, Kiron is perceived as "a connection to the outside world" (I15). Especially during

the initial time after arriving in the host country, students experience Kiron as the only place to go when they do not know anyone yet:

> I2: "They were always in touch with me and they asked me if I need anything else. One time we went to Thanksgiving dinner, they all were kind, they were nice, they introduced me to other refugees, and they introduced me to Kiron team. It was something nice because at first I didn't know anyone here in Germany, I was alone. I am here without my family. Also, I got to know other refugees and we exchanged our numbers. We talked after that and we shared all our experiences here in Germany."

The local Kiron community can also serve as "refuge" when students experience social rejection within the host society. As another positive factor of joining offline support specifically, students mention an increase in online study motivation. However, as these offers are rare and only last at the maximum for a weekend, students can "loose this spark [of motivation] afterwards" (I10) very fast.

*Mentors & Buddies*
As mentioned before, Online Mentoring is very popular among interviewees. The program usually starts with one initial offline meeting with all mentors and mentees and then continues with nine additional weekly online sessions in which mentoring partners meet independently. Students' valuation of Online Mentoring is strongly connected with social integration. One reason is the chance to get a personalized, one-on-one support that focuses on a student's specific needs. At the same time a mentor is considered a potential friend:

> I8: "I wanted to sign up for mentoring because I need a guide because I was filled with frustration because my initial expectation was to get admitted into university last year in 2018, but it was quite unfortunate. I was frustrated. I really need a mentor, someone who will say never give up, keep trying."

Besides motivational and emotional support, students value Online Mentoring because it helps them integrate into the host society:

> I15: "It's really important when we can be able to connect with somebody from the society and then we can also talk on this level, how does the society really picture us, because then you get this feedback from a native. Also, what do I do to integrate myself? I really talked on this matter, I really discussed it with him from day one. He gave me a lot of tips, how to integrate, the things I can do."

For students who suffer from a lack of social contacts within the host society the mentor becomes a main contact person or the only friend they can talk to about private things. After experiencing disinterest and rejection from locals, the mentor appears as someone who is interested, "very open" (I1) and a "good listener" (ebd.). Another benefit students may get from the Mentoring is to improve their language skills: "When I used this mentoring I had a jump in my language level […], you can speak easier." (I13) When mentoring partners reached a personal, friendship-like character it is likely that this contact remains after the official Mentoring program has ended. Sometimes student and mentor changed from online to offline meetings or to other mediums like WhatsApp or phone calls. This flexibility for many students is important to create a more individualized and personal character of the relationship which also fits their tight schedule.

Students' experiences with the Buddy Program are slightly different. The Buddy partnership is usually between a Kiron student and a university student. Other than the Mentoring Program, this support measure has no explicit organization and thus depends on the self-organization of Kiron student and Buddy. On the one hand, Kiron students made good experiences as their buddy partner were very nice and they occasionally even met in person. On the other hand, students also stated that having a buddy partner did not really help much as they expected something else and in most cases contact was unsteady.

*What Limits the Effects of Support?*
While participation in the Mentoring Program on one hand can help students to improve their language skills, on the other hand, students must have a sufficient level of either German or English to be able to communicate with their mentor at all. Thus, language barriers can also limit the use of the Mentoring Program. One student, for example, mentions he had to end his mentorship as he struggled expressing himself. Limited time capacities on both sides, local distance, no regular access to internet and health issues can lead to an early termination in each of the measures. Although both measures are supposed to be online, locality did matter in both the Online Mentoring and the Buddy Program as the willingness of both parties to keep up online meetings is not always given. The Buddy Program is less popular among the interviewed students, which seems to be due to its unstructured nature and no facilitation. Another reason for termination of the Buddy partnership lies in the matching of refugee student expectations and what the Buddy is able to provide. Interviewees, for example, mention their need for guidance, which can be difficult to manage for a Buddy, who is a university student him-/herself. In addition to that, Kiron students who are participating in

welcome programs[5] at German universities, prefer to use Buddy Programs within these welcome programs as this enables them to connect with prospective peers.

*Continuity of Kiron Contacts*

While meeting other refugees and Kiron staff as part of Study/ Orientation weekends can be exciting, this does not necessarily lead to persisting and stable contacts or friendship, which is so highly desired by many students. Often these contacts are exclusively embedded in support measures and do not continue outside of an offer. As regards interaction between Kiron students, this seems to hold true for online support measures where the purpose of students' communication is specific and limited to "just typing" (I3) and without "any face call" (ebd.). The chances that contacts remain after support measures ended are higher for measures such as Study/ Orientation Weekends which include physical presence and can go beyond a purely functional character. To sustain the new connections, a proactive student self-organization of further meetings and communication is required. In most cases, students then use established communication channels like WhatsApp instead of the Kiron platform. From this, peer learning and other study supporting communication can emerge.

Although some students see support staff as "good company" (I2) and "good friends" (ebd.), none of them mentions any continuity of these contacts outside of Kiron. Their positive evaluation results from the fact that they receive help from Kiron in the form of fast response to their requests for example. Other aspects such as personality, which are actually relevant for a friendship, seem to be less important. Despite many positive experiences, students also meet distanced and uncommunicative people at Kiron offline events, which they interpret as a singularity of the German culture that prevents them from developing intense relationships with local people.

## 4.2.3 Social Integration at University

*Students & Lecturers*

Whether students' participation at Kiron and specifically in the support measures has a positive impact on social integration into the university environment cannot be finally assessed at this point of research. Interviews with four students who

---

[5] Such programs have increased at German universities after the German Academic Exchange Service (DAAD) started the Integra-Program, which is meant to support the integration of refugees into higher education. The program funds several measures of study preparation and language courses at German universities (DAAD 2019).

already studied at university during the time of the interview, however, give a first impression of refugees' social situation at university. All interviewees experience professors and lecturers as friendly and helpful whereas interaction with local students is reported to be difficult. The chances of making social contacts among German peers is often limited by students' communication skills:

> I14: "The language is still difficult because I cannot discuss with other German student in fluent way. I need time to organize my idea, I need time to speak it correctly. German students are active, in hurry."

Although single positive experiences with mixed study groups for example are reported, contacts with other students usually seem to remain on a sporadic and functional level whereas friendships do not develop. When students face rejection as they for example seek help from peers, they consequently make more contacts with other refugees and international students at the same university. Rejection can also influence students' well-being and mental health. One of the interviewed students who sought help from his peers got rejected repeatedly which frustrates him a lot and even makes him question his stay in Germany: "I think most people do not feel comfortable in Germany. That's my opinion. […] I don't care if I find work here for example or earn a lot of money, if I don't feel good." (I1).

*Influence of Life Situation*
Interviews also point towards external influence resulting from students' life situation. One student for example explains that she has no contact with peers outside of university because she has to travel between her home and university two hours a day and because she suffers from a bad health. After university admission, specific life challenges remain such as finding a job in order to improve the legal status and cover life expenses as well as the need to continue language studies. Students constantly need to balance between different tasks resulting both from their individual goals and between formal necessities. Thus, students with an insecure legal status often terminate other integration efforts to work full time in order to improve their chances of staying in Germany. Legal status can also influence social integration as it limits mobility outside the country and students may not be able to join excursions to other countries. Thus, "this status thing is keeping [them] away from the group" (I15).

## 5 Discussion

In order to answer our research questions for this paper, we will discuss the following four issues: 1) online education vs. the need for offline social interaction; 2) social integration vs. other needs, 3) microcosm Kiron vs. higher education system in Germany, 4) locality vs. translocality.

### 5.1 Online Education vs. the Need for Offline Social Interaction

Providing educational opportunities for refugees is often seen as a psycho-social intervention (Grüttner et al. 2018; Crea 2016; Morrice 2013). As shown elsewhere (Halkic and Arnold 2019a), Kiron's offer as such is considered valuable by students. Kiron's offer seems to positively affect students' well-being especially after arrival in the host country when refugees are often challenged by isolation and no connection to the host society. This perception may also show as part of an overall positive evaluation of the Kiron support (see Fig. 2). However, as a closer look revealed, a positive impact on students' social situation mainly results from (offline) social interaction with peers, Kiron staff and Mentoring/ Buddy partners. Students only study a few online courses and instead try to get as much as possible from support measures that allow for social interaction. It seems that online education, especially in the form of MOOCs as the main part of the Kiron offer, does not foster social integration. Support measures are used as tools for social interaction and come into effect as a stand-alone offer. Although there may be several reasons, why students do not study as many online courses as intended by Kiron (cf. Halkic and Arnold 2019), their conscious choice of support measures may reflect a priority setting in favor of social interaction and the benefits presumed with it. Needs resulting from students social situation may then limit the effects of online education. At the same time, as Kiron's online education program does not guarantee access to university, interacting with locals and other Kiron students seems to be a more promising investment within students' often very tight schedules and needs that go beyond education itself.

### 5.2 Social Integration vs. Other Needs

Refugee students' life situations are often characterized by a complex interplay of individual needs and available resources which manifests in a flexible use of

Kiron's offer. As Grüttner et al. (2018) point out there are interrelations between the social situation of refugees and other aspects of their life situation. While priority must be given to language learning as this "influences to what degree other everyday tasks become demanding" (Grüttner et al. 2018, p. 125), securing housing is of even higher priority as it can limit efforts for language studies (Grüttner et al. 2018). At the same time, refugee students' social life can affect their well-being and motivation to study and well-working social interaction can unfold valuable effects such as access to information (Naidoo 2015; Morrice 2013) and other resources. Despite structural barriers, language skills and dealing with cultural disparities and stereotypes are highly relevant for making social contacts and building networks of support. For refugees who do not speak German, support in English can be useful. However, not all refugees interested in higher education necessarily speak English, some live in remote areas in Germany, without internet access and no options to travel. Within higher education, the conflict between English as the tool of internationalization on one hand and German as the language of social integration on the other hand was already identified as problematic for international students (Morris-Lange 2017).

## 5.3 Microcosm Kiron vs. German Higher Education System

Kiron can be especially useful in the initial time after arrival and can serve as social anchor and "safe space" for those who lack contacts within the host society. Contacts made at Kiron can have further positive effects on students' access to information and orientation within the host society. In addition to that, mentors and interaction with other Kiron students seem to be useful in terms of emotional support. However, the scope of social contacts made as part of Kiron support measures seems to be limited. Contacts only sustain in few cases where stable relationships can be maintained outside of the Kiron context. Consequently, social integration at Kiron does not necessarily mean social integration at university and into other parts of society. Kiron can serve as a starting point where the foundation for persisting social contacts can be built by providing a platform and facilitation. Once students enter university, however, they often need to build relations from scratch. One dilemma that seems to arise as part of this process is the required transition from refugee (at Kiron) to student (at university) on one hand and the remaining need for additional assistance and help on the other hand which, as a consequence, can challenge social interaction with peers.

## 5.4 Locality vs. Translocality

The idea of a transboundary online education and online student communities is limited by refugees' life situations, which are strongly influenced by locally embedded circumstances. Be it legal frameworks that differ between countries or the need to speak the local language and become familiar with a specific local culture, refugee students' integration process is locally framed. Thus, individual integration efforts such as the use of support measures are influenced by locality instead of being transboundary as it is inherent to Kiron's online environment. At the same time, for many refugees whose residence is not or may not be permanent, a re-conceptualization of what integration, both academic and social, should look like for people who are "on the move" seems to be necessary. Therein, questions on the transferability of locally gained social capital as well as the potential of digital technology to build and preserve social contacts (e.g. Dahya and Dryden-Peterson 2016) arise.

## 5.5 Limitations

Our study comes with some limitations: The investigation of social integration needed to be contextualized to one host country. Our interpretation as well as the qualitative data refers solely to Germany as a host country and the German higher education context. However, Kiron's offer is available worldwide and the SUCCESS cohort consists of students in many different host countries, wherefore our results cannot be transferred to the general group of Kiron students. In addition, the process of sampling interviewees was limited due to reachability of specific student groups and might be slightly skewed towards the more invested students with Kiron. Furthermore, language barriers restricted verbal self-expression in the case of several interviews which in turn can limit interpretation of the interview material.

## 6 Conclusions

The results of this study show that pre-university support measures within online education environments can help refugees acquire needed information and make first social contacts within the host society. Low threshold and flexibly usable support can have positive effects for refugee students. Especially facilitated mentoring programs that can help social integration into the host society seem to be a useful complementation to other available support in Germany. Social integration into higher education with support measures such as provided by Kiron, however, is limited if transferability from the support context to the wider social life of refugees is not realized. Priority should therefore be given to equipping students with sustainable resources such as language, orientation and understanding of the local culture instead of building strong but exclusive communities, which are primarily built on the use of a specific offer. Furthermore, the interplay of refugee students' challenges and needs must be considered when designing support in order to create maximum effectivity and to reach less privileged refugee subgroups. Further research is required to get the full picture on refugees' social integration within higher education, for example by applying ethnographic field research and consideration of other actors involved. Therein, emphasis should be put on how refugees' specific life situations affect their social integration at university and by this possibly (re)produce social inequalities among university students.

## References

Apolinarski, B. & Poskowsky, J. (2013). Ausländische Studierende in Deutschland 2012. Ergebnisse der 20. Sozialerhebung des Deutschen Studentenwerks durchgeführt vom Deutschen Zentrum für Hochschul- und Wissenschaftsforschung (DZHW).

Arnold, P., L. Kilian, & A. Thillosen. (2002). „'So lonely?!' - Online-Betreuung als kritische Erfolgsbedingung beim telematischen Studieren. Ergebnisse einer Befragung von Studierenden und Mentoren in der Virtuellen Fachhochschule für Technik, Informatik und Wirtschaft (VFH)". In G. Bachmann, O. Haefeli, and M. Kindt (Eds.), *Campus 2002: Die virtuelle Hochschule in der Konsolidierungsphase*, (18), 334–344. Münster: Waxmann

Arnold, P., Lars, K., Thillosen, A. & Zimmer, G. (2018). *Handbuch E-Learning. Lehren und Lernen mit digitalen Medien*. 5. erw., und aktual. Aufl., Stuttgart: UTB

Bajwa, J. K., Couto, S., Kidd, S., Markoulakis, R., Abai, M. & McKenzie, K. (2017). Refugees, Higher Education, and Informational Barriers, *Refuge: Canada's Journal on Refugees*, 33(2), 56–65.

Baker, S., Ramsay, G., Irwin, E. & Miles, L. (2017). 'Hot', 'Cold' and 'Warm' Supports. Towards Theorising where Refugee Students go for Assistance at University, *Teaching in Higher Education*, 37(1), 1–16. DOI: https://doi.org/10.1080/13562517.2017.1332028

Baxter, J. (2012). Who am I and what keeps me going? Profiling the distance learning student in higher education. *The international review of research in open and distance learning*, 13(4), 107–129.

Bauer, E. & Knauf, H. (2018). Subjektorientierte Feedback-Kultur als Kommunikations- und Lerngelegenheit im Online-Studium. In P. Arnold P, H. Grieshop & C. Füssenhäuser (Eds.), *Profilierung Sozialer Arbeit online* (pp. 165–182). Wiesbaden: Springer VS. DOI: https://doi.org/10.1007/978-3-658-17088-2_10

Bean, J. P., & Metzner, B. S. (1985). A Conceptual Model of Nontraditional Undergraduate Student Attrition. *Review of Educational Research*, 55(4), 485–540. https://doi.org/10.3102/00346543055004485

Beins, A. (2016). Small Talk and Chit Chat. *Transformations: The Journal of Inclusive Scholarship and Pedagogy* 26(2), 157–175. DOI: https://doi.org/10.5325/trajincschped.26.2.0157

Berg, J., Grüttner, M., Schroeder, S. (2018). Zwischen Befähigung und Stigmatisierung? Die Situation von Geflüchteten beim Hochschulzugang und im Studium. Ein internationaler Forschungsüberblick. *Zeitschrift für Flüchtlingsforschung*, 2(1), 57–90. DOI: https://doi.org/10.5771/2509-9485-2018-1-57

Berthold, C.; Jorzik, B.; Meyer-Guckel, V. (Hg.) (2015): Handbuch Studienerfolg. Strategien und Maßnahmen: Wie Hochschulen Studierende erfolgreich zum Abschluss führen. Stifterverband für die Deutsche Wissenschaft. Essen: Edition Stifterverband.

Colucci, E., Smidt, H., Devaux, A., Vrasidas, C., Safarjalani, M. & Muñoz, J.C. (2017). Free Digital Learning Opportunities for Migrants and Refugees. An Analysis of Current Initiatives and Recommendations for their Further Use. European Commission JCR – Science for Policy Report. Retrieved December 20, 2017 from https://publications.jrc.ec.europa.eu/repository/bitstream/JRC106146/kjna28559enn.pdf.

Crea, T. M. (2016). Refugee Higher Education. Contextual Challenges and Implications for Program Design, Delivery, and Accompaniment, *International Journal of Educational Development*, 46, 12–22.

Crea, T. M. & N. Sparnon. (2017). Democratizing education at the margins: Faculty and practitioner perspectives on delivering online tertiary education for refugees, *International Journal of Educational Technology in Higher Education*, 14(43). DOI: https://doi.org/10.1186/s41239-017-0081-y

DAAD (German Academic Exchange Service) (2014). *Ergebnisbericht zur Evaluierung des DAAD-Programms „STIBET I und STIBET III Matching Funds*, Bonn: DAAD.

DAAD (German Academic Exchange Service). (2017). *The integration of refugees at German higher education institutions: Findings from higher education programmes for refugees.* Bonn: DAAD.

DAAD (German Academic Exchange Service) (2019). Integration von Flüchtlingen ins Fachstudium - „Integra", DAAD. Retrieved December 13, 2019 from https://www.daad.de/de/infos-services-fuer-hochschulen/weiterfuehrende-infos-zu-daad-foerderprogrammen/integra/

Dahya, N. & Dryden-Peterson, S. (2017). Tracing pathways to higher education for refugees: the role of virtual support networks and mobile phones for women in refugee camps, *Comparative Education*, 53(2), 284–301, DOI: https://doi.org/10.1080/03050068.2016.1259877

Dryden-Peterson, S. (2016). Refugee Education: The Crossroads of Globalization, *Educational Researcher*, 45(9), 473–482.

Dryden-Peterson, S., Dahya, N. & Adelman, E. (2017). Pathways to educational success among refugees: Connecting locally and globally situated resources, *American Educational Research Journal*, 54(6), 1011–1047.

Fincham, K. (2017). Complex barriers to refugees accessing university, *University World News* 463, June 9. Retrieved March 21st 2019 from https://www.universityworldnews.com/article.php?story=20170606133740246

GIZ (Deutsche Gesellschaft für internationale Zusammenarbeit). (2016). Education in conflict and crisis: How can technology make a difference? *A landscape review*. Bonn: GIZ.

Grüttner, M., Berg, J., Schröder, S. & Otto, C. (2018). Refugees on their way to German higher education: A capabilities and engagement perspective on aspirations, challenges and support. *Global Education Review*, 5(4), 115-135.

Halkic, B. & Arnold, P. (2017). MOOCS for Refugees: Access and Success in Higher Education? ICERI2017 *Proceedings*, 1271-1280. https://library.iated.org/view/HALKIC2017MOO

Halkic, B. & Arnold, P. (2019). Refugees and online education: Student perspectives on need and support in the context of (online) higher education. *Learning, Media and Technology*, 44(3), 345-364. DOI: https://doi.org/10.1080/17439884.2019.1640739

Halkic, B. & Arnold, P. (2019a). Who sets the agenda? Supporting refugees' pathways to higher education. *CIRN Prato Community Informatics Conference 2019 Proceedings*.

Haythornthwaite, C. (1998). A Social Network Study of the Growth of Community among Distance Learners. *Information Research (Online Journal)* 4(1). Retrieved May 1, 2002 from https://informationr.net/ir/4-1/infres41.html

Heublein, U.; Ebert, J.; Hutzsch, C.; Isleib, S.; König, R.; Richter, J.; Woisch, A. (Hg.) (2017): Zwischen Studienerwartungen und Studienwirklichkeit. Ursachen des Studienabbruchs, beruflicher Verbleib der Studienabbrecherinnen und Studienabbrecher und Entwicklung der Studienabbruchquote an deutschen Hochschulen. Hannover: Deutsches Zentrum für Hochschul- und Wissenschaftsforschung (DZHW).

Isphording, I., & Wozny, F. (2018). Ursachen des Studienabbruchs – eine Analyse des Nationalen Bildungspanels (IZA Research Report No. 82). Bonn: IZA.

Kuh, G. D., Kinzie, J., Buckley, J. A., Bridges, B. K., & Hayek, J. C. (2006). What matters to student success: a review of the literature (commissioned report for the national symposium on postsecondary student success: spearheading a dialog on student success). Washington, D.C.: National Postsecondary Education Cooperative.

Lambert, L., von Blumenthal, J. & Beigang, S. (2018). *Flucht und Bildung: Hochschulen*. State-of-Research Papier 8b, Verbundprojekt ‚Flucht: Forschung und Transfer', Osnabrück: Institut für Migrationsforschung und Interkulturelle Studien (IMIS) der Universität Osnabrück / Bonn: Internationales Konversionszentrum Bonn (BICC), April 2018.

Mergner, J.; Ortenburger, A.; Vöttiner, A. (2015). Studienmodelle individueller Geschwindigkeit. Ergebnisse der Wirkungsforschung 2011-2014. Projektbericht. Hg. v. Deutsches Zentrum für Hochschul- und Wissenschaftsforschung (DZHW). Hannover. Online verfügbar unter https://www.dzhw.eu/pdf/21/bericht_wirkungsforschung_2015.pdf, zuletzt geprüft am 19.07.2017.

Morris-Lange, S. (2017). *Allein durch den Hochschuldschungel. Hürden zum Studienerfolg für internationale Studierende und Studierende mit Migrationshintergrund*. Retreived November 25, 2018 from https://www.svr-migration.de/publikationen/hochschuldschungel/

Morrice, L. (2013). Refugees in Higher Education. Boundaries of Belonging and Recognition, Stigma and Exclusion, *International Journal of Lifelong Education*, 32(5), 652-668. DOI: https://doi.org/10.1080/02601370.2012.761288

Moser-Mercer, B. (2014). MOOCs in fragile contexts, *European MOOC Stakeholder Summit 2014*, Université de Genève: n.a.

Naidoo, L. (2015). Educating Refugee-background Students in Australian Schools and Universities, *Intercultural Education*, 26, 210–217.

Neugebauer, M.; Heublein, U.; Daniel, A. (2019): Studienabbruch in Deutschland: Ausmaß, Ursachen, Folgen, Präventionsmöglichkeiten. In: Zeitschrift für Erziehungswissenschaft 22(5), S. 1025–1046. DOI: https://doi.org/10.1007/s11618-019-00904-1.

Paloff, R. & Pratt, K. (1999). Building Learning Communities in Cyberspace. Effective Strategies for the Online Classroom. San Francisco: Jossey-Bass.

Pilcher, A. J. (2017). Virtual learning community: Utilizing learning communities in hybrid and online graduate programs. *Graduate Theses and Dissertations*. 15604. Retrieved November 25, 2018 from https://lib.dr.iastate.edu/etd/15604

Plasterer, R. (2010). Investigating Integration. The Geographies of the WUSC Student Refugee Program at the University of British Columbia, *Refuge: Canada's Journal on Refugees*, 27(1), 59–74.

Putz, P. & Arnold, P. (2001). Communities of Practice: Guidelines for the Design of Online Seminars in Higher Education, *Education, Communication, Information*, 3/2001, 181–195.

Preece, J. (2000). Online communities: designing usability, supporting sociability. Chichester: Wiley.

Reinhardt, F., Zlatkin-Troitschanskaia, O., Deribo, T., Happ, R. & Nell-Müller, S. (2018). Integrating refugees into higher education—the impact of a new online education program for policies and practices. *Policy Reviews in Higher Education, 2*(2), 198–226. doi.org/https://doi.org/10.1080/23322969.2018.1483738

Salmon, G. (2011). E-Moderating – The Key to Teaching and Learning Online, New York: Routledge.

Schreier, M. (2012). *Qualitative Content Analysis in Practice*. London: Sage Publications.

Spady, W.G. (1970). Dropouts from higher education: An interdisciplinary review and synthesis. *Interchange 1*, 64–85. DOI: https://doi.org/10.1007/BF02214313

Streitwieser, B., Brueck, L., Moody, R. & Taylor, M. (2017). The Potential and Reality of New Refugees Entering German Higher Education: The Case of Berlin Institutions, *European Education*, 49, 231–252. DOI: https://doi.org/10.1080/10564934.2017.1344864

Tinto, V. (1975). Dropout from Higher Education: A Theoretical Synthesis of Recent Research, Review of Educational Research, 45(1), 89–125. DOI: https://doi.org/10.3102/00346543045001089.

Unangst L. & Streitwieser B. (2018). Inclusive Practices in Response to the German Refugee Influx: Support Structures and Rationales Described by University Administrators, In A. Curaj, L. Deca, & R. Pricopie (Eds.), *European Higher Education Area: The Impact of Past and Future Policies*, 277–292, Springer Cham. https://doi.org/10.1007/978-3-319-77407-7_18

UNESCO. (2018). *A Lifeline to Learning. Leveraging Technology to Support Education for Refugees*. Paris: UNESCO. https://unesdoc.unesco.org/images/0026/002612/261278e.pdf.

Zlatkin-Troitschanskaia, O., Happ, R., Nell-Müller, S., Deribo, T., Reinhardt, F. & Toepper, M. (2018). Successful Integration of Refugee Students in Higher Education: Insights from Entry Diagnostics in an Online Study Program. *Global Education Review*, 5(4), 158–181.

# Refugee Students in German Higher Education: How Perceptions of *Time* and *Language* Impact on Academic Experiences

Anika Müller-Karabil and Claudia Harsch

## 1 Introduction

The challenges that all international students face when entering unfamiliar academic contexts are well-known, be it with regard to getting accustomed to new academic teaching and learning cultures (e.g. Wu et al. 2015), or be it with regard to mastering academic language demands in a foreign language (e.g. Harsch et al. 2017). This situation also applies to students from refugee backgrounds (SFRB), one subgroup within the group of international students that often gets overlooked and that will be in the focus of this paper. In addition to challenges that all international students may face, refugee students also have to deal with a complex array of pressures arising from issues such as their often unresolved immigration status, their often precarious financial situation, suffered trauma, or the insecure family situation in their home countries (e.g. Grüttner et al. 2018).

One important further challenge for students entering higher education (HE) from "outside" which has been somewhat neglected so far are time-scopes in HE systems, as pointed out in a recent study by Baker et al. (2019). HE is governed by a tight time structure, which is often stamped by an internally contradictory tempo: Research and teaching are operating with increasing time-pressure, while the bureaucratic pacing often imposes long processing times. Baker et al. (ibid.) state that HE time-scopes are often invisible and highly unfamiliar especially to

SFRB. They conclude that "time is a central aspect of this diversity that often gets overlooked" (ibid., p. 4).

In this contribution, we adapt the approach by Baker et al. and examine the perceptions of *time* and its interaction with *language* amongst first-year students from refugee backgrounds in the German academic context. We argue that *time* and *language* are factors that greatly influence the pathways of SFRB into HE and beyond. Already before starting their academic studies, SFRB have to deal with competing tempi: On the one hand, they want to take up or continue with their studies as soon as possible. On the other hand, they first have to invest more time to acquire a new language at a high proficiency level in order to meet the official language requirements of German universities. After having entered HE, SFRB have to get accustomed to unfamiliar academic requirements in a foreign language, which include the aforementioned hidden and often contradictory time structures. In order to investigate the role and interconnection of *time* and *language*, we follow a twofold focus in this paper: On the one hand, we look into the impact time has on students' language learning and academic experiences, as well as their self-perception and personal well-being. On the other hand, we investigate the impact language has on students' perception(s) of time, academic experiences and well-being. We aim to deduce recommendations for students and higher education institutions (HEI) with a view to empowering students to effectively handle different time concepts and perceptions.

## 2     Context

### 2.1    Background of the Study

The study we are reporting here was situated in the north of Germany, within a preparatory language programme for students from refugee backgrounds.[1] Students in our study started the intensive language programme either in April (n = 60) or October 2016 (n = 20). For these students, the language programme ended in summer 2017 with a proficiency test targeting the level C1 of the Common European Framework for Languages (Council of Europe 2001). The language programme comprised intensive classes delivered by the Goethe Institute (15 h

---

[1] The language programme is the key component of the :here studies, a full-time, free of charge programme preparing future students from refugee backgrounds for academic studies in the federal state of Bremen (Higher Education Entrance for Refugees: www.aheadbremen.de/en/here-studies). The language programme within the :here studies is (partly) financed by the Germany Academic Exchange Services' (DAAD) *Integra* programme.

per week) and a tutoring programme focusing on autonomous language learning strategies and language usage in academic contexts delivered by the Languages Centre of the Universities in Bremen (20–30 min per week). In addition, students were expected to study German autonomously for about 8 h per week, using the self-access centre of the Languages Centre that offers a range of workshops and resources.

Out of the 80 participants in this cohort, 52 reached the C1 level and took the C1 language test in July 2017. 47 Students successfully passed the C1 language test, and 33 of these took up academic studies in autumn 2017. The academic year in Germany is organised in two semesters, with the so-called winter semester running from autumn to spring (October–March) and the summer semester covering late spring and summer (April-September).

## 2.2  Students from Refugee Backgrounds in (German) Higher Education

The body of research on refugee students' transitions into and pathways through the Higher Education context has increased in recent years. Most research is conducted in traditional immigration countries like the United States of America, Canada, the United Kingdom, and Australia. Many of these studies focus on experiences of SFRB in schools or pathways into universities; less have investigated the actual journeys of SFRB through their academic career. Generally, qualitative (case) studies are dominant for research on the topic (for summaries of existing research see Berg et al. 2018; Mangan and Winter 2017; Ramsay and Baker 2019). In Germany, researchers only recently started to investigate the pathways of SFRB into and through HE (see Lambert et al. 2018, for an overview). Currently, information is available on the engagement of universities at an institutional level (e.g. Schamann and Younso 2016) or the role of national programmes funding the transition phase, mainly through language courses and counselling (see e.g. Fourier et al. 2018, on the programmes *Integra* and *Welcome*, which are funded by the German Academic Exchange Service (DAAD)). Reports and surveys shed light on numbers and the general situation of SFRB in the academic context (e.g. SVR 2019) and a number of individual research projects and resulting publications investigate aspects such as study preparation, the role of language or individual experiences of inclusion/exclusion in HE.[2] Hence,

---

[2]The project "WeGe" investigates the preparation phase of SFRB for HE (https://wege.dzhw.eu); the project "ErgeS" (University of Bremen, https://www.fb12.uni-bremen.de/interkulturelle-bildung/forschung/erges.html) aims at making experiences of inclusion/exclusion

our insights into the experiences of SFRB in the German HE context are still limited.

Many researchers credit SFRB with high aspiration for HE (Baker et al. 2019; Morrice 2009; Naidoo 2018). At the same time, research shows that they encounter various challenges when actually entering academia (Stevenson and Baker 2018). Language proficiency is acknowledged to be one of them, but its effects have only been partly researched specifically for SFRB in German tertiary education. The role and perceptions of time as experienced by SFRB in HE (Baker et al. 2019) have so far been neglected for the German context. With our contribution, we address this gap by shedding light on experiences of SFRB related to both language and time. We argue that investigating the multiple connections between time and language adds a new perspective to existing research in the field and can foster better understanding of the multifaceted experiences and also challenges of SFRB in academic settings. We focus on the following research questions:

RQ1: What impact does time have on students' language learning, their academic experiences as well as their self-perception?

RQ2: What impact does language have on students' perception of time, their academic experiences as well as their self-perception?

## 3 Methodology

### 3.1 Study Design

This contribution draws on a longitudinal mixed-method project that investigated pathways of students with a refugee background into German Higher Education, supported by the Central Research Fund of the University of Bremen. Within this larger project, we explored the (language learning) experiences of students with refugee backgrounds during a preparatory language programme for academic studies (e.g. Müller-Karabil and Harsch 2019). A small group of students (see above Background section) was further accompanied during their first three academic semesters with the aim of shedding light on linguistic, social and academic experiences and mechanisms during the transition phase from language classes to academic lectures. Figure 1 gives an overview of the overall study design:

---

of SFRB in German HE visible; the aforementioned project at Bremen University (https://www.fremdsprachenzentrum-bremen.de/uploads/media/Projektinfo_01.pdf) investigates experiences of SFRB in their first semesters at HEI in Germany, with a focus on the role of language and linguistic preparation (e.g. Müller-Karabil and Harsch 2019).

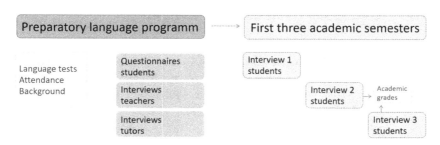

**Fig. 1** Overall study design

For the current contribution, we draw on the interviews conducted with the students during their first three academic semesters.

## 3.2 Instruments and Participants

Data were collected via a series of interviews at three points (first, second and third semester). All 33 students who passed the language programme in summer 2017 and took up academic studies in autumn 2017 were invited; participation was voluntary. In total, 21 students participated in 49 interviews; within the study reported here, we will concentrate on a data set from 14 participants who took part in at least two of the three interviews, with one of them being the last one. We analysed a total of 39 interviews. All participants come from countries of the Middle East, mainly Syria (n = 13) and most are male (n = 13). The median age of the group members is 24 (min. = 22, max. = 39). Participants are enrolled at four different universities in the north of Germany and study in three different academic clusters: Engineering (n = 7), Natural sciences (n = 4), Humanities (n = 3).

The interviews were conducted in a semi-structured way, audio-recorded and transcribed verbatim. Since the investigation of *time* was not within the scope of the original study, (individual) concepts, frames and experiences of time and their social meanings were not explicitly asked for or brought up as a topic as such in the interviews. Interestingly, the concept of time and its intertwinedness with language emerged to such a degree that we consider it worth analysing here.

## 3.3 Conceptual Frame and Data Analysis

The interviews were analysed inductively and deductively, following Kuckartz's (2018) approach to qualitative content analysis. For the deductive analysis, we adapted the analytic approach used by Baker et al. (2019), who selected the first three categories from the social time-typology suggested by Liao et al. (2013) for their study and adapted them the following way:

- *Compressed time*: perception of urgency arising from issues related to meeting deadlines and managing studies alongside the competing demands of students' time; also cultural practices and understandings of time;
- *Time as a goal*: referring to a person manipulating time, trying to gain back control over time, e.g. by taking several courses at the same time;
- *Wasted time*: perception of time not being used productively, for reasons outside one's control.

We initially used these three themes as deductive codes. Given that the role of language was one of the main project foci, we complemented them by two further codes, which we developed inductively and which are related to the interaction between time and language. After the first round of coding, we adapted the code definitions to account inductively for our interview data. Since the two codes regarding language and time turned out to comprehensively cover the data on a more general level, they were defined as umbrella themes. Table 1 summarizes our coding scheme.

For our final analysis, we considered all coded interview segments that proved to be related to both language and time. Consequently, all segments that were coded with our two umbrella themes were included. Codings regarding the three subthemes were only considered if coinciding locally—and thus also with regard to content—with segments coded for the two umbrella themes. By following this approach, we reduced the original amount of codings from 1462 instances in 39 documents to 469 instances in 39 documents and ensured a clear focus on the research questions.

Half of the interviews were double-coded by both authors with the finalised coding scheme. All discrepancies were resolved in discussion. The remaining interviews were single-coded. Both authors collaboratively conducted the analysis of the coded data and the interpretation.

It is important to stress that our work was guided by the principles of thematical content analysis only. We did not pursue a typology-constructing approach

**Table 1** Coding Scheme

| Code | Definition |
| --- | --- |
| Language impacting on time *(umbrella theme)* | External (language demands) and internal (proficiency, personality) perspective:<br>– impact of studying in a L2[a] on timing in academic studies, e.g. advancing slower than L1 peers, additional time pressure due to higher preparation time<br>– impact of (low) L2 proficiency on time pressure (including anxiety, lack of interaction with peers) |
| Time impacting on language *(umbrella theme)* | External time constraints and internal time management impacting on one's language proficiency/learning pathways<br>– increase of language proficiency over time (taking away pressure, facilitating social contacts)<br>– time pressure or time management impacting (negatively/positively) on language learning (and interaction with peers) |
| Time constraints | Cultural, contextual and institutional constraints (external constraints, based on "compressed time" in the typology proposed by Baker et al. (2019)):<br>– study pressure<br>– work pressure, family pressure, money pressure, etc.<br>– cultural differences that are impacting on time/timing |
| Time management | Internal perspective (individual perception and management of time, individual reactions to time pressures and demands, based on "time as a goal" in the typology suggested by Baker et al. (2019))<br>– management/organising studies<br>– personal aims (on a timeline)<br>– personal work ethics<br>– personal phases of rest, amusement, hobbies, etc.<br>– comparison of personal "time budget/expenditure of time" to L1 students<br>– investing time in social relations/contacts |
| Wasted time | Perception of time not being used productively for reasons outside one's control (based on Baker et al. (2019))<br>– situations, were the feeling of "wasted/wasting time" is described<br>– also instances of activities/situations that are considered the opposite, i.e. not a waste of time, but well invested time |

[a]Languages that are acquired after the first language (L1) are usually termed as second languages (L2) (Hammarberg, 2001). In this paper, we will therefore refer to German as (one of) the participants' L2. All students who grew up in Germany and learned German as a first or very early second language will be referred to as "L1 peers", even if they have different family and linguistic backgrounds

and consequently did not comprise of the stages which usually guide such approaches, e.g. the development of relevant dimensions of analysis, the creation of an attribute space, the grouping of the cases and the characterisation of the developed types (see Kluge 2000). The two prototypes suggested in Sect. 4.2.3 are therefore not the result of a full-blown typology-construction process, but rather a helping tool to present the results of this chapter in a comprehensible way.

## 3.4 Limitations

First, our sample is limited to mainly male participants from the Middle East studying in the north of Germany. Hence, the results will not be generalizable, but rather provide first insights which have to be carefully interpreted. In addition, only a very small number of the participants have to provide for a family or family members, which could particularly influence the perceptions of time constraints and time management. Furthermore, as mentioned in Sect. 3.3, we only included subtheme codings coinciding with the umbrella themes in our analysis. At the same time, the high amount of single codings for the subthemes *time constraints*, *time management* and *wasted time* clearly point out that these time concepts play a crucial role also beyond the language focus. They relate in many ways to other topics within the participants' personal and academic situations, such as their immigration status, financial and family situation, personal health, study subject or study success (in terms of academic grades). While all these aspects are surely worthwhile analysing to further complement the picture of SFRB's academic experiences and to help establishing more profound typologies, their consideration proved beyond the scope and the main goal of the present paper and is to be dealt with in future research.

## 4 Results

When our participants, i.e. the graduates of the preparatory language programme start their academic studies, a vast majority is dealing with two dominant experiences: the (constant) feeling of 1) insufficient language proficiency and 2) time pressure. In many instances, these two experiences seem to be intertwined. Participants often relate the feeling of having (too) little time to manage and master academic studies to their L2-identity, hence attributing the perceived time pressure at least partly to their (insufficient) language proficiency. At the same time, many participants relate the encountered linguistic challenges to issues of time and timing.

We will introduce our results by starting with our two umbrella themes: 1) the *impact of language on (perceptions of) time* and 2) the *(perceived) impact of time on language*. The additional subthemes—*time constraints, time management* and *wasted time*—are then integrated and discussed under the respective umbrella themes.

## 4.1  The Impact of Language on (Perceptions of) Time

The factor language plays an important role in the "time budget" of all interviewed SFRB. They almost unanimously mention that many study-related activities are not only difficult to perform due to linguistic struggles, but also take longer due to studying in an L2. Consequently, the subtheme of *time constraints* is of great relevance for this umbrella theme. Additionally, the data show that the individual reaction to this challenging situation and the employed strategies to dealing with time pressure due to low language proficiency can have an impact on individual self-perception and corresponding (time) management strategies. Consequently, the subtheme *time management* also connects to this umbrella theme.

## 4.2  Increased Time Effort due to (Low) Language Proficiency

On a general level, many students indicate that acting within a new academic environment in a new language imposes excessive demands and leaves them overwhelmed, especially in the first two semesters (008_1[3]; 020_1; 026_1_2; 028_1; 029_1; 031_1; 048_2). They stress that coping with their academic studies requires great time investments (e.g. preparing and wrapping-up lectures and seminars at home), and mainly attribute them to low language proficiency. For instance, reading texts is considered extremely costly in terms of time by many, partly because students feel the need to engage in time-consuming translating activities while reading, not only, but especially when beginning their studies (008_1; 013_1_2; 016_1_2; 020_2; 026_2; 031_1; 043_2; 048_1; 051_1):

---

[3] The first three numbers represent the participants' project ID in the study, the number(s) after the underline character provide(s) information on the interview, e.g. "_1" stands for interview 1, "_3" for interview 3. "008_1" consequently refers to participant 8's statements in interview 1.

> If I have to read something, I need to, what's it called? I need to search for these words. What does this mean, and not only the words, but also within the sentence. In the text. Mh, yes. And this takes time. You need to be patient (048_3).[4]

During exams, a slow reading pace, e.g. of instructions, can increase time pressure and even impact on grades (031_2; 038_2_3). In addition, many report the need to re-read and revise lectures at home, since they feel not capable of processing content and language simultaneously. Some say that they just cannot keep up concentration long enough, since following lectures in the L2 consumes too much energy (008_1; 043_2). Others report on losing track of the talk due to the lecturer's way of speaking (rate, dialect or low voice; 020_1; 026_1; 028_2; 031_1; 043_3; 040_3; 051_1) or unfamiliar terminology and new content (020_1; 016_1_2; 023_2; 038_1_3; 043_2). The importance of making scripts of lectures available is stressed:

> If you do not understand one specific term, (…) then you get lost right away (in a lecture situation, ed. note) and I hated this. In the first semester, I always had to work through the script afterwards, and this was exhausting (038_3).

Many of the interviewed SFRB refrain from note-taking, most of them simply because they feel that they cannot engage in listening, processing and writing at the same time (008_3; 013_1; 016_1; 026_2; 040_1; 048_2; 051_1_3). Preparing presentations and writing assignments is assumed to take long(er) (023_3; 028_3; 029_2; 048_2; 23_3; 028_3; 029_2; 031_2; 051_3). However, in these cases language issues seem to be mixed with other aspects, such as unknown genres and conventions in writing (e.g. a "protocol"), or personal factors like being nervous during presentations.

### 4.3 Self-perception and the Role of L1 Peers

While long working hours and feelings of stress and time pressure are not unusual also with traditional students, many of the SFRB experience their L2 as an extra burden that increases regular time pressure. The comparison with L1 peers is explicitly drawn by many SFRB: Some find it reassuring that L1 peers deal with similar challenges (013_2; 016_2; 020_1; 028_1); others, however, feel disadvantaged and stress that they have to invest more time to reach the same goals (008_1_3; 013_1; 026_2; 028_2; 031_2; 051_3):

---

[4] All the interviews were conducted in German. The quotes were translated by the authors.

(…) I try to study a lot. Because I need more time to study compared to the others. That is a fact, yes (051_3).

This awareness can create or reinforce feelings of inferiority or frustration and leaves some of the student with the impression that the additional language burden makes it difficult for them to catch up no matter how hard they try (008_1_3; 013_2; 026_1_2_3; 028_2; 029_2; 048_2_3).

The role of language, its impact on time or timing and the comparison with L1 peers also plays a role in situations where SFRB need to react quickly and spontaneously, i.e. in group discussions or (study-related) talks with peers. In such situations, many of our participants feel that their perceived lower language proficiency disadvantages them. This relates not only to the speech of peers, which is considered (too) fast and often unfamiliar, i.e. colloquial, and thus inhibits understanding (013_2; 031_2; 048_2). Many SFRB also feel that they cannot share knowledge and thoughts since they are too slow in composing answers or statements (023_3; 038_1; 048_1_3; 051_1). Interestingly, some attribute this to a personal (obstructive) focus on linguistic correctness (013_1; 020_1; 029_1; 048_1). Additionally, a perceived lack of patience of L1 counterparts can increase pressure and lead to silence (013_2; 020_1; 051_1). Accordingly, many participants express a reluctance or even fear to speak in lecturers, seminars, or group-work situations, mainly at the beginning of their studies. Some students also report worries that their "deficient" language proficiency will lead others to consider them as deficient students in general (008_1_3; 013_1; 016_1; 028_3; 040_2; 043_2; 048_1):

But I cannot continue asking questions, so that it's not/so that the others don't find it funny when I make mistakes (laughs) (048_1).

With regard to establishing social contacts with their L1 peers, many SFRB experience challenges, especially in the first semester. Some attribute these challenges to language. Ohers, however, hold a range of different factors responsible for this situation, amongst them linguistic and cultural factors, pressure and competition or a perceived general disinterest on behalf of L1 students to become engaged, presumably since they already have existing networks (013_1_2; 020_1_2; 028_1_2; 043_2; 048_1; 051_2). At the same time is support by L1 peers—if existent—highly appreciated and considered as time-saving:

Yes. You always study, but if I do it on my own, it takes long. But if the others tell me [how to do it, ed. note], it's easier (031_3).

As a consequence of limited contacts, many of the interviewed SFRB feel alone, alienated and unsupported by their L1 peers, mainly in the first semester. After having unsuccessfully tried to establish contacts, some participants even consider it a *waste of time* to spend further effort on connecting with fellow L1 peers:

> In the first two semesters, I tried to find a friend, because this helps so much. But I realised that the Germans are very nice, (…) but they do not want to be your friend (008_3).

It is noteworthy that many of the interviewed SFRB stress that it feels easier for them to establish contacts with L1 peers who have a migration background themselves or with other international students (008_3; 020_2; 031_2; 051_3).

## 4.4 Additional Time Pressure Due To Language: Effects and Reactions

In sum, our data show that many of the SFBR we interviewed experience how insufficient language proficiency increases their time pressure and affects their schedules in many ways; some explicitly express that they are losing time in their academic pathway because of language issues:

> Because (…) also my language is not so good and I have lost a lot of time in my studies due to this, and, yes (020_3).

This delay concerns some of our participants, particularly since they feel that they have lost enough (life) time already; many refer to themselves as "old" compared to peers (008_1; 013_2; 026_2; 029_1; 038_2; 043_2). A consistent feeling of compressed time, language struggles and low peer support can, for some students, lead to phases of decreasing motivation, high frustration and a fear of failure (013_1; 026_2_3; 028_1; 029_1_2; 048_2). These students struggle to employ personal coping and (time) management strategies, which—amongst other factors—leaves them dissatisfied and possibly affects negatively on their self-esteem. This cycle is depicted in Fig. 2:

While this picture may seem rather gloomy, our data also do show that many students over time develop successful coping strategies and gain new perceptions. A number of the participants succeed in shifting their attention to empowering aspects, amongst them the perception of growing language proficiency over time. This goes hand in hand with (or supports) the incorporation of pro-active self-

**Fig. 2** Language impacting on time

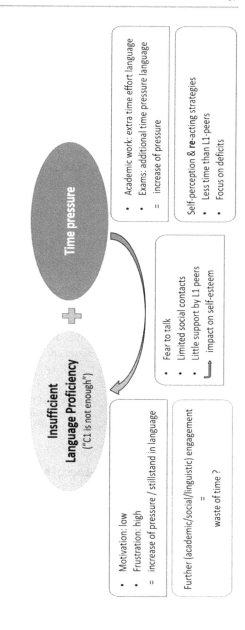

and time management strategies. These aspects, under the umbrella theme *time impacting on language,* will be described next.

## 4.5 The (Perceived) Impact of Time on Language

The theme *time impacting on language* is twofold. One major aspect concerns the linguistic changes over time (i.e., three semesters) and according to our data coincides with the subtheme *time management.* A second aspect deals with a generally perceived lack of time throughout academic life which can impact negatively on language learning as well as on meaningful interaction with peers. This aspect is closely related with the subtheme *time constraints.*

Language proficiency is dynamic and its development is influenced by many factors, e.g. personal motivation, the amount of active learning, exposure to or meaningful interaction within the target language. Our participants started their academic studies after having passed a C1 test, i.e. after having mastered the official linguistic entrance requirement for German HE. The term "entrance" makes it very clear that continuation of language learning is both expected and understood as a prerequisite to master the academic pathway successfully. Nevertheless, nearly all our participants seem surprised by this fact: They expected to "be done with" their language learning after the long preparation programme and only gradually come to realize that their academic language learning journey has only just begun (008_1; 016_2; 031_1; 028_1):

> We have passed C1, okay, and now start our academic studies. This is real C1. This [the language classes, ed. note] was a game. Really, a game or a joke. And now the real language and the real studies start (016_2).

## 4.6 Time Pressure (and other Factors) Inhibiting Language Learning

Our data show that none of the interviewees participate in further language classes after having taken up academic studies—a situation inconsistent with the fact that all of them experience linguistic struggles and a certain level of stress connected to this. Many attribute this non-participation to time pressure: they feel that they have to deal with so many new things to meet the academic requirements that there is no time to actively take language classes (008_1_3; 020_1_2; 031_1; 038_1_2;

043_3). Others feel that they have concentrated for long enough on learning German; despite experiencing language challenges, they report on low motivation to continue their language education and would like to use their time for other private or study-related activities (029_2_3; 040_3; 043_3). In addition, many consider their academic studies and their constant exposure to German a legitimate substitute for actual language classes (008_1; 028_1_2; 029_1; 051_1). Besides, time pressure also indirectly impacts negatively on language development: Many SFRB report that their full schedule leads to decreasing time invested in (establishing) social contacts with L1 speakers, which, in turn, leads to a lack of meaningful interaction, and thus to a lower degree in linguistic automatization (008_1_3; 040_1; 051_1_3).

## 4.7 Language Development Over Time

Considering their linguistic coping, most participants, after an initial shock in semester 1, do report on perceived improvements over time. Such improvements may not take place equally in all skills, and also not necessarily on a linear line, but many share the experience of a certain degree of automatization. Many students feel that following lectures becomes easier (016_2; 020_3; 026_2; 028_2; 038_3, 040_2_3) or report on their reading speed increasing (016_2; 023_2; 029_2; 043_3; 048_3; 051_3). Others still read papers in English even in semester 3 if they need to do it quickly or if they want to understand everything (029_3; 040_3). Some interviewees see their spontaneous speaking improving (020_2; 023_2; 026_2; 038_3; 040_2; 043_3). Enhancements in writing quality, however, are hardly mentioned. Some report improvements in understanding of specific terminology, which supposedly impacts positively on reading and listening performances (023_3; 026_3; 031_2; 038_3). When asked about their satisfaction with the development of their language proficiency, several of the participants seem to have a somehow positive tendency during the second and third semester; most of them, however, add limitations:

> Good question. (…) Rather yes. I am satisfied ok, but not that much. I could also do a lot better (026_3).

Some also accept that their learning process is ongoing and will be for some more time:

> Every day we learn something new. Every day we learn something new. Endless this language (031_3).

## 4.8 (Time) Management and Personal Approach

The above quotes indicate that the perception of linguistic development is twofold and that language—despite a general increase—remains a topic. So do external time constraints. What changes, at least for some of the interviewees at some points, is the personal evaluation of their situation and their coping strategies, especially related to time and language challenges. The subtheme *time management* (next to other factors) reflects this personal approach and, as mentioned at the end of Sect. 4.1, the data display two distinctively different ways of reacting to the aforementioned pressures.

Some students succeed in employing pro-active management strategies and seem to be changing their mind-set in various ways, especially towards the second and within the third semester. They have developed their own management strategies and learning styles fitting the new system (020_3; 023_3; 043_3; 051_3); they remind themselves, or let them be reminded by others, of recent achievements (in general and in terms of language learning) and try to shift their focus on positive things in order to move ahead with their studies (020_3; 016_2; 026_2; 028_3; 029_2). Some integrate the thought that language needs time and that it might take them longer to graduate, also due to language (031_3; 028_3; 040_3; 051_3):

> Well yes / well, it is a crisis for me that my studies will take longer than 3 years. But I slowly come to accept this fact (040_3).

This attitude often is related to the strong wish to finish one's studies, in combination with a clear plan for the future (work, doing a Master's degree; 023_3; 040_3; 043_3). Many also report to concentrate less on language in general or linguistic correctness specifically; this often goes hand in hand with a general rise in self-esteem (016_3; 028_3; 043_3) or growing contacts and activities (023_3; 026_3; 028_3; 029_2_3; 031_2; 038_3):

> (…) but in the second term the situation changed. I met a lot of people, and they invited me over and I invited them over and things like this (023_3).

Others, particularly but not only at the beginning of their studies, experience a lot of frustration due to the overwhelming demands of academic life and their lacking language skills. The recurring theme of "not understanding" relates to the feeling of *wasting time*, not settling in or of starting over and over again (008_3; 026_3; 029_2_3):

> I have been here for 3 years now, 3 years, and I go to University and I hear a lot of German and I also have groups at university, friends and stuff. We always talk German to each other. And they always try to teach me how to speak in a colloquial way (laughs). But still, it's difficult. (…). Always like a, I have a new start. Like, I actually always lose, and then I start again from scratch (029_2).

Some struggle to get used to the new learning system (031_2; 048_3; 051_1_3), are upset for not being able to display their real abilities due to language (008_3; 013_2; 029_2; 048_2) or are generally tired of being expected to adapting themselves (013_2; 031_2):

> Yes, but for me, since I also have a lot of [working, ed. note] experience, a lot, I was always expected to fit in, fit in, fit in, fit in. Then I maybe do not have, well, the will is not as strong as before (013_2).

In short, some participants at times feel not empowered or capable of coping, which, in turn, leads to low motivation, frustration and higher (time) pressure. Fig. 3 displays the two seemingly opposing approaches to coping with pressure:

We consider these two approaches as prototypes at opposite ends of a continuum. Even if these prototypes are not the result of a systematic typology-constructing analytical approach (see e.g. Kelle and Kluge 1999; Kuckartz 2018), they clearly emerged from the date and help to structure approaches and strategies employed by the participants. The two types share blurry boundaries, and most of the participants change their type of approach or certain features of it over the course of the interviews, some even switch within the same interview. Such changes can be explained by further factors, which go beyond the scope of this paper, such as personal study situation (learning preferences, work ethics, study subject, grades), financial resources, additional responsibilities (family, work), leisure activities or general well-being. However, these two types do point towards possible ways in which SFRB deal with and react to pressure and challenges. Thus, our schematic Fig. 3 can help formulate recommendations for supporting and enabling SFRB to develop confidence and coping mechanisms, in order to navigate the academic context self-assured and autonomously—under time pressure and in a L2.

**Fig. 3** (Time) management approaches

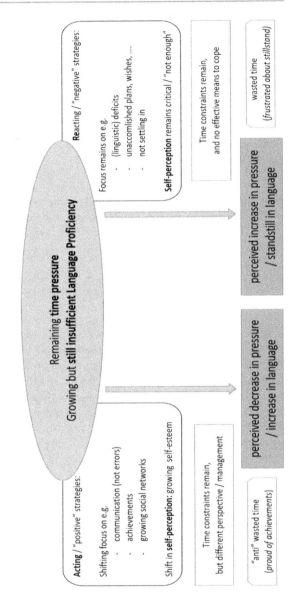

## 5 Discussion and Recommendations

First, our results show that the two themes *time* and *language* impact on the academic pathways of SFRB, both independently and in combination. On the one hand, SFRB who take up academic studies in the German HE context experience additional time pressure in many situations due to their (low) L2 proficiency. On the other hand, the feeling of general time pressure inhibits further engagement in continuing targeted language learning, despite the fact that all participants report struggles with the academic L2. Based on our findings, and in line with existing suggestions in the literature for international students (e.g. SVR 2017), we recommend including language classes into regular curricula and adjusting the workload accordingly for all students who study in a L2. This would ensure that these students participate in study-oriented L2 classes without having to invest extra time. We assume that this, in the long run, can enhance study results and foster feelings of belonging.

Secondly, our data point towards the fact that the *language-time-scope* can affect other areas of SFRB's study situation, e.g. their social networks. Perceived time pressure inhibits not only language learning, but it also limits leisure time and social contacts. At the same time, L1 peers are not perceived as very social and encouraging counterparts by SFRB. These realities, in turn, can lead to feelings of social isolation, less exposure to conversation and, hence, potentially less linguistic development. Additionally, personal and study-related interactions are lacking automatism due to limited exposure to meaningful interaction with L1 peers, and thus stress and time pressure in conversations with peers remain. As a conclusion, it seems reasonable that universities take additional measures to encourage L1 students and staff to fill the widely announced "welcoming culture" with more life. Buddy or mentoring programmes are helpful, but should ideally be expanded and supplemented with events and activities that bring together the differing personal, cultural and study-related realities within a diverse student body.

Furthermore, we conclude from our findings that personal perceptions of *language* and *time* play an important role in developing appropriate coping strategies. At the same time, our longitudinal approach made visible that personal perceptions of language development and time constraints are dynamic and subject to both internally and externally stimulated change over time. In conclusion, this means that universities and their members can foster such positive coping mechanisms and strategies by providing a supporting infrastructure for this endeavour. On an institutional level, it could be beneficial to provide more systematic counselling for SFRB, at least at the beginning of their studies. Such support structures could include topics like the choice or change of study subjects, or transparent information on exam accommodation procedures in terms of language. Another important feature is transparency concerning academic expectations in general and also in terms of time investment, management strategies and cultural aspects. On a more personal level, it seems to be important that peers and lecturers support active empowerment, also through acknowledging the achievements and past academic careers of SFRB instead of focusing on their deficits. Here, support could be also provided for L1 students and lecturers, e.g. by mentoring them on SFRB's, or, more generally, international students' needs, perceptions and challenges. As a result, L1 students and staff could engage deeper in further opening the way for true a internationalisation of (German) HE.

Despite the aforementioned limitations of our explorative study, our findings yield important insights into how SFRB could be supported in their transition into HE both on an institutional and on a personal level. We hope that by networking with colleagues in Germany and beyond, we will be able to share best-practice examples of such support endeavours.

**Acknowledgements** We would like to thank all our participants, who took the time and had the courage and confidence to share their experiences with us. We learned so much from you and wish that you all may reach the goals that you have set for yourselves.

## References

Baker, S., Irwin, E. & Freeman, H. (2019). Wasted, manipulated and compressed time. Adult refugee students' experiences of transitioning into Australian higher education. *Journal of Further and Higher Education* 7(1), 1–14.

Berg, J., Grüttner, M. & Schröder, S. (2018). Zwischen Befähigung und Stigmatisierung? Die Situation von Geflüchteten beim Hochschulzugang und im Studium: ein internationaler Forschungsblick. *Z'Flucht: Zeitschrift für Flüchtlingsforschung: the German journal for refugee studies* 2(1), 57–90.

Council of Europe (2001). *Common European Framework of Reference for Languages: Learning, teaching, assessment.* Cambridge, UK: Cambridge University Press.

Fourier, K., Kracht Araújo, J., Latsch, K., Siemens, A., Schmitz, M. & Grüttner, M. (2018): *Integration of refugees at German institutions of higher education.* Report on the higher education programmes for refugees. Bonn: DAAD

Grüttner, M., Schröder, S., Berg, J. & Otto, C. (2018). Die Situation von Geflüchteten auf dem Weg ins Studium. Erste Einsichten aus dem Projekt WeGe. *DZHW-Brief* 5, Hannover: DZHW.

Harsch, C., Ushioda, E., & Ladroue, C. (2017). *Investigating the predictive validity of TOEFL iBT scores and their use in informing policy in a U.K. university setting* (TOEFL iBT

Research Report TOEFL iBT – 30, ETS Research Report RR – 17–41). Princeton, NJ: Educational Testing Service.

Hammarberg, B. (2001). Roles of L1 and L2 in L3 production and acquisition. In J. Cenoz, B. Hufeisen, & U. Jessner (Ed.): *Cross-Linguistic Influence in Third Language Acquisition. Psycholinguistic Perspectives.* Clevedon et al.: Multilingual Matters, 21–41.

Kelle, U. & Kluge, S. (1999). *Vom Einzelfall zum Typus. Fallvergleich und Fallkontrastierung in der qualitativen Sozialforschung.* Opladen: Leske + Budrich

Kluge, S. (2000). Empirically Grounded Construction of Types and Typologies in *Qualitative Social Research. Forum Qualitative Sozialforschung / Forum: Qualitative Social Research,* 1 (1). Retrieved from: https://www.qualitative-research.net/index.php/fqs/article/view/1124/2499

Kuckartz, U. (2018). *Qualitative Inhaltsanalyse. Methoden, Praxis, Computerunterstützung.* Weinheim: Beltz Juventa.

Lambert, L., Blumenthal, J. von & Beigang, S. (2018). *Flucht und Bildung: Hochschulen* (State-of-Research-Papier 8b). Retrieved from: https://flucht-forschung-transfer.de/wp-content/uploads/2018/04/SoR-08-HS-04-2018.pdf

Liao, T. F., Beckman, J., Marzolph, E., Riederer, C., Sayler, J., & Schmelkin, L. (2013). The social definition of time for university students. *Time & Society* 22 (1), 119–151.

Mangan, D. & Winter, L. A. (2017). (In)Validation and (Mis)regonition in Higher Education: The Experience of Students from Refugee Backgrounds. *International Journal of Lifelong Education* 36(4), 486–502.

Morrice, L. (2009). Journeys into higher education. The case of refugees in the UK. *Teaching in Higher Education* 14(6), 661–672.

Müller-Karabil, A. & Harsch, C. (2019). Sprachlernwege geflüchteter Menschen im Vorbereitungsstudium. *Fremdsprachen und Hochschule 94*, Themenschwerpunkt Deutsch und andere Sprachen für Geflüchtete, 31–61.

Naidoo, L., Wilkinson, J., Adoniou, M. & Langat, K. (2018). *Refugee Background Students Transitioning Into Higher Education. Navigating Complex Spaces.* Singapore: Springer Singapore.

Ramsay, G., & Baker, S. (2019). Higher Education and Students from Refugee Backgrounds. A Meta-Scoping Study. *Refugee Survey Quarterly* 38(1), 55–82.

Schammann, H., & Younso, C. (2016). *Studium nach der Flucht? Angebote deutscher Hochschulen für Studieninteressierte mit Fluchterfahrung.* Hildesheim: Universitätsverlag Hildesheim.

Stevenson, J., & Baker, S. (2018). *Refugees in higher education. Debate, discourse and practice.* First edition. Bingley, UK: Emerald Publishing (Great debates in higher education).

Sachverständigenrat deutscher Stiftungen für Integration und Migration (SVR) (2017). *Allein durch den Hochschuldschungel. Hürden zum Studienerfolg für internationale Studierende und Studierende mit Migrationshintergrund.* Studie des SVR-Forschungsbereichs 2017-2. Berlin: SVR.

Sachverständigenrat deutscher Stiftungen für Integration und Migration (SVR) (2019). *Bewegte Zeiten: Rückblick auf die Integrations- und Migrationspolitik der letzten Jahre.* Jahresgutachten 2019. Berlin: SVR.

Wu, H., Garza, E., & Guzman, N. (2015): International Student's Challenge and Adjustment to College. *Education Research Internationa* (20), 1–9.

# From Refugee Programmes to a Benefit for All: The Extension of University Study Preparation Programmes to Other Target Groups in Germany

Steffen Beigang

## 1 Introduction

In the summer of migration in 2015, many people in Germany supported the newly arriving refugees, and this commitment included the universities. Many members of the universities, students as well as staff, volunteered: They offered German courses, organised opportunities to get to know the university and the local environment and thus offered the refugees meaningful activity (Schammann and Younso 2016, pp. 20–23).

After this short phase of this mainly unorganised and non-targeted support, a second phase began, which was characterised by the institutionalisation of the activities. Instead of focusing on all refugees, the universities now focused more and more on their core task: Academic training. The new target group were refugees who had already studied or had a university entrance qualification and had good prospects of staying in Germany (Schammann and Younso 2016, pp. 26–28). This also changed the nature of the activities: Many universities introduced study preparation programmes designed to offer refugees orientation in the German higher education system. In addition, German language courses were offered that bridged the gap between the B1 language level as taught in integration courses and the B2/C1 level which is required for studying (Schammann and Younso 2017a, p. 12). The study preparation programmes also offer intercultural training and provide subject-specific knowledge (Blumenthal et al. 2017; Schammann and

S. Beigang (✉)
Deutsches Zentrum für Integrations- und Migrationsforschung (DeZIM-Institut), Berlin, Germany
E-Mail: beigang@dezim-institut.de

© The Author(s), under exclusive license to Springer Fachmedien Wiesbaden GmbH, part of Springer Nature 2021
J. Berg et al. (eds.), *Refugees in Higher Education*, Higher Education Research and Science Studies, https://doi.org/10.1007/978-3-658-33338-6_5

Younso 2016, pp. 23–25). In addition, most universities set up coordination offices for their activities for refugees (Blumenthal et al. 2017, pp. 20–23). This commitment was supported by programmes at the state level (Steinhardt and Eckhardt 2017, p. 33) and, in particular, by the Federal Ministry of Education and Research (BMBF) providing 100 million euros for the period from 2015 to 2019.

After the intensive commitment of students and university staff, the extensive efforts of the universities and the enormous financial investment, the question arises, what remains of those efforts? Apart from the important support for refugees that has been given so far, is there a sustainable effect of opening the universities that goes beyond the group of refugees? Was the enormous commitment of the universities only a short-term reaction to a social challenge, or did it set in motion mechanisms that will change the universities in the long term? In view of the positive effects that the study preparation programmes have for refugees, it would seem reasonable to extend them to other groups. This is because international students and non-traditional students often have greater problems starting their studies, which could be countered by such programmes.

In this paper, the institutional factors that made learning possible—in the sense of transferring the experiences made with refugees to other target groups—will be explored in order to address these questions. For this reason, three university organisations have been selected which, in addition to study preparation courses, offer similar courses for other groups of students. The results show that the transfer to other international students is particularly obvious, but that possible learning effects go far beyond this.

## 2   Change as the Counterpart of Institutional Stability

At the same time, a theoretical argument will be made: If "institutional reproduction and change are flip sides of the same coin" (Campbell 2009, p. 108), then the explanations for both phenomena must also be in a consistent relationship. In other words, change should be explained by overcoming the factors that generate stability. Based on the assumption that institutions are always faced with different requirements that are not fully compatible with each other, it can be assumed that they are always under pressure to adapt and change.

In order to analyse this, the reproductive mechanisms must be conceptualised appropriately. Mahoney (2000) elaborates in his path-dependency model four different reproduction mechanisms, each of which has different implications (Mahoney 2000, pp. 517–525). They can be used for this purpose:

- *Utilitarian reproduction* is characterized by the fact that the costs of institutional change exceed those of maintaining the institution. The maintenance of the institution can thus be understood as the result of rational consideration of the actors (Mahoney 2000, pp. 517–519).
- *Functional reproduction* considers the integration of an institution into an overall system. The preservation of the institution is important because other institutions of the overall system depend on it (Mahoney 2000, pp. 519–521).
- *Legitimation-based reproduction* of an institution is possible when "actors believe it is morally just or appropriate" (Mahoney 2000, p. 517). This is the normative assumption that the institution is indeed 'good' and therefore the actors reproduce it (Mahoney 2000, pp. 523–525).
- *Power-based reproduction* occurs because a group with power supports the institution (Mahoney 2000, pp. 521–523).

In contrast to Mahoney, here the mechanisms are considered not only as reproductive mechanisms for path dependencies, but as fundamental mechanisms of change and stability. In addition to their reproductive effect on the institutions, three other functions are imaginable. Contrary to reproduction, they can make change necessary and be causally responsible for it if they occur in the opposite form to the existing institution, i.e. if only a different institutional form satisfies the utilitarian, functional, legitimatory or power-oriented demands. In these two extremes, the maintenance or change of the institution can be explained almost deterministically by the mechanisms. But these mechanisms can also create opportunities in which change becomes possible but does not necessarily occur. This can happen a) when existing reproductive mechanisms become less important and therefore can no longer fully protect the institution from change, or b) when demands for change become more important but cannot yet force change. In these cases, further institutional development is contingent.

Whereas in Mahoney's work these reproductive mechanisms are regarded as discrete explanatory patterns, here their combined effect will be considered (similar Edelstein and Nikolai 2013). In principle, each of them can contribute to the stabilization of the institution. The difficult question, however, is at which point the reproductive mechanisms will have eroded to such an extent that they can no longer protect the institution from the pressure to change. This question arises on two levels: 1) For each reproductive mechanism its individual effectiveness must be examined. This is a spectrum that cannot be reduced to "effective" or "ineffective". 2) If at least some reproductive mechanisms are no longer fully effective, the question arises whether they all contribute equally to institutional reproduction. This is not the case: If institutional change is understood as an actively brought about decision on the structure of the institution, then the power to decide is central. In a similar way, decision-making power in the form of veto power is just as essential to be able to stop institutional change. In fact, organisations can also be sufficiently complex that the decision-making power rests with different actors, each of whom can cause changes either individually or collectively. Although subordinate actors do not have the possibility to change the existing institutional regulatory systems, they can add their own institutions—unless higher authorities intervene—which in turn change the way the established institutions operate. Such forms of institutional change are discussed under the term layering (Mahoney and Thelen 2010; Streeck and Thelen 2005).

For the evaluation of the reproductive mechanisms the perspective of the actors with decision-making power must be adopted. This means that even if existing institutions are not functional, legitimate or utilitarian from the perspective of actors without decision-making power, this does not mean that there is direct pressure to adapt. This pressure must first be communicated to the actors with decision-making power. As strategically acting actors, they can also decide to make concessions at certain points, i.e. to allow or prevent institutional change, even though the nature of the reproductive mechanisms does not require this from their point of view.

To understand why these reproductive mechanisms are so important, it is necessary to focus on the view of the human being behind the approach. In historical neo-institutionalism, the actors—insofar as they are addressed—are granted a rationality that is, however, also limited (John 2012, p. 55; Peters 2012, pp. 70–89). This can best be grasped with the concept of bounded rationality, as it is used, for example, in the Multiple Streams Framework. It is characterised by the fact that the actors have the ability to find solutions but that it is limited by temporal, economic and cognitive resources. They are therefore mostly reactive to societal challenges, have to rely on heuristics in their approach and apply their problem-solving competence especially to those challenges that appear to them to be manageable and solvable (Kingdon 1984). This means that reproductive mechanisms can not only increase the pressure to adapt but can also lower the barrier to change. Already established structures, newly legitimised practices, positive evaluations of existing ones and the provision of appropriate resources can make problems that previously seemed insurmountable more manageable.

## 3 Study Design

The study has an exploratory character. It aims to explore the possibility of institutional change in universities based on their experience with the programmes for refugees. The extension of the programmes to other target groups is used as a hard indicator. Low-threshold learning effects, such as increased sensitivity and attention to certain problems faced by students regardless of their residence status and the resulting improved counselling, and stronger intercultural skills are not taken into account. They are not reflected in the established institutional structures of the universities and are therefore much more difficult to identify.

The possibilities of institutional change shall be identified based on the four mechanisms of change and stability (utilitarian, functional, legimatory, and power). These will be explored through interviews with representatives of three selected universities: In four qualitative interviews, persons responsible for these processes who have been involved in the programmes for several years—e.g. heads of department or coordinators—have explained how the process of transferring experiences to other target groups in their universities has worked. In this way their narratives of institutional change can be captured. The aim of these expert interviews is to identify the factors that made institutional change possible from the perspective of strategically responsible actors, i.e. actors with decision-making powers. Semi-structured expert interviews were conducted, with guidelines adapted to the specific university programmes and the situation on the ground. This was supplemented by documents, self-descriptions and publications of these universities.

The universities were selected based on the dependent variable. Universities were selected that have a joint programme for refugees and other international students or that have implemented a similar programme to the one they set up for refugees for other international students. These cases can show what opportunities exist for learning from experiences with refugees and how this process works.

Higher education institution 1 (HEI-1) is a comparatively small university that does not have its own Studienkolleg. The proportion of foreign students is in the range of 5 to 10%. It had no programme for refugees until 2016. Then a one to two semester preparation programme was set up, which includes both language and subject preparation. Since 2019, international students without refugee background can also participate in the programme. In the future, it will be extended to include German students. Participation results in a bonus on the final school grade, thus increasing the chances of admission to the university. The expansion to other target groups was a step-by-step process, which took place incrementally and did not follow a master plan.

HEI-2 is a network of several universities that do not have their own preparatory college and perceive this as a disadvantage. Various programmes were jointly set up, ranging from a guest lecture to a real preparatory course. The programme was planned as a role model for a similar programme for other international students. This programme for international students was launched in 2019 and, similar to the program for refugees, includes linguistic and professional preparation as well as an introduction to the chosen study programme. Overall, the proportion of non-German students in participating universities is slightly below 15%. In order to obtain information about different phases of the programme, two different people were interviewed.

HEI-3 is different from the other two HEIs. In 2015, a study preparation programme for international students had already been started here. Thus, unlike in the other two cases, an already existing program was extended to refugees. This will support the argument that support programmes for different target groups can be compatible and show which components are transferable between international students and refugees. The focus of the programme is on language preparation, but study competences and subject-specific knowledge are also to be taught. For foreign students, there is an independent program for the subject-specific preparation. The proportion of foreign students at this HEI is also just under 15%.

In all three HEIs, the number of refugee students represents a very small minority of the total number of international students.

## 4 Factors Making a Transfer to Other Target Groups More or Less Likely

### 4.1 Utilitarian-Supported Persistence, Necessity for Change and Opportunities for Change

As utilitarian reproduction represents the rational choice of the actors, first the utility must be identified. From the point of view of the actors with decision-making power, three forms of utility are particularly relevant to the issue at hand:

1. Profile building of the university: In order to compete nationally and internationally, most universities try to give themselves an individual profile. This is supposed to help in the acquisition of external funding and in the competition for the best scientists. However, the focus of such a profile is primarily on research and less on teaching (Schneidewind 2016, pp. 14–15).

2. Financial resources for the university: Financial resources are an important instrument for strengthening one's own organisation and implementing changes within the institution. For this reason, decision-makers have a great interest in acquiring additional financial resources—be it third-party funds or budget funds.
3. Competition for the (best) students: Combined with the allocation of funds from the university authorities, but also as an independent goal in itself, it is important to fill existing programmes to capacity. The universities have an interest in attracting and training especially highly qualified students.

Internationalisation is expected of universities as a part of both profile building and competition for the best students. It consists of two interdependent pillars: Internationalisation abroad and internationalisation at home (Knight 2012, pp. 34–36). An important driving force for the internationalisation of higher education is globalisation. Based on this the higher education system aims to not only prepare students for the international labour market where intercultural competence is needed, but also to position itself successfully in the international competition for attention and the best brains (Knight 2012, pp. 32–34). At the same time, a higher education organization can improve its reputation by hiring international experts or forming international partnerships. In the competition for the best brains internationalization can be a brand essence in attracting potential students (Bloch et al. 2014, pp. 255–257). At the same time, this can serve society's overall need for skilled workers (Morris-Lange and Brands 2015). HEI-3 is an exception: There is no coherent internationalization strategy there. This is the reason why some actors in the university did not perceive the necessity for a program to prepare international students.

For the Länder, which are the federated states which are responsible for most state universities, the provision of financial resources is one of the most important governance mechanisms. In many cases, funding is provided at least in part—even within universities—through indicator-based budgeting. In this context, aspects of teaching are of particular importance (Henke and Dohmen 2012; Jaeger 2006). Success in teaching can be measured in many ways, for example in terms of economic usability on the labour market, the successful transfer of specialist knowledge or personality development. In addition to the difficulties to measure success in terms of content, successful completion of studies is an easily quantifiable indicator. This is also used in many forms of performance-based budgeting. A counterpart, and thus a problem from the point of view of the relevant decision-makers, is the dropout. In order to be able to identify the situations more precisely, statistics of drop-out rates by subject or by individual student groups are useful.

Heublein and Schmelzer (2018, pp. 6–8) have evaluated the drop-out rates for bachelor's degree courses at universities for German first-year students from 2012/2013. The results show significantly lower dropout rates in law, economics and social sciences (24%) compared to mathematics/natural sciences (41%), humanities and sports (37%) or engineering (36%). The universities are also aware of this. For example, HEI-1 also justifies the special need for study preparation courses with the lower study ability, which is particularly visible in the technical subjects.

Among the groups of students who are the most likely to drop out are students who do not meet the institutional norm of white, non-disabled, male, young, middle or upper class, non-working etc. students. These include very different groups, including students with disabilities. Students with non-academic parents are also more likely to drop out of university (Heublein et al. 2017, pp. 59–61). Students who did not acquire their university entrance qualification at a Gymnasium are also significantly more likely to drop out of their studies (Heublein et al. 2017, pp. 66–67; Wolter et al. 2017, pp. 35–53). The reasons cited for discontinuing their studies are often performance problems that occur early in the course of their studies (Heublein et al. 2017, pp. 71–72; Wolter et al. 2017, pp. 35–53). Similarly, German students with a migrant background are less likely to graduate (Ebert and Heublein 2017, pp. 13–18).

International students, meaning students who have immigrated to Germany to study, also have an above-average rate of dropping out (Lokhande 2017, p. 10). Heublein and Schmelzer (2018, pp. 19–20) also point to differences among foreign students depending on their region of origin: The drop-out rate for Bachelor's degree courses is particularly high among students from Western Europe (53%), Asia (except East Asia: 48%) and Latin America (48%). One reason for the high drop-out rates is that international students often arrive in Germany very late due to bureaucratic obstacles and therefore sometimes miss the important introductory phase of their studies (Morris-Lange 2019, pp. 16–17).

In principle, the introductory phase of the study proves to be central for further progress. The academic overload and lack of orientation that occur quickly accumulate into a challenge that can be hard to overcome (Heublein et al. 2017, pp. 123–124). Therefore, support offers in the introductory phase of studies such as introductory events, bridging courses or courses for scientific research, play an important role. Attendance alone does not protect against dropping out of a study programme, but those people who find the preparation courses useful are less likely to drop out (Heublein et al. 2017, pp. 130–134). In some cases, however, it is precisely those who need a course more urgently that participate less frequently (Heublein et al. 2017, p. 133). The study preparation programmes for refugees which many universities offer address exactly this point. With the teaching of necessary German language skills participation is almost a necessary requirement for studying, increasing the chance of success. This is especially emphasized in HEI-1: The refugees from the preparation program mastered the introductory phase of their studies better than other students. This is because they have already become familiar with essential elements of the higher education system and study management during the preparation programme. This enabled them to concentrate on the professional challenges. These effects can be expected regardless of the refugee background. The positive evaluation of the programme for refugees thus reduces the risks and thus the potential costs of extending the programme to other target groups.

Regarding international students, there are several research findings that support the introduction of similar programmes to those for refugees. At the beginning of a program there are sometimes supplementary courses and preparatory programs but they are much more infrequently used than would be necessary (Morris-Lange 2017, pp. 28–29). Adequate time to correct knowledge deficits, help to self-organize their new life, and German language intensive courses should be offered to all students, especially international students, at the beginning of their studies (Morris-Lange 2017, pp. 28–29). During the program it is important that international students have access to low-threshold advice (Lokhande 2017, p. 33). Furthermore it is essential to bring them into contact with local students (Lokhande 2017, p. 35; Morris-Lange 2017, pp. 29–30).

Given the demographic change in Germany with a declining number of young people, some universities are also facing problems. Some small and medium-sized universities of applied sciences in particular have seen their student numbers decline in recent years (Morris-Lange 2019, pp. 6–7). However, many of these universities have in parallel made increasing efforts to attract international students (Morris-Lange 2019). This makes it possible to fill study places that might otherwise remain empty. Increased utilization of study capacities is in the self-interest of the university management to demonstrate the relevance of their university.

Beside the German language barrier, the university entrance qualification is often an obstacle for international students. These are often not regarded as equivalent to a German higher education entrance qualification. It is therefore only an indirect higher education entrance qualification. In order to be able to study at a university in Germany, persons with an indirect higher education entrance qualification must pass an assessment test. In preparation for this test, most Länder have Studienkollegs (Schröder et al. 2019, pp. 70–72). Universities that do not have a Studienkolleg have disadvantages in recruiting international students.

None of the three universities examined has a Studienkolleg. As HEI-2 reports, those students who have indirect university entrance qualifications often move first to a city with a Studienkolleg. Afterwards, it is natural for them to begin their studies in this city and not to move to another city. When developing the programme for refugees, HEI-2 therefore planned from the very start to open it up to other international students later. In this way, the access to studies was also to be regulated directly by the universities, even in the case of indirect university entrance qualifications. The same applies to HEI-1, where students with indirect university entrance qualifications are to be issued a certificate that entitles them to study at least at their own university. In contrast, there are currently no plans for an expansion of HEI-3, as this is not possible under the current legal situation and no political interest for it is apparent.

All these challenges have existed for a long time and are not directly related to the universities' commitment to refugees. Since 2015 they have not changed significantly. From a utilitarian perspective, it is therefore important to question why they were not addressed before. One reason is that the priorities between teaching and research are clearly divided in the German higher education landscape: Teaching is a compulsory task which in most cases only plays a subordinate role both at the level of the university as a whole and of the individual scientist (Schneidewind 2016, pp. 14–15). In the rational choice considerations of the decision-relevant actors, questions of teaching sometimes tend to be neglected because of the limited time and material resources available. Thus, if the achievable profits are low, action becomes likely only when the costs of action decrease. In fact, the development of offers for refugees can be interpreted as a reduction in the costs of institutional change for other groups of students. In this respect, the establishment of functioning structures and routines that can be transferred to other groups should be considered. This integration of new offers using existing structures is explained in more detail in the following chapter from the point of view of functional mechanisms.

## 4.2 Functional-Supported Persistence, Necessity for Change and Opportunities for Change

Functional reproduction explains the survival of institutions through their integration into broader institutional contexts. As a mechanism of change, however, it can also explain the need for change within the institution, which is necessary to prevent drift through changes in the institutional environment. The institutional environment communicates the need for change to the relevant decision-makers within the universities. This is done by establishing standards, setting criteria for competition between universities, providing financial incentives etc. As a result, functional adaptations are often included as costs and benefits in the rational-choice considerations of the relevant actors. This is illustrated for example by the shortage of skilled workers and the resulting need for universities to train more students. This is also the reason for the even stronger orientation of funding towards the number of graduates and the call to make greater efforts in recruiting international students.

While the maintenance of existing institutions or the establishment of new ones can be explained by their integration into the functional context, it seems much more difficult to explain the lack of institutions in functional terms. One approach to this can be the functional division of tasks. Most of the offers for students examined here represent a preparation for studies. Ideally, a direct higher education entrance qualification is a certificate for a preparatory training that qualifies for a study programme. Hence, such a certificate is issued by educational institutions, especially Gymnasien, or, in the case of international students, evaluated by the responsible recognition office. In the higher education system the need for further preparation for university studies is especially recognized in the case of those with indirect university entrance qualifications. Otherwise, in principle all persons coming to the university are sufficiently qualified for a course of study.

The universities have already broken through this strict functional division of tasks by offering propaedeutic courses, bridging courses and courses for scientific work. The universities are trying to prepare their first-year students even better for further studies, but these are measures that are already integrated into the course of study. The study preparation programmes for refugees, which were often designed for one or two semesters, go far beyond this (Blumenthal et al. 2017). The fact that these study preparation programmes were made possible at all depends on the one hand very much on the commitment of the members of the universities and the will to support the refugees. On the other hand, it also depends on the fact that the refugees—unlike other international students—had no opportunities to prepare for studying in Germany. This is especially true for language skills, which are a central component of nearly all study preparation programs (Blumenthal et al. 2017). At the same time, the existing Studienkolleg capacities would have been overstretched by the number of refugees. The regional distribution of refugees with only a few central Studienkollegs would also cause problems. Decentralised solutions therefore proved to be extremely reasonable.

With the establishment of the programmes for refugees, universities that previously did not have study preparation programmes or a Studienkolleg were also able to establish new structures and accumulate experience and knowledge. The programmes for refugees served as laboratories. This is described particularly by HEI-2: It was possible to test the entire study preparation programme, the additional courses, the use of test procedures, the application procedure and the completion of the courses. Here it was examined what is functional and useful. Coordination between the participating universities could also be implemented. Perfecting these processes is in the view of HEI-2 especially important because international students without a refugee background have to raise a lot of money to study in Germany and therefore have high expectations.

Thus, the development of study preparation programmes for refugees has not yet set the course that would make an extension to other target groups imperative, but at least this path is recognisable as a possibility. The study preparation programmes for refugees functioned as laboratories in which processes, instruments and structures could be tested, adapted and evaluated. At the same time, the university staff gained special experience and knowledge. Extensions to other target groups have the opportunity to benefit from the structures established. Thus, functional structures are established into which the extended programmes could be integrated.

The decisive factor for the feasibility of transferring the structures and knowledge to other target groups is their specific character. In fact, three dimensions of what has been learned can be differentiated: 1) Refugee-specific knowledge: By dealing with refugees, employees gain knowledge about the refugees' countries of origin, residence and asylum laws. Some of the support processes developed are also tailored to the specific legal situation of refugees. This knowledge and processes cannot be transferred to other groups. 2) Specific knowledge for international students: Part of the knowledge of residence law, contacts with authorities for foreigners and civil society groups that support migrants can also be used in the context of international students. This also applies to questions concerning the specifics of German university admission in international comparison and non-German university admissions. Regarding intercultural openness and intercultural skills, the teaching of language skills and the difficulties of starting studies in another country, a large part of the knowledge and measures can also be transferred very easily to international students without refugee background. 3) Knowledge related to the preparation of studies: This part can be transferred to all students. As shown in the previous chapter, the introductory phase of studies poses a challenge for very different groups of students in terms of orientation in the new place of study and at the university, in terms of basic knowledge and in terms of academic work. This applies for example to orientation courses, taster courses, buddy or tandem programs, study ability tests and the like. Very different groups of students can benefit from this.

This indicates that the transfer to international students is particularly obvious. Comparatively much of the acquired knowledge and established structures can be transferred to them. In addition, the refugees themselves are considered as international students because they acquired their education in a third country. In addition, the coordination of services for the refugees in many universities is institutionally the responsibility of the International Offices (Blumenthal et al. 2017, p. 22; Schammann and Younso 2016, p. 32). Their focus is on international students. If universities are viewed as complex organizations based on the division of labor, learning from experience with programs for refugees is easier within those organizational units that were responsible for these programs. Transferring such programmes to other students than international students would therefore require much more effort. The reason why this has worked in HEI-1 is that it is a very small university and the International Office and other student service departments are under the authority of the responsible actors. This also helps to minimize institutional frictional losses. In HEI-3, the International Office is responsible for organizing the program. The International Office argues against extending the program to include native students, arguing that on the one hand, a preparation program is already available for them, and on the other hand, due to the focus on language learning, the content of the program is not suitable for extension to this group.

## 4.3 Legitimation-supported Persistence, Necessity for Change and Opportunities for Change

Legitimacy-based explanations for change and persistence are also closely intertwined with the other mechanisms. Regarding the legitimacy of the absence of preparatory courses, reference can be made to the functional division of labour between university and school. The actors seem to find it legitimate to refrain from further study preparation courses because they see corresponding tasks as the responsibility of the schools. Whether and to what extent these persistent forces can be overcome also depends on whether and under what conditions transferability to other groups appears legitimate.

One could consider refugees as a special group. Support for refugees, for example, enjoyed a particularly high degree of legitimacy in view of the looming humanitarian tragedy in 2015 (Streitwieser and Brück 2018). Moreover, unlike other international students they had no chance to prepare for studying in

Germany in their countries of origin. And unlike German students, they had not attended school in Germany. Given the basic assumption underlying the question of the recognition of foreign educational qualifications, it must first be proven that their qualifications are equivalent to German qualifications (in general Sommer 2014, pp. 7–9). Therefore, the assumption that foreign students need more time to prepare for their studies does not contradict the assumed functional division of school and university, as the discussions at HEI-1 have shown.

So, the transfer of experiences from refugees to other international students seems appropriate, even if higher education standards are considered. Refugees are considered international students because of their foreign university entrance qualification. Thus, two groups of international students appear: Refugees and others. Since 2015, a variety of offers have been made available to refugees, be it the waiver of fees at Uni-Assist, the study preparation programmes or special tandem and buddy programmes. A recurring point of discussion was that the other international students should not be disadvantaged in comparison to the refugees (Schammann and Younso 2016, pp. 41–42). Accordingly, from the perspective of higher education policy actors, it seems obvious to open up offers for refugees to other international students in order to avoid possible debates on fairness.

## 4.4 Power-supported Persistence, Necessity for Change and Opportunities for Change

As far as can be assessed so far, no relevant group of actors is fundamentally and with full conviction opposed to the extension of programmes for refugees to other target groups. Rather, power-based resistance can take place for the reasons already described, namely that such a change is not recognised as necessary, is not wanted normatively in the self-image of the university or is not deemed worth the effort in terms of time and resources.

At the same time, however, there is no powerful actor who forces a transfer of the experience with refugees to other target groups. But there may still be power-based opportunities for change. Three aspects are particularly relevant in this case: First, decisions from higher levels can open a window of opportunity. Secondly, financial resources can be used as an instrument to promote certain courses of action. Thirdly, the universities can create semi-autonomous spaces in which actors other than those with university-wide responsibility can exert and shape influence.

A higher-level decision was the resolution of the Standing Conference of the Ministers of Education and Cultural Affairs of the Länder on the handling of missing documents in the case of refugee university applicants. HEI-2, in whose Land no Studienkolleg exists, reports that the obligation imposed by the resolution that all Länder offer at least one examination or assessment procedure (Kultusministerkonferenz 2015, p. 2) had a strong influence because it forced the Land to implement such a procedure. This resulted both in a legal change and in a window of opportunity to introduce more extensive study preparation programs for international students with indirect university entrance qualifications.

The questions of financing and semi-autonomous spaces are closely related. It is important to note that in most cases the original commitment to the refugees did not come from the university management but from the university members. This engagement was then taken up and institutionalised by the universities. Even though conflicts repeatedly arose between voluntary work and university bureaucracy, some of the voluntary spirit was retained (Schammann and Younso, 2016, pp. 31–32). HEI-1, for example, reports how the joint programme design with volunteer students generates enormous innovative potential. By allowing students to contribute their own experiences, the program can be specifically targeted at addressing challenges at the beginning of their studies. This is supported by the German Academic Exchange Service's (DAAD) promotion line Welcome funded by the BMBF which supports student assistants for the support and coordination of student engagement.

In general, almost all study preparation programmes for refugees at German universities were implemented with the help of third-party funding (Blumenthal et al. 2017, pp. 17–18). The DAAD programme Integra (Fourier et al. 2018), which is financed by the BMBF, proves to be particularly relevant in this respect (Blumenthal et al. 2017, pp. 17–18). The funding programmes have an explicit focus on refugees, however, this has also opened up to international students in the course of the calls for proposals. While such an expansion is virtually irrelevant in the calls for proposals in 2015 and 2016, it is explicitly desired in the 2018 call for proposals. At the same time, the universities are supposed to evaluate whether the goals for refugees and other international students can be achieved equally. In the call for proposals published in 2019, it is even more clearly stated that the offers should be opened to other international students according to a university-defined distribution key. This is also perceived by the universities, as the statements from HEI-2 prove. For offers such as those from HEI-3, which explicitly address refugees and international students, this presents a difficulty if they have mixed financing with different logics (participant or course orientation). Since they do not know how many refugees and how many other international students are enrolled, it is difficult to estimate in advance how far the funding will go.

If the applying body is also responsible for the implementation and disbursement of funds, this gives it a certain degree of autonomy. This is also reported from HEI-1, where the programmes for the various target groups are financed by third-party funds (e.g. DAAD, foundations etc.) and therefore do not burden the university budget. This allows the university to act largely autonomously and independently. At the same time, however, this sometimes leads to a lack of overall conceptual integration (Unangst and Streitwieser 2018, pp. 286–287).

In addition, the external financing of the programmes also has a cost-reducing effect in the utilitarian sense. This applies both to the financial impact of the programmes and the pressure on them to succeed. Success can be understood here—according to the memorable explanations from HEI-3—as an informed decision for or against a course of study as well as an educational unit preceding the course of study. Thus, the decision against studying or the informed choice of another place of study is also a success. However, what makes sense from a macroeconomic perspective is hardly justifiable if the university itself must pay for the costs of the programmes. Then only the successful enrolment at one's own university counts as a profitable investment. These concerns from HEI-3 are central when it comes to the possible financing of an expansion of the programmes and make clear the necessity of financing by actors with a perspective for society as a whole, such as a federal ministry.

## 5 Conclusion

Regarding the theoretical objective to explain change and stability by the same factors and thus show chances for change and tendencies of persistence, it can be stated that the four mechanisms named by Mahoney open up a helpful perspective. Utilitarian, functional, legitimation- and power-based mechanisms draw attention to various causal relationships that enable or hinder institutional change. One important insight, however, is how closely the various mechanisms are interrelated: For example, legitimatory arguments about the inequality of foreign educational qualifications are reflected in functional contexts of the education system with the outsourcing of study preparation to preparatory courses in Studienkollegs. To systematically formulate such connections between the mechanisms of action and to examine their effectiveness seems a worthwhile theoretical undertaking. The study also makes clear that the perspective from which the mechanisms are evaluated must be made explicit. In this case it was from the perspective of the decision-relevant actors.

The analysis gives also important empirical results. The starting situation in 2015 was contingent. As also emphasized by HEI-2, the previous lack of offers for international students has been an advantage at that moment. The actors were not trapped in existing structures in a path-dependent manner but were able to react directly to existing needs. The challenge could be addressed with structures that were developed for international students without a refugee background. This close connection with internationalisation (Berg 2018; Schammann and Younso 2017b) makes an extension of the existing programmes to international students an obvious choice. There is a particularly large overlap in terms of the drop-out rate, the institutional location of the programs, the knowledge acquired, and the structures tested. Nevertheless, there are also significant differences between the two groups of students (for a systematic overview Berg et al. 2018) which must be reflected in the program design in order to adequately address the individual target groups. These include, for example, the opportunity to prepare for studying and learn German in Germany, the security of their residence status, restrictions associated with the residence status such as a residence obligation, or the prevalence of traumatic experiences. An extension to other target groups can also be a very important instrument to maintain the structures even if the number of refugees declines and to keep the ability to reactivate them if necessary. For the funding bodies as well as the university's sponsors, this also means the necessity to switch from project funding to structural funding in the medium term (Beigang et al. 2018, p. 4; Unangst and Streitwieser 2018, p. 286).

However, the analysis of the various mechanisms of action shows that there is no inevitable transfer of experience gained from the programmes for refugees to those for international students. Instead, a window of opportunity for further fundamental reforms is emerging. In order to make use of this, either a proactive commitment on the part of the universities or increased political governance is required. The DAAD funding programmes financed by the BMBF have proven to be extremely important and effective in the case of the programmes for refugees. It is therefore all the more important that they already include the demand for an extension to other international students.

The various factors that indicate an extension to international students are shown in Table 1. In particular, the understanding of the role of the universities, which do not consider the preparation of studies to be anchored in their own institutions, and the time and resources required for this are inhibiting factors. It is therefore necessary that more attention be paid to teaching as a core task of the universities.

**Table 1** Factors from different perspectives that indicate an extension to international students

|  | Utilitarian | Functional | Legitimate | Power |
|---|---|---|---|---|
| Perspectives on responses to existing needs | Reduction in dropout rate, | System-wide shortage of skilled workers, |  | Indicator-based university funding with graduate numbers as an indicator |
|  | Full utilisation of the study programmes | Role of universities as training institutions |  |  |
| International perspectives | Internationalisation as profile building | Globalisation |  | National and global competition |
| Financial perspectives | No burden on the university budget |  |  | Third-party funding, |
|  |  |  |  | Semi-autonomous spaces |
| Risk perspectives | Reduced risks through positive evaluations | Tried and tested structures and knowledge gains through programmes for refugees |  |  |
| Fairness perspectives |  |  | Unequal starting conditions of different student groups |  |
| Equal treatment perspectives |  |  | Avoidance of unequal treatment within the group of international students |  |

The problem remains, however, that the preparation for international students is not part of the actual course of study. This means that they are always considered to have a deficit. However, if one looks at the fundamental problems that many first-year students have, the question arises whether a corresponding offer would be useful for everyone. This would require the introductory phase to be more flexible. This phase could then include the teaching of required specialist knowledge, scientific work, orientation at the university as well as the teaching of language basics and even offer the possibility to get a taste of different subjects. For these events, creditable study points would then also have to be awarded.

After all the limitations of the present exploratory study are the small number of universities examined as well as the small number of interviews. Therefore, this paper offers only a starting point for considerations regarding the transferability of the experiences from refugee programmes to other target groups. A study that reaches a greater number of universities is needed, with a special focus on those that have not transferred their programmes to other target groups. At the same time, however, it is also necessary to critically monitor the transfer that has taken place in order to better identify target group-specific factors and thus be able to show the limits of a successful application to other target groups.

## References

Beigang, S., Blumenthal, J. von, & Lambert, L. (2018). *Studium für Geflüchtete: Aufgaben für Hochschulen und Politik* (Flucht: Forschung und Transfer Policy Brief 08b). Osnabrück, Bonn. https://flucht-forschung-transfer.de/wp-content/uploads/2018/04/PB-08b-04-2018.pdf.

Berg, J. (2018). A New Aspect of Internationalisation? Specific Challenges and Support Structures for Refugees on Their Way to German Higher Education. In A. Curaj, L. Deca, & R. Pricopie (Eds.), *European Higher Education Area: The impact of past and future policies* (pp. 219–235). Springer Open. https://doi.org/https://doi.org/10.1007/978-3-319-77407-7_15.

Berg, J., Grüttner, M., & Schröder, S. (2018). Zwischen Befähigung und Stigmatisierung? Die Situation von Geflüchteten beim Hochschulzugang und im Studium. Ein internationaler Forschungsüberblick. Zeitschrift für Flüchtlingsforschung, 2 (1), 57–90.

Bloch, R., Kreckel, R., Mitterle, A., & Stock, M. (2014). Stratifikationen im Bereich der Hochschulbildung in Deutschland. *Zeitschrift für Erziehungswissenschaft, 17* (S3), 243–261. https://doi.org/https://doi.org/10.1007/s11618-014-0531-4.

Blumenthal, J. von, Beigang, S., Wegmann, K., & Feneberg, V. (2017). *Institutionelle Anpassungsfähigkeit von Hochschulen: Forschungsbericht*. Berlin. Berliner Institut für empirische Integrations- und Migrationsforschung. https://www.bim-fluchtcluster.hu-berlin.de/de/11-institutionelle-anpassungsfaehigkeit-von-hochschulen/forschungsbericht_institutionelle-anpassungsfaehigkeit-von-hochschulen/at_download/file.

Campbell, J. L. (2009). Institutional Reproduction and Change. In G. Morgan, J. L. Campbell, C. Crouch, & Pedersen, Ove K. Whitley, Richard (Eds.), *The Oxford Handbook of Comparative Historical Analysis* (pp. 87–116). Oxford University Press.

Ebert, J., & Heublein, U. (2017). Ursachen des Studienabbruchs bei Studierenden mit Migrationshintergrund: Eine vergleichende Untersuchung der Ursachen und Motive des Studienabbruchs bei Studierenden mit und ohne Migrationshintergrund auf Basis der Befragung der Exmatrikulierten des Sommersemesters 2014. Hannover. Deutsches Zentrum für Hochschul- und Wissenschaftsforschung; Stiftung Mercator. https://www.dzhw.eu/pdf/21/bericht_mercator.pdf.

Edelstein, B., & Nikolai, R. (2013). Strukturwandel im Sekundarbereich: Determinanten schulpolitischer Reformprozesse in Sachsen und Hamburg. *Zeitschrift für Pädagogik*, *59*(4), 482–495.

Fourier, K., Kracht Araújo, J., Latsch, K., Siemens, A., Schmitz, M., & Grüttner, M. (2018). *Integration of Refugees at German Institutions of Higher Education: Report on the Higher Education Programmes for Refugees*. Bonn. https://static.daad.de/media/daad_de/pdfs_nicht_barrierefrei/infos-services-fuer-hochschulen/expertise-zu-themen-laendern-regionen/fluechtlinge-an-hochschulen/p15_geflu%CC%88chtete_en_rz_webpart2.pdf.

Henke, J., & Dohmen, D. (2012). Wettbewerb durch leistungsorientierte Mittelzuweisungen? Zur Wirksamkeit von Anreiz- und Steuerungssystemen der Bundesländer auf Leistungsparameter der Hochschulen. *die hochschule*, *21*(2), 100–120.

Heublein, U., Ebert, J., Hutzsch, C., Isleib, S., König, R., Richter, J., & Woisch, A. (2017). Zwischen Studienerwartungen und Studienwirklichkeit: Ursachen des Studienabbruchs, beruflicher Verbleib der Studienabbrecherinnen und Studienabbrecher und Entwicklung der Studienabbruchquote an deutschen Hochschulen. Hannover. Deutsches Zentrum für Hochschul- und Wissenschaftsforschung. https://www.dzhw.eu/pdf/pub_fh/fh-201701.pdf.

Heublein, U., & Schmelzer, R. (2018). *Die Entwicklung der Studienabbruchquoten an den deutschen Hochschulen: Berechnungen auf Basis des Absolventenjahrgangs 2016*. Hannover. Deutsches Zentrum für Hochschul- und Wissenschaftsforschung. https://www.dzhw.eu/pdf/21/studienabbruchquoten_absolventen_2016.pdf.

Jaeger, M. (2006). Leistungsbezogene Budgetierung an deutschen Universitäten: Umsetzung und Perspektiven. *wissenschaftsmanagement* (3), 32–38.

John, P. (2012). *Analyzing Public Policy* (2nd ed.). Routledge.

Kingdon, J. W. (1984). *Agendas, Alternatives, and Public Policies*. Little, Brown and Company.

Knight, J. (2012). Concepts, Rationales, and Interpretive Frameworks in the Internationalization of Higher Education. In D. K. Deardorff, de Wit, Hans, J. D. Heyl, & T. Adams (Eds.), *The SAGE Handbook of International Higher Education* (pp. 27–42). SAGE.

Kultusministerkonferenz. (2015, December 3). Hochschulzugang und Hochschulzulassung für Studienbewerberinnen bzw. Studienbewerber, die fluchtbedingt den Nachweis der im Heimatland erwor- benen Hochschulzugangsberechtigung nicht erbringen können. o.O. https://www.kmk.org/fileadmin/Dateien/veroeffentlichungen_beschluesse/2015/2015_12_03-Hochschulzugang-ohne-Nachweis-der-Hochschulzugangsberechtigung.pdf.

Lokhande, M. (2017). *Vom Hörsaal in den Betrieb? Internationale Studierende beim Berufseinstieg in Deutschland*. Berlin. Sachverständigenrat deutscher Stiftungen für Integration und Migration. https://www.svr-migration.de/wp-content/uploads/2017/12/SVR-FB_Study_and_work.pdf.

Mahoney, J. (2000). Path Dependence in Historical Sociology. *Theory and Society, 29* (4), 507–548.

Mahoney, J., & Thelen, K. A. (2010). A Theory of Gradual Institutional Change. In J. Mahoney & K. A. Thelen (Eds.), *Explaining institutional change: Ambiguity agency and power* (pp. 1–37). Cambridge University Press.

Morris-Lange, S. (2017). Allein durch den Hochschuldschungel: Hürden zum Studienerfolg für internationale Studierende und Studierende mit Migrationshintergrund. Berlin. Sachverständigenrat deutscher Stiftungen für Integration und Migration. https://www.svr-migration.de/wp-content/uploads/2017/05/SVR_FB_Hochschuldschungel.pdf.

Morris-Lange, S. (2019). *Dem demografischen Wandel entgegen: Wie schrumpfende Hochschulstandorte internationale Studierende gewinnen und halten*. Berlin. Sachverständigenrat deutscher Stiftungen für Integration und Migration. https://www.svr-migration.de/wp-content/uploads/2019/03/SVR_FB_Schrumpfende_Hochschulstandorte.pdf.

Morris-Lange, S., & Brands, F. (2015). *Zugangstor Hochschule: Internationale Studierende als Fachkräfte von morgen gewinnen*. Berlin. Sachverständigenrat deutscher Stiftungen für Integration und Migration.

Peters, B. G. (2012). Institutional Theory in Political Science: The 'New Institutionalism' (3rd ed.). Continuum.

Schammann, H., & Younso, C. (2016). *Studium nach der Flucht? Angebote deutscher Hochschulen für Studieninteressierte mit Fluchterfahrung*. Empirische Befunde und Handlungsempfehlungen. Universitätsverlag Hildesheim. https://www.hrk.de/fileadmin/redaktion/Studie_Studium-nach-der-Flucht.pdf.

Schammann, H., & Younso, C. (2017a). Endlich Licht in einer dunklen Ecke? Hürden und Angebote für Geflüchtete im tertiären Bildungsbereich. *Zeitschrift für internationale Bildungsforschung und Entwicklungspädagogik, 40* (1), 10–15.

Schammann, H., & Younso, C. (2017b). Zwischen Kerngeschäft und Third Mission: Angebote deutscher Hochschulen für Studieninteressierte mit Fluchterfahrung. *Die Deutsche Schule, 109* (3), 260–272.

Schneidewind, U. (2016). Die „Third Mission" zur „First Mission" machen? *die hochschule* (1), 14–22.

Schröder, S., Grüttner, M., & Berg, J. (2019). Study Preparation for Refugees in German 'Studienkollegs' – Interpretative Patterns of Access, Life-wide (Language) Learning and Performance. *Widening Participation and Lifelong Learning, 21* (2), 67–85. https://doi.org/https://doi.org/10.5456/WPLL.21.2.67.

Sommer, I. (2014). *Ist das Anerkennungsgesetz ein Verkennungsgesetz? Der umkämpfte Wert ausländischer Berufsqualifikationen in Deutschland*. Berlin. Heinrich Böll Stiftung. https://www.boell.de/sites/default/files/e-paper_anerkennungsgesetz.pdf.

Steinhardt, I., & Eckhardt, L. (2017). 'We can do it' - Refugees and the German Higher Education System. In J. Jungblut & K. Pietkiewicz (Eds.), *Refugees Welcome? Recognition of qualifications held by refugees and their access to higher education in Europe - country analyses* (pp. 25–42). Brüssel: The European Students' Union.

Streeck, W., & Thelen, K. A. (2005). Introduction: Institutional Change in Advanced Political Economies. In W. Streeck & K. A. Thelen (Eds.), *Beyond Continuity: Institutional change in advanced political economies* (pp. 1–39). University Press.

Streitwieser, B., & Brück, L. (2018). Competing Motivations in Germany's Higher Education Response to the "Refugee Crisis". *Refuge, 34*(2), 38–51. https://doi.org/https://doi.org/10.7202/1055575ar.

Unangst, L., & Streitwieser, B. (2018). Inclusive Practices in Response to the German Refugee Influx: Support Structures and Rationales Described by University Administrators. In A. Curaj, L. Deca, & R. Pricopie (Eds.), *European Higher Education Area: The impact of past and future policies* (pp. 277–292). Springer Open. https://doi.org/https://doi.org/10.1007/978-3-319-77407-7_18.

Wolter, A., Kamm, C., Otto, A., Dahm, G., & Kerst, C. (2017). *Nicht-traditionelle Studierende: Studienverlauf, Studienerfolg und Lernumwelten*. Berlin. Humboldt-Universität zu Berlin; Deutsches Zentrum für Hochschul- und Wissenschaftsforschung. https://www.dzhw.eu/pdf/21/pdf/22/Nicht-traditionelle%20Studierende_Projektbericht%202017.pdf

# Refugee and Third-Generation Migrant Students in Comparison: Class Position and Integration Discourse

Emre Arslan

## 1 Introduction

In recent years, refugee movements have increased to a certain extent due to the civil war that started in Syria in 2011. Germany, which has a relatively more liberal refugee policy compared to other European countries, has received over a million refugees since 2015. Although this process strengthened the existence of nationalist and racist parties and movements, which completely denied the right to asylum, the idea that refugees should be integrated into society and be granted asylum has been accepted in wide parts of the population (Bendel 2017). While the defence of the idea of integration against nationalist exclusion is based in part on a universalist humanist attitude, its narrative is rather predicated on a pragmatic or utilitarian perspective. Especially in mainstream politics and media in Germany, it is most common to emphasize the importance of bringing refugees to education and then to business life as a remedy for the determination of the lack of experts (*Fachkräftemangel*) in certain professions (Geis 2017).[1] Although this kind of utilitarian approach criticizes political nationalism, it is at least methodologically

---

[1] In the media, the news about the question whether the refugees are helpful for the lack of experts are common. There are sometimes optimistic (for example https://www.dw.com/de/mehr-fl%C3%BCchtlinge-finden-eine-arbeit/a-50040261) or pessimistic (for example https://www.welt.de/wirtschaft/article181754410/Einwanderungsgesetz-Fluechtlinge-lindern-den-Fachkraeftemangel-nicht.html) reports about it.

E. Arslan (✉)
IU - Internationale Hochschule, Düsseldorf, Germany
E-Mail: emre.arslan@iu.org

nationalist[2] because its main presumptions are based upon the interests of the nation-state.

In this article, it will be claimed that a framework based on a class analysis is a meaningful and helpful perspective in understanding and explaining the education processes of immigrants and refugees. The discourse of integration, which is frequently used in the context of immigrants and refugees, prevents understanding of the real situation of these groups when it is not based on a relational class position analysis. Pierre Bourdieu's concepts such as habitus, cultural capital, symbolic violence, and social space can serve as suitable tools for this perspective of relational class analysis (especially Bourdieu 1974, 1991, 1998a, 1998b, 2012 and Bourdieu and Wacquant 1992).

In the first part of the article, the relationship between class positions and discourse of integration will be discussed. In the second part, I will give a short account of the literature on the subject and the methodological background of the study. In the third part, the education biography of two university students from Syria who have to take refuge[3] in Germany, and began to study there, will be analysed in terms of habitus and cultural capital transfers. These students have a family habitus that can be categorised middle class in their own country. While they have to change the country and therefore the social space due to migration, they do not experience a change in class position as they study at the university in Germany. The fourth part deals with another profile of educational biography for comparison: third-generation immigrant university students from families with low educational capital. In the last two sections, a comparative analysis of these two groups, and brief pedagogic suggestions as a result of the study will be formulated.

## 2 Class Position and Social Equality as the Core of Integration Process

The concept of integration is widely accepted in society and scientific research as a tool to explain the process of immigrants becoming part of society. In general, the concept of integration is understood as a process of adaptation of the newcomers or foreigners to the society and the established social system. The most

---

[2] For the discussion about the term, see Wimmer and Glick Schiller (2003).

[3] In this study, the term "refugee" is not used in a strictly juristic sense. Because the sociological analysis, especially the social class mobility, is the focus of the study, also the asylum seekers without a legal refugee status are a part of the study.

well-known representative of this understanding in the field of social science in Germany is Hartmut Esser, who has done extensive research on integration, migration, education system and multilingualism (Esser 2001, 2003, 2006, 2009). In his understanding, foreigners coming to the system from the outside will go through certain stages as individuals and groups and will experience different forms of integration depending on the situation. Esser sees assimilation and abandoning the mother tongue in the education system as the most functional strategies for immigrants (Esser 2003).

In general, the problems in Esser's work concerning integration, education system, multilingualism and methodology[4] stem from the fact that he reduces the scientific operation to describe the existing phenomena and the doxas they generate without seeing the relational and historical dimension of social reality.[5] By statistical method Esser describes the reality of a certain historical moment and place (for example Germany today) and posits that English and French, for example, are the only valuable languages for cultural capital (Esser 2006). Instead of seeing it as a product of certain historical social relations, he suggests giving up the opportunity to immigrant children to learn their mother tongue at school, as if it was a never changed and universal validity. He does not consider that educational institutions are the most effective scales that increase or decrease cultural capital. Thus, he contributes, in the name of science, to the devaluation of the language of migrants in society and further decreases their already low cultural capital.

The discourse of integration sets positive targets and shining promises for immigrants: If you pass certain stages, you will become integrated (or assimilated by Esser's terminology).[6] However, even if an immigrant with a black skin

---

[4]For a strong critique of Esser and Karl Popper's philosophy, which forms his methodological basis, see Norbert Elias (1985).

[5]Even when Esser uses sociologically meaningful and valuable concepts, those seem misleading and hollow because they are detached from their context. The idea of cultural capital conceptualized by Bourdieu is an example of this. For Bourdieu, 'cultural capital' can only be understood as a depiction of inter—class relations within a social sphere (for example Bourdieu 1974, p. 42, 2012, p. 229). Esser, on the other hand, reduces this concept to an isolated quantity of human-capital of an abstract individual, which makes the real value of the concept pointless (z. B. Esser 2001, pp. 8, 15).

[6]Esser claims that with ethnic assimilation, a full social equality will be achieved in terms of ethnic relations (Esser 2003, p. 9). In the same way, he claims that gender equality needs a process of gender assimilation. He does not explain what gender assimilation looks like in practice. However, while talking about ethnic assimilation processes, he focuses on the processes that immigrants should experience, who are in a minority and in a less powerful position. When the ethnic assimilation process is based on the idea that the minority should

colour or a Muslim name has been living in Germany for generations and underwent all of the integration stages, there is no guarantee of being accepted as a part of the German identity.[7] As long as the implicit definition of 'German' identity is made according to a certain skin colour or religious belief in the collective subconscious, the promise of integration is doomed to remain empty and false.

Ludger Pries defines this type of integration as the idea of monist integration and instead defines that a pluralistic and open-ended integration approach is more realistic and meaningful (Pries 2015a). Pries, known for his transnationalism studies (especially Pries 2008; 2015b), declares that the concept of integration is not an imperative to remain within the borders of the nation-state. For Pries, integration is an open-ended and pluralist process, where immigrants and the non-immigrants will develop in an ongoing negotiation rather than a single goal to be reached. Pries criticizes approaches that completely reject the concept of integration and instead find the framework of democracy more meaningful. He contradicts the motto "democracy instead of integration" with his proposition of "democracy through integration or integration through democracy" (Pries 2015a, p. 23). In general, he points out that, rather than the cultural adaptation duties of immigrants, the state and the host community should provide opportunities for the integration of immigrants. As such, a Pries-type understanding of integration focuses in general on the realities and needs of many immigrants. However, the understanding of 'integration of immigrants', even in its most advanced forms, involves a certain culturalism because of the implicit assumption of an homogenous host society with an identical ethos and imaginary core (Czollek 2020, p. 64), which in turn leads to misconceptions in understanding social reality.

In this article, it will be argued that class positioning is more than just an important dimension of integration, but the very essence of the discourse on integration. When it is discussed about the integration of immigrants in a particular social space and in a given time, it is not actually the adaptation process of every individual that migrates. The subject of the discussion is always the groups under a certain economic, social, cultural and symbolic resources (like so-called "guest workers" since the 1970s) and the relations of these groups with the majority

---

reach the norms of the majority ethnic group, it is clear that this will bring burden and debt to the minority group. Interestingly, Esser does not talk about the processes that the German identity must go through. How to achieve the social equality in such an unequal division of duties in the process of the integration is a mystery.

[7]Hence the frustration of many third generation students at the universities, who are often exposed to the question "Where do you actually come from?" (for an analysis of this question from the point of migration sociology, see Mecheril, P. et al. 2010, p. 41).

society. Groups and individuals with a high economic, social, cultural and symbolic capital but migrated to another country are excluded from the integration discussions: If a person with a high level of economic, cultural and social capital from a rich country decides to live in Germany, the integration problems of this person or their children in terms of education and language are not discussed. This person is called normally as an expatriate (or expat) rather than an immigrant, although he actually emigrated.

The class analysis in this article takes a broader definition of the concept of class. Not only the income and educational degree, but also the asymmetrical relationships due to ethnic, religious, sexual or other factors are components of class positioning. Concepts such as symbolic capital, symbolic violence, and symbolic order in particular, are tools capable of showing the class character of apparently out-of-class phenomena and group identities, essentially based on the sharing of social resources. For example, the stigma of belonging to certain ethnic and religious groups is often explained by the concepts of prejudice or ignorance. However, such explanations, as Norbert Elias discusses, are misleading explanations that do not see the systematic figuration and power relations behind this definition (Elias and Scotson 2010, pp. 253–4). It is also possible to explain the stigma processes within the framework of the concept of symbolic capital and symbolic violence. Stigma is the process of marking a group with negative symbolic capital, i.e. symbolic debt, and thus forming symbolic violence. This is not only intellectual and emotional but also a materialistic process. Groups with a substantial symbolic capital can be seen as starting already off with a loan before reaching a socially valuable opportunity or position, while stigmatized groups have to spend more time, energy and efforts for reaching the same position. Due to the stigma certain negative properties are attributed to people. Therefore, any person from this group must deliver extra proof for their suitability for a valuable position.

## 3 Literature Review and the Research Design

The most important obstacles for refugee students are insecure socio-economic situation, problems with residence permits and asylum procedures, problems with recognition of diplomas and limited institutional support (Lambert et al. 2018, p. 9). In average, refugees need one and a half years after their arrival to apply to a department or a preparatory program at the university (Fourier et. al. 2017, p. 24). It is estimated that more than half of the refugees who want to study cannot enter university (Lambert et al. 2018, p. 8). In some cases, refugees who have sufficient qualification are rejected by the university itself because of their juridical vulnerability. The possible juridical problems contradicts with the administrative logic of the universities based on the predictability and the long-term planning (Lambert 2018, p. 360). In addition to the problems of stigma and discrimination, refugee students who can enrol have problems such as learning the language and adapting to the German academic system and the learning culture (Bouchara 2019, p. 54).

Research on the educational process shows that immigrants in Germany, particularly the parents originated from Turkey, have more educational aspirations for their children than non-immigrant parents (Vodafone 2011; Becker 2011). However, this higher educational aspiration is not sufficient for children to become successful in the education system. Especially Turkish students in primary school are relatively less often sent to *Gymnasium* which is in general a big (and nearly the only) stepping stone for university (Autorengruppe Bildungsberichterstattung 2016, p. 173; Statistisches Bundesamt 2017, p. 181).[8] The inverse relationship between the high level of educational aspiration and the low educational success shows that desire and determination are not enough for educational success. Research based on Bourdieu's sociology exposes that the educational capital of children is influenced mostly by the cultural capital and habitus they receive from the family (Büchner and Brake 2006; El-Mafaalini 2012; Thiersch 2014; van Essen 2013 etc.).

The third-generation immigrant students do usually come from working class families (Fürtjes and Arslan 2016, p. 180) and do not feel themselves at home at the university (Fürtjes and Arslan 2016, pp. 184–5). They have lower-class habitus because most of them have a working class origin and additionally their cultural values (for example Turkish language) are seldom recognized as cultural capital in Germany. This article aims at exploring and extending this result of the above-mentioned study with qualitative data mainly stemming from former research projects (with migrant parents and students) and new interviews for this article (with refugee students in two universities). During my interviews, I followed the three stages of on the autobiographic narrative interview as outlined by Fritz Schütze: 1) initial request for an autobiographical narrative (without interruption) 2) new questions for the further narration 3) other questions like opinions or arguments (Schütze, 1983: 285). In the analysis of the interviews,

---

[8] There are basicly three school forms in Germany: Gymnasium, Realschule and Hauptschule. Usually, only students attending Gymnasium are entitled to go to university. Out of these schools, there is also *Förderschule* (earlier named as *Sonderschule*), for those labeled as "learning disabled" (*lernbehindert*).

the methodological reflections of the "sociology of knowledge" seemed to be the mostly helpful (Mannheim 2015; Bohnsack 2014; Nohl 2013; Schittenhelm (2012). Because the knowledge of a person is more than what the people verbally can communicate, focusing on the manner of the expressions (not only on the content of the interviews) is important to reach into the layers of practical or implicit knowledge of a person (Nohl 2013, p. 4).

An important limitation of this article is the absence of statistical data about the class position of the refugee students in Germany. Refugee university students examined in this article are people who have started already university in their home country or have at least qualified for enrolling in university in their home country. The problems mentioned in the literature like the lack of knowledge of German university system and language, uncertainty of the residency status seem to have led to both delays and shrinkage in educational objectives. However, there is one aspect missing in most of the academic works about this subject. When refugee students at the universities have enough cultural capital to go to university in their home country and thus internalized the habitus of the educated class, such as appreciating reading and believing in the value of art and science, they *could* get better positions at the university in Germany than the immigrant students who have parents without academic grades. The refugee students I spoke to had a particularly high motivation and self-consciousness at the university. For these reasons, contrary to my expectations, they feel more at home at the university in Germany than the third generation immigrant students. The examples in part three (Jiyan and Mahmud)[9] will depict this type of refugee students.

The paradox between the high educational aspiration of the migrant parents and students and their relatively unsuccessful career in the education system as depicted in the literature (Vodafone 2011; Becker 2011) can also be understood from the perspective of habitus and cultural capital. Third-generation immigrants from Turkey in Germany have mostly parents with a low cultural capital due to their foreign and subclass origins. They have often open and implicit conflicts with school institutions due to the lower class habitus and so they lose a lot of time and energy to achieve the goal of higher education because of the systemic obstacles. The first example (Can) described in detail in part four can be seen

---

[9]All names of the interview partners and cities in this article are anonymised. In the transcription, the bold letter indicates the loud expressions, and the length of the pause during the speech is shown in brackets. All the interviews with the refugees in this article were carried out in German. The interviews with third-generation immigrant students were partly in Turkish and in German. In the English translation, I tried to keep the original forms of the interview passages with their grammatical and stylistic peculiarities.

as relatively a stronger example of these processes, whereas the second example (Yasemin) is a relatively soft version.

## 4 Refugee Students: Educational Trajectories Beyond the Nation-State Boundaries

### 4.1 Jiyan: "I have no Time to Think About the Integration"

Jiyan, a 27 year old woman from Syria, has been in Germany for about five years. As soon as she finishes high school in her home country, she starts studying engineering. In the 5th semester, when the civil war began in Syria, she migrates to Iraq. Since she is of Kurdish origin, she goes to the Kurdish region of Iraq. By then her brother had already been living in Germany, which is why she could migrate to Germany in 2014 due to the family reunification law. After learning German for a year, she enters university. Instead of continuing to study engineering, she switches professions and enrols in the Social Work department:

> I only applied for social work I didn't want to finish my former degree because after the war I really wanted to do something with people. I actually wanted to study international law but because of the level of my language skills social work seemed to me the more realistic choice.

The problem, that Jiyan speaks about throughout the whole interview, is learning the German language. After a year of language preparation school, she passes the C1 level exam, which is mandatory for studying at university. In her first year at the university, she spends more time studying grammar and vocabulary than dealing with the content of the courses. She is mostly disappointed with the grades she got during that period. She points out that in her first semester, she got the score of 2.7,[10] which was slightly above the average in her class because of her limited knowledge of the language. She is still very upset about this. In her second semester, she tries applying for extra time in the exam, which is an exceptional privilege for disabled people. Lack of language was not considered a disability, which is why she had to finish the exam in the same time as her native speaker colleagues. Nevertheless, she manages to get the best grade in this exam, being the only student passing with a 1.0. After this exam result and a very good

---

[10] The German academic rating system starts with 1.0 being the best grade one can get, to 6.0 being the worst grade. At the university, one is passing a test only with the grades 1.0 to 4.0.

grade from another oral exam, she feels reassured of expressing herself accurately in the German language in exams. However, she still considers the language as a problem that will always remain, even if she gets the best grades and succeeds:

> I think studying here is not difficult compared to my previous studies. My only difficulty is the language. I have to learn so many new words every day and sometimes you have to read a very small section ten times, and you still have the feeling that, sometimes, you have the feeling that you will **never** get native speaker level (...) sometimes very difficult for me to accept (laughs).

In the passage above, the fact that she emphasizes the word "never" can be considered as a way of emotionally underlining or stressing the statement that comes later, "it is very difficult for me to accept this situation". Since Jiyan is used to being always the first and the best in the field of education back in Syria, getting the best grade in the courses is not enough for her. The passage given below shows the approach of her family and herself to a successful education in Syria:

> In 9th grade, I was the best in my school but not all over town. There were two or three that got more points than me, more than me. That was, I felt like I was the worst, including my family, they didn't recognize that I was good, that wasn't important. You always had to get a 1, 1 plus or the full points. If only one point was missing, they didn't say, we didn't say I had to learn. But this trust, and these expectations they have from you, resolve in a lot of stress, although they don't really say anything, but you always feel that you, always have them, even here (laughs) I always get 1, funny (laughs), but not always (laughs)

Jiyan stresses that her family does not have a lot of money, which is why they see education as the only chance for a better future. Her father is a lower office clerk, and her mother has neither degree nor literacy. While a family with the same educational level can be seen as having a low cultural capital in any large city of Germany, in a small town in Syria, this family is a part of the middle-upper class level regarding the point of cultural capital in this social space.[11] Here, it should be reminded again that cultural capital is based on relational resources that can be activated in the social sphere rather than absolute wealth. In the example of Jiyan, she has brothers and sisters who are older and have university education, who transmitted her a trained class habitus in the social field in which she grew up.

---

[11] As Bourdieu puts it, the upper class of a small town shows typical behaviors of the middle class of a big city, especially because their economic, cultural, and social traits have now different position in the new structure (Bourdieu 1974, pp. 45–46).

> We are seven children. I am number six. My eldest sister is a math teacher. Then my brother comes, who did not graduate. And my niece is only working and then my sister is a computer scientist, then a brother who studied English literature. But then when he went to Germany, he worked as a tailor and another sister who is a civil engineer and I am and then my little brother who studies ethnology at Heidelberg University.
>
> My oldest sister was already 12 years old when I was born. She is my mom, too.

Especially the fact that her older siblings are in continuous education and helping her like parents leads Jiyan to think and feel about education in accordance with a habitus of middle-upper classes. Aiming a higher level in education and learning new things without focusing any other purpose (such as money, profession or status) is a basic indicator of this kind of habitus. It is possible to see some kind of playful enjoyment and enthusiasm in education in the following passages:

> When I have free time, I can, I actually don't have any free time (laughs)
>
> I don't even think about it, I'm trying here when I've started… social work here, I don't really think much about what grade I get, or so, um, but, I try, I like the topics. I am interested in the content. I also try to improve my language and whenever I read, I like anyway, I read anyway. Most of the topics that I choose are interesting for me, um, that's why, actually, I think studying here is not difficult compared to my previous studies.

She has internalized the idea that the subjects are interesting and valuable independently of the grades, and that the grades are only the natural results of this interest. She also has built up a critical attitude as a constant part of her habitus towards herself, her work, or even her own department, which is important in university life:

> I'm probably very critical, because if you're studying, you're more likely to be critical. I don't know, but sometimes I think I can't. This course of study is very nice, but that's not enough, at least for me.

Jiyan states that studying at the university is a good thing for her but does not suffice. From childhood on, she considers studying at a university as a stage to be experienced. "I have never thought of a life in which I wouldn't be studying at university," she says. Studying at the university and being very successful (even more the best) is a dominant feeling installed in her since childhood. She concerns not on being a successful student, but rather on being in a higher position for helping the other people. Accordingly, in her narrative, she mentions more about did what she did for others rather than the help she received from the university and from her colleagues as a refugee. For example, she actively works in *Allgemeiner Studentenausschuss* (AStA)[12] and provides legal aid to many foreign students. She helps refugee children with their job applications.

Her answer to the question of whether she has a big enough circle of friends in university and laughs, "I am not complaining about the lack of friends but the overflow of friends". She assures her satisfaction with the university, even more, as there is an official who takes care of almost everything and loves his job very much. She claims that she has never encountered any racist attitude in the university, but she mentions several racist situations on the streets and elsewhere:

> Unfortunately, I suffer from knowing so many people (laughs). I feel very, really good here at the university. I have encountered no problem at university so far. I mean, not a racist... (...) When I wanted to pick up my bike on the street, an old woman scolded me: "Why are you wearing a headscarf, why don't you go to school? I said I'm studying." (laughs) They're just prejudices. I realize that prejudices are everywhere. I was a Kurd in Syria, and in Aleppo, and I was a Syrian in Iraq.

In fact, she states that the headscarf is not very important for her, that people attach more importance to it than necessary. She does not want to engage in discussions on the headscarf and its view as a symbol because she is concentrated on her educational targets:

> At some point, I decided that I no longer wanted to wear a headscarf, that I simply didn't want to show a symbol at all. I just want people not to put me right in that category. But that's also, even that it's not easy to do.

The dilemma, which is stated in the passage above, stems from the difficult position of women wearing a headscarf as being a highly controversial object. She formulates her strategy as trying not to let the outside comments block her or distract her. Her observation about the situation of third-generation students who grew up in Germany can also be helpful to understand her self-concept:

> My friends who have a Turkish migration background and were born here, um, they suffer more, but I have no problem if people want to call me a foreigner or if they want to call me a refugee. I don't really care because I've already fled. But they were born here and they are then called foreigners, which is not true because they were born here and they feel at home here. But I, I don't know where my home is.

---

[12] *Allgemeiner Studentenausschuss* (AStA) is the legal institution of student participation in Germany.

"Not knowing where your home is" usually can be seen as a negative and tragic thing. Jiyan refers to this as the reason why she is in a relatively better condition than the students of Turkish origin who grew up in Germany. Because, unlike the third-generation migrant students, she did not experience any difference between her own reality and the reaction and perception from the outside. Turkish students experience disappointment because they are perceived as foreigners even though they are born and raised in Germany. Jiyan thinks that, as in the case of the headscarf, spending too much for debating the concept of integration is not beneficial:

> At work, I hear that I am very well integrated, but I don't know what they mean by that. I don't really know at any point in time, I don't really think about it, I don't care what the others under, whether I'm integrated or not, I'm just me and I always try (2) to improve, and to develop myself personally, mentally and just like that, I don't really care, the whole ethnic or linguistic or I don't know, they are not important to me. Because I know that we are all **human**. I know that one, I mean, I've always said this since I, with this topic, since I was 15-16, because I knew that there was something, I always think that it wasn't decided that you belong to this ethnic group, or to this religion ...

Jiyan compares the discussions on integration with the discussions on ethnicity and religion she had heard in Syria. She had already encountered the topic in her childhood at a certain age, but she does not allow these issues to set her own agenda. She thinks that aspects such as identity, ethnicity and religion are a kind of fate that cannot be chosen by herself. She has a strategy of concentrating on the areas that she can influence instead of the subjects like identity discussions where immigrants, minorities, or refugees are objectified.

## 4.2 Mahmud: "if you want to achieve something, you feel at home"

Like Jiyan, Mahmud comes from a family with a relatively strong accumulated cultural capital in Syria, whereas the economical capital was on a lower level. Compared to Jiyan, it can be observed that he is less ambitious academically although he is also successful in his classes. In this sense, Mahmud and Jiyan can be seen as two types of variations of the same educational process. Mahmud is 27 years old and comes to Germany in 2015, a year after Jiyan. He has been trying for a long time not to leave his country and school:

After graduating from high school, I got a place for psychology in Damascus. I actually wanted to hold out. I wanted to finish my BA there. Without escaping, I mean. I studied 6 semesters. I had to do 4 semesters. At some point I had the feeling that it couldn't go on. If I had stayed there, you couldn't, so you don't know what's going on, but I made the decision to just stay here, so maybe for a better future because we had bad experiences.

He says that the situation became more difficult especially for male students at that time. It was necessary to apply to extend the military service. He had often heard news about male students being recruited or imprisoned. He thinks that an irresistible point has been reached after a certain experience:

We also had experiences. We were arrested even though we were not taken by anything because we rented an apartment. And those who were in front of us, that is, in the apartment before, caused problems. They just took us. In the end we said we didn't do anything, just study there. But anyway, if you go there you have to get something. ... Because you didn't do anything, it was more difficult feeling, and then I made the decision to just go away.

Like Jiyan, Mahmud's parents did not study at university. But his father is a civil servant who represents a certain cultural capital in the small city where he lives. Another similarity with Jiyan's social situation is the fact that he grew up in a family with many sisters and brothers (a total of 10 siblings), many of whom study at universities. As a younger child of the family, he is supported by his older brothers who are studying at university. Mahmud describes studying at a university is a natural goal for all family members. Due to the university experience of his older siblings, even if the parents did not study, Mahmud does not feel as if he is part of the first generation to go to university in the family. Being asked he explains that his grandfather did not study and that he had fields and a farm. He then recalls that both brothers of his grandfather had received university education, one of them in Egypt. "I didn't think about that, but I think the family has been giving importance to education since ancient times".[13]

When he came to Germany, he participated in a language course as a first step. He points out that he was constantly trying to get information about the university education system, especially from the social worker responsible for him during this period.

---

[13] For an enlightening study on the decisive effects of the grandfather and grandmother generations in the transmission process of cultural capital, see Gohlke and Büchner 2006.

> I have asked again and again what subjects are good or what content they have. ... So my primary department was psychology, and secondary social work. I didn't apply for anything else.

He had wanted to continue studying psychology in Germany. Although he had had good grades, the university he applied for did not accept him. "I don't understand why," says Mahmud disappointingly. As a result he began studying social work. Being interviewed why he did not try to apply at other universities for psychology he answers:

M: I tried again, actually I got a place. But since I chose social work. .... We spoke on the phone. I have also thought for a long time. But I was here. I still want to do something, maybe later. A master, or combination ... It was a difficult decision. And it still is. Getting a place in psychology is difficult, I realized.
I: Are you regretting the decision now?
M: Yes, **completely,** because, as I found out, social work is on the one hand, you know the system, social system in Germany, education system, system everywhere, you can also deal well with people. But psychology is different.

Mahmud raises his voice when he says "yes **completely**" to the question of whether he regrets. However, he then lists the interesting aspects of the Social Work department. His expression "It was a difficult decision. And it still is" also carries a paradox in itself. While using the past tense in the first sentence implying that the difficult process of the decision was ended, he uses present continuous in the next sentence, as if the process of decision has not yet been completed. The expression 'I found out', which he frequently uses in this context, implies his earlier thought as somehow naïve and illusory. In fact, it is still theoretically possible to leave the social work department and enrol in the psychology department, but this means a waste of time. Due to the lack of information about the education system in Germany, he has already lost time to a certain extent and decided to turn to his second, not his first choice. Thus, he faces the situation of losing some of his active and potential cultural capital. Although Mahmud struggles with his decision to stay in the social work department, he has formed an inner compromise of the possibility to follow his degree in social work by a master in psychology. This would combine his desire to finish his degree in psychology with efficient use of time (including the time invested already in social work). As Bouchara (Bouchara 2019, p. 54) stated, educational differences and language problems between countries are also a problem for Mahmud:

> I am in the 3rd semester. I did a pre-internship and language course beforehand. 1st and 2nd semester I had difficulty. The content was easy. But the preparation for the exam was difficult. .... I knew for housework. But not exams. In Syria you had a book for a module. But here, there is a lot of literature. Even when expressing language. (...) The lecturers want exactly that you write correctly. And then describe correctly. If you are not completely good at the language, you get difficulties. Especially due to the time pressure in the exam, you have to write quickly. If you write quickly, you put stress. When you're under stress, you're doing wrong (laughs)

Fleeing the war and leaving their home country has led to a loss of certain amount of cultural capital in both cases, complying with the general tendency of the migration from the South (Nohl et al. 2006). Both the type of exam, the expectations of the teachers in the exam and the language problems lead refugee students to get smaller rewards and recognition for their efforts than they would have gotten in their own country. However, both cases in this article (especially Jiyan), show that if these students came from their own country with a middle-class habitus, they were more likely to compensate the loss of cultural capital throughout the migration. In the statements above, Mahmud stresses not the content, but the format of the exam is difficult for him. He is optimistic that he will surmount this obstacle as time goes by: "I had to read a page three times or four times last year, now only twice." He also points out that many classmates and lecturers have helped him in this process.

The concept of integration is one of the issues that keep your mind busy to a certain degree.

M: I have always tried to integrate here.
I: What does integration mean for you, and integration?
M: That you know everything here and always ask.
I: Is integration relevant to you?
M: Integration, yes, it is very relevant for me because it describes that you want to integrate in another country, so you have to integrate. It's difficult. Not everyone can do it.

Unlike Jiyan, he stresses that the concept of integration is important for him. He also tells that he observed or heard some discriminatory words of teachers at the university. He gives two examples of a concrete situation of students wearing a headscarf and a student who has difficulty speaking German have to hear:

> There was a topic about racism and National Socialism, there was a film, the topic is exact, they also talked about Islam and, oh, terrorism, something like that. And the

lecturer said that women with a headscarf can answer that. So this question, they can answer that. (…) A fellow student, he speaks German, but he writes really well, but he is not good at talking. And the lecturer told him that he should repeat the language course again because his German is not so good for the university. So he just took it, but if you think about it, if you think to hear something from a lecturer, it's a bit difficult.

Even though he deals with more racism and integration issues than Jiyan, Mahmud's approach is similar to Jiyan's in a certain way. As Jiyan, he does not feel weak and paralysed. He comments on the situation from a higher position of normative judgement instead of a role as a victim: "My classmates with headscarves experienced discrimination and racism. You wouldn't expect something like that at a university, especially in the field of social work." Towards the end of the interview, he answers the question of how he felt in Germany and at the university and how far racism affected him:

Now is better. I understand the language better. Racist things were only a small part of my life. (…) I think if you want to achieve something, you feel at home here. If you don't feel at home, you don't get everything...

Mahmud sees Germany's future positively. He predicts that Germany will be stronger in the economic field and will be more effective in world politics. Mahmud attributes special importance to legal issues, both due to his experience as a Kurd in Syria and as a refugee in Germany.

We were always excluded as Kurds in Syria. We weren't allowed to speak Kurdish at school. My uncle is not a Syrian citizen. If he had studied, he wouldn't have gotten a job. Not just civil servants, but other jobs. If I could get citizenship because of that, I would feel like a complete person.

Mahmud assumes that if he got citizenship, he would feel like a complete person. This statement implies at the same time that he does not feel like a full person in Germany yet.

## 5 Third-Generation Migrant Students: Exhausting Investment for more Cultural Capital

### 5.1 Can: "Somehow Like an Internal Fight"

The education life of Can starts with substantial problems at the very beginning of his education because of the habitus disparity between his family and educational institutions:

> I just went to the after-school care center and spent the time there until my parents came to pick me up. Exactly, that was childcare for schoolchildren. There I was, I (hmm) got into the first class (hmm) in community elementary school (*Gemeinschaftsgrundschule*) (hmmm) there I have (..) how can I say, there I couldn't cope (hmm) with the class, with the way of teaching, just not (.) yes, how can I say (2) with teachers and such. I was used to **rules** at home, but my mother was not a particularly authoritarian person, so (.) raised us children almost anti-authoritarian, is very rare for Turks of their generation. (hmm) that's why I couldn't manage and was downgraded to school kindergarten. I had the problem that I was (3) quite bright and intelligent child, but because of my (hmm) I should say, underestimated foreign roots from the beginning, and rather (.) underestimated and not encouraged. Because of that I also cancelled the time in the school kindergarten (hmm) I was threatened at the time, you are coming to the school for kids with special needs (*Sonderschule*)...

Can is found to be inadequate in the first year of primary school and sent back to kindergarten. The education system does not take into consideration changing or questioning the habitus of school and its compatibility with the habitus of the student, when there is a disturbance caused by children's behaviour in daily school life. As an explanation, the child is assessed to be developmentally back and not yet ready for normal education. Putting the child back in kindergarten, however, does not solve the problem. If there had been developmental problems, the child would have to get special support that cannot be given in this kindergarten. Furthermore, such a degradation leads to a stigma that has a much bigger effect on the social status of the child in primary school. It is not a coincidence that the word "rules" is stressed by voice in the passage above. Can's behaviour at home is in fundamental contrast with his behaviour at school. Like all children, he internalized certain rules with the socialization he acquired in the family. Classmates who adopt the habits such as sitting together at the table, listening to others quietly and reading books, which are generally applied in the lifestyle of an educated middle class, do not have a problem when they come to school and feel at home there. On the other hand, Can is in a situation of an outsider because of both the class position and ethnicity roots. At school, not only the language spoken at home, but also the way of behaviour conducted at home is foreign.

Can is threatened to be sent to '*Sonderschule*', where most of the students diagnosed as learning disabled (*Lernbehindert*) are sent in the early years of school. The educational life of Can passes with a tension between the efforts of teachers to create an order in school, and the habitual resistance of Can and his family against them. Therefore, Can speaks about an internal struggle with teachers:

> I had a class teacher who was unable to support myself. However, she had an ear for me, I learned a lot from her. Today, even in my professional life, I benefit from the things she taught me at the time. However, at that time there was also an effort to remove me from school and at the same time (..) so just, so somehow like an **internal** fight, somehow there were teachers who just said that they liked me best want to get out from school.

Can then gives an example of the expression "somehow like an internal fight", where a teacher wants to send him politely and courteously to the youth workshop (*Jugendwerkstatt*).

> I was suggested in the eighth grade, I should go to the youth workshop. Youth workshop, there are children who are difficult to educate, handicapped children or young people, who just work for Ford's automotive suppliers, for example, or anything else that assemble car doors that still have bla bla lessons. Something not endowment (hmm) back then, a teacher had told me (imitated in a nice voice), well you like cars too, yes, sure and tell me, don't you want to go to a youth workshop, you can see cars all day. Then I said, ok, tell me more, 'yes you do something like that and then you can go straight to an apprenticeship', then I said, 'do you have a child?' and she says' yes ', I said,' Boy or girl? A boy, how old is he? Just as old as you. I said ok, did you suggest it to him too?, then she was quiet. Then I said I wish you a nice day.

The story told by Can is basically trying to explain that behind the kind and supportive behaviour of the teacher there is a belittling way of looking on him. The phrase 'I wish you a good day' at the end of it is intended to show how ridiculous this supposed politeness is. In Can's narrative, the parties are extremely polite towards each other, but the conflict between them is definitely felt. In this narrative, he says the last word with a subtext that he understood the underlying intent of her kindness, and rejects it with the same strategy of being nice.

Can states that both his father and his mother could not support him adequately although they were interested and willing. He realizes a deep resistance against his father's strict attitude and often makes decisions against his wishes. He starts after work high school (*Abendrealschule*) because a cousin was there.

In many occasions he left the job he did and started something else, only because of the suggestion of friend or acquaintance. When he was looking for a place for vocational training after *Realschule*, a friend of him asked why he does not go to the military instead of waiting. Although his father and siblings were completely against this idea, he decides to enlist. After the military, he goes to a vocational school in the field of Computer Science (*Informatik*). After finishing this school, he finds a job in which he earns very little money although he had applied for many jobs. In this job, one of the bosses asks, why he does not study abroad. He then started a vocational college in Germany because he could not afford it abroad. The college process does not go exactly as it intended:

> I just wanted to (2) study at a university with a monumental buildings and was unfortunately somewhat disappointed by the school system that was schooled, because sitting in class and doing homework as it was in school, I did not imagine it like that. (2) hmm, so during my studies I went into business for myself on the advice of a friend, who told me you are **such a smart guy,** why do you let the whole company fool you? I said, hmm, what should I do, I'm already working. He said be independent, do something of your own. It's really easy. You may have to start small and then rise big Start your own business. Then I went through my head and asked my father. My father wasn't for it, he didn't want to.

Despite his father's unwillingness, he leaves school. The expression "you are such a smart guy" voiced by Can loudly in the section above is an important leitmotif in his general narrative. Being "talented" and "clever" in the understanding of meritocracy, which is generally dominant in the discourse of the German education system, is seen as the basis of educational success. Since the beginning of elementary school, he is confronted with the teachers' idea sending him to *Sonderschule,* where usually students with learning difficulties and lower intelligence go to. He stresses that almost every child of immigrant origin he knows in primary school was sent to either *Hauptschule* or *Sonderschule*. He admits he thought immigrants were stupid at that time. He also has difficulties and is sent to psychotherapy sessions by teachers on grounds that his behavioural problems are a sign of psychological disturbances.

During that same time, he takes an intelligence test at school, and it turns out he had an "unexpectedly" high IQ. He describes this test as a turning point in his perception of himself. Although it makes a positive contribution in terms of self-perception, this information does not lead to the improvement of his participation in school lessons because he got the *Hauptschule* diploma, which is not enough for studying at a university. While the education system is based on the idea that intelligence is decisive for success, the education process cannot provide a high-intelligence student determined with a straight educational path. Although this information increases Can's self-confidence, it does not guarantee the kind of education career he wants.[14]

> Yasemin: "...because my father knew nothing about science,"

At first glance, it can be said that the educational lives of Can and Yasemin are at almost opposite directions. Compared to Can, Yasemin's education life was more calm and successful. Unlike Can, at the time of the interview, she did not leave university and seemed determined to finish it. However, the common decisive effect of having a family with a low cultural capital for Germany but a high educational motivation is also seen in Yasemin's educational biography. Like Can's father, Yasemin's father is concerned with his child's educational success. However, Yasemin's father approaches in a less oppressive and more supportive manner. Instead of punishing or arguing with his child, he tries to give her ideas. Nevertheless, he can support his daughter very little because of his limited cultural capital:

> If I have to do any homework, um, my father always tries because he himself can't write that much in German or something. He tries to give me some ideas in Turkish now, of course, but because he doesn't have the scientific skills, he tries to communicate with his acquaintances who studied and then I send my homework accordingly, um, and they control it and then I have it.

Yasemin's father is very interested in his daughter's educational life and helps her. Yasemin feels the need to say that her father has no scientific thinking and written language proficiency, which is very important for the educated middle-class habitus. But she also adds that he is trying to overcome this deficiency by

---

[14]Can is an example that empirically falsifies the following statements of Hartmut Esser: "In secondary schools, the disadvantages of migrant children are largely lost, mainly due to the selectivity according to intelligence." (Esser 2001, p. 75). Esser himself regards the work done by the qualitative method per se non-scientific. (Esser 2006, p. 4). It would therefore also be worth noting that the sentence is irrational in itself. Esser says that in the German school system, selections are decided according to intelligence in accordance with the meritocratic principle. If it is true, it would be pointless to talk about the exclusion of migrant children in the same sentence. Esser says that the migration age of children and social factors such as ethnic concentration affect the educational success (Esser 2001, p. 63). If social factors such as above are decisive in the child's success, it is not meaningful to claim that selection in the school system is based on intelligence.

mobilizing his own social capital. Yasemin briefly summarizes her education life as follows:

> I started in kindergarten when I was three years old, when I was six years old I then switched to elementary school and after four years I went to Realschule I went and after the tenth grade I went to comprehensive school (*Gesamtschule*) and there I graduated from high school and then I studied in Gießen for a year, not really studied, rather a tried to study (laugh) because the subjects didn't suit me because I did um history and English started again as a teacher for secondary, junior high school and comprehensive school. But I didn't like the subjects at all, so I later switched to another University because I always wanted to study Turkish.

The expression of Yasemin above "not really studied, rather I tried to study" (*Was heißt studiert, ich hab versucht zu studieren*), and her laughter afterwards show that university life was difficult for her at that time. Even if it is in a weaker form, like Can, Yasemin had an experience with teachers who reject the suggestion for access to the Gymnasium:

> So I can say that I was the only Turkish girl in first grade and of course you felt a little bit, that you were marginalized a bit or so. Maybe that's how I felt I don't know. So on the whole, and it was actually doable. Only at the end of the fourth class is the recommended, recommendation, and so it was said because I am more reluctant to go to *Gymnasium*, even though I was student, who had always 1 or 2.

Unlike Can, Yasemin gets good grades when she starts primary school. In the case of Can, it creates a problem that the student is very active and wilful, whereas in the case of Yasemin, it is suggested that being closed and silent prevents her from going to Gymnasium. While Can relates to the school and teachers in a more rebellious and contentious manner, Yasemin accepts the authority of the teacher and acts accordingly. After her father is having a discussion about her future with the teacher, she finds it more appropriate to follow the teacher's decision. One of the common points of Yasemin and Can is their critical attitude towards their father's suggestions. Unlike the two refugee cases discussed above, the father represents a negative orientation in the existing education system. Although Yasemin's relationship with her father is much better than with Can's father, her father's idea is less important than the teacher who is the representative of the school system, just like Can's father.

> My father insisted that I go to *Gymnasium*. But then I always said **no** with the teacher's recommendation that I want to go to *Realschule* now. That is **my** decision and she even

suggested the school to which secondary school I should go and accordingly I also relied on the teacher and then attended the secondary school anyway.

Yasemin, like Can, is generally distant from his father's suggestions. Although the styles of the two fathers are different, they both serve as a negative orientation framework for students in terms of the German education system. While she prefers the decision of the teacher, Yasemin describes it as her own decision. When I talk about her decision, she expresses the words "**no**" and "**my** decision" aloud shows that there is a certain tension here. When I ask why the teacher chose his decision, she gives the answer:

> Because the parents always want the child to achieve the best, and then the teacher got so back, or, suppressed (*zurück, ähm unterdrückt*) so not exactly suppressed but umm (3) yes always told into (*eingeredet*) me no you can't do it.

While Yasemin expresses that the teacher has a decisive effect on herself, she has difficulty in defining what effect this is. The fact that she uses the words "back" and then "suppressed" until she finds exactly what she wanted, and then she does not know what to say for three seconds shows an ambivalent feeling about it. The expression '*eingeredet*' also shows that the decision is not exactly with her own will and persuasion. Yasemin goes to *Realschule* at the suggestion of the teacher and says that she later saw that this was the right decision:

> I am also satisfied that I attended Realschule and not Gymnasium. That was great I think and yes there were more foreigners. At the gymnasium that's not the case, there are more Germans and it gets a little more difficult anyway, I say.

Yasemin says that the advice given by the teacher is very correct and her own experience supports this. However, there is a significant difference between the reason why the teacher recommends *Realschule* and the reason that she later found *Realschule* well. Contrary to the teacher's prediction, Yasemin does not find *Realschule* good because it is relatively easy, it is mainly positive that she is a student of immigrant background. While defining *Gymnasium* as a place where Germans go, she shows it as the reason of the difficulty in that place. Here, as the teacher said, *Gymnasium* is described as more difficult. However, the difficulty is not due to the more challenging lessons in *Gymnasium*. The main difficulty stems from being the only student of immigrant background who is in primary school and not feeling at home.

## 6   Discussion: A Comparison of the Habitus and Cultural Capital of the Refugee and Third-generation Migrant Students

The basis for the comparison made within the framework of this article forms the continuities and changes in the class positions of the interviewees across generations. In all the examples described, families have high educational motivation for their children. However, refugee students have been able to study in highly respected departments in their own country without considerable barriers. In the case of immigrant children, the process of studying a university was more difficult. The difference is that the families of refugee students can transfer sufficient cultural capital from their home country as a particular social space to their own children. If we take Germany as a social space, parents and families of immigrant children have not been able to transmit a substantial cultural capital and educated class habitus to their children. Students from immigrant backgrounds with a lower class habitus are channelled into the German education system to school forms that deprived them of their right to university at a very young age.

The migrant students are not as comfortable as refugee students, when they criticize the university in general because they have reached that point with an intense effort. Two refugee students described above perceive their department in Germany (Social Work) lower than the departments they studied in their own country. Therefore, they are more comfortable and self-conscious when they criticize the curriculum of the department. Migrant children, on the other hand, criticize the difficulties of the department (Yasemin) or the teaching techniques of teachers (Can). Their criticism is from a lower position, as they have experienced a rise in class position. Refugee students, on the other hand, experience the feeling of falling from height due to the department they studied and the cultural capital they lost (time, language, legal conditions).[15]

The examples above have important paradoxes in terms of culturalist presumptions in the debate on integration in Germany. We can say that the following three ideas constitute these presuppositions: 1) German language is the key to integration 2) Recognition and adaptation of German culture are decisive 3) Immigrants must show a special effort for integration. When we compare the situation of the

---

[15] Ruzgar, another Syrian immigrant student I spoke to during the research, said that while she was studying art in Syria, when she came to Germany, she thought that art education was far from life and that she started to study social work after the refugee experience. Her parents, who are doctors, belonged to a high class in Syria and were enrolled in the faculty of art because she considered to be a painter herself. She said she saw that it is more important to help people because of their urgent problems in Germany.

newly arrived refugee students from Syria and the situation of the third generation students socialized in Germany, we face a situation that contradicts these pre-admissions: For the third generation immigrant children that I have evaluated in this study, German is the language they know best, they grew up in the German culture and they show a special effort for integration. Although they suit more to the pre-assumptions of the integration process, they feel less free in the university space. Jiyan, who feels mostly at home at university and is the most successful in her lessons, speaks less German than third-generation students, shows less interest in adapting to German culture (she wears headscarves and do not attach special importance to this). Refugee students in this article have characteristics such as having confidence in themselves, coming from families with a relatively higher cultural level and seeing education as an object of desire on its own, apart from achieving a specific goal.

These empirical examples show that mainstream integration perceptions and debates are insufficient to explain reality because of not taking into account the class relations. It seems that, efforts for the integration in the German culture mean unnecessary burden rather than a substantial benefit for the young third-generation immigrants. The following expression, which I mentioned above, can also be interpreted in this respect: "I just wanted to (…) study at a university with a monumental building and was unfortunately a little disappointed by the school system that was schooled because sitting in class, doing homework, was just like at school". While a national cultural indicator (monument) is guiding in Can's university preference, he does not see the idea that sitting in lessons and doing homework as valuable and desirable as means of reaching more culture and education. The relation of education with habitus, and cultural capital is not explicitly shown to students in the education system (Fürstenau and Niedrig, 2011). Instead of this explicit education, an ideology of talent and intelligence mystifies the real processes of the educational and cultural improvement.

## 7 Pedagogical Inferences for the Higher Education

An important limitation of this article is the absence of the statistical data about the class positions of the refugee university students in Germany. The refugee students discussed in this article had, however, a relatively higher cultural capital in their homeland and are prone to scientific study style from their own country. Even if they lose their cultural capital to a degree in the new country, they incorporated a habitus of middle class, so that they do not feel 'out of place' at the university space. Such refugee students need counselling services such as language courses, residence and work permit problems, psychological support, and knowledge of the education system in the short term (Grüttner et al. 2018, p. 130). Especially the knowledge about the differences between the systems in their own countries (for example Syria) and Germany can be effective for realizing their preferred educational path. The refugees with higher cultural capital need mostly a general information about the possibilities and obstacle in the university system.

Third-generation migrant students do not need to learn German language, education system and culture. What such students need is not an ordinary German course, but rather learning German as a scientific language (Brandl et. al. 2013). In addition, workshops in which the scientific study style are shown are of special importance for such students. Such lessons are important not only for immigrant origin but also for all the other students as well, including refugees without higher cultural capital. Explicitly or implicitly, third-generation immigrant students have been given by their education system a feeling of being out of place in the field of higher education and they can reach the university level only with a great volume of personal effort because of their lower-class habitus. Socio-analytical reflections (not only in relevant sociological seminars, but also in all level of university administration and campus) sensitive to habitus and class positions can help for discharging the burden of seeking integration and identity and finding a self-conscious position that is in accordance with its own reality for the third-generation migrants in the education system.

## References

Autorengruppe Bildungsberichterstattung (2016). *Bildung in Deutschland 2016: Ein indikatorengestützter Bericht mit einer Analyse zu Bildung und Migration.* Bielefeld: Bertelsmann.

Becker, Birgit (2010). Bildungsaspirationen von Migranten: Determinanten und Umsetzung in Bildungsergebnisse Mannheim. *Arbeitspapiere - Mannheimer Zentrum für Europäische Sozialforschung*; 137.

Bendel, P. (2017). Alter Wein in neuen Schläuchen? Integrationskonzepte vor der Bundestagswahl APuZ 27–29/2017 pp. 4–9

Bohnsack, R. (2014). *Rekonstruktive Sozialforschung: Einführung in qualitativen Methoden.* Opladen: Verlag Barbara Budrich.

Bouchara, A. (2019). Bildungsbedürfnisse und Hindernisse von Geflüchteten in Deutschland: eine empirische Studie zu sozialen Netzwerken von Geflüchteten an deutschen Hochschulen. *interculture journal: Online-Zeitschrift für interkulturelle Studien* 18(31), 53–72. https://nbn-resolving.org/urn:nbn:de:0168-ssoar-62767-2.

Bourdieu, P. (1974). *Zur Soziologie der symbolischen Formen.* Frankfurt a. M: Suhrkamp.

Bourdieu, P. (1991). *Language and Symbolic Power.* Cambridge, MA: Harvard University Press.
Bourdieu, P. (1998a). *Masculine Domination.* Cambridge: Polity Press.
Bourdieu, Pierre. (1998b). *Practical Reason: On the Theory of Action.* Stanford, CA: Stanford University Press.
Bourdieu, P. (2012). Ökonomisches Kapital, kulturelles Kapital, soziales Kapital Ullrich Bauer et al. (ed.) *Handbuch Bildungs- und Erziehungssoziologie.* Wiesbaden: VS-Verlag S. 229–242.
Bourdieu, P., & Wacquant, L. J. (1992). An invitation to reflexive sociology. Chicago, Il.: University of Chicago Press.
Brandl, H., Arslan, E., Langelahn, E., & Riemer, C. (2013). *Mehrsprachig in Wissenschaft und Gesellschaft.* Bielefeld: Universität Bielefeld.
Büchner, P. & Brake, A. (Hrsg.) (2006). *Bildungsort Familie: Transmission von Bildung und Kultur im Alltag von Mehrgenerationenfamilien.* Wiesbaden: VS Verlag für Sozialwissenschaften.
Czollek, M. (2020). *Desintegriert Euch!* München: Carl Hanser Verlag.
Elias, N. (1985). Wissenschaft oder Wissenschaften? Beitrag zu einer Diskussion mit wirklichkeitsblinden Philosophen. In Stichting, N. E. (ed.) *Aufsätze und andere Schriften III Gesammelte Schriften Band 16,* (pp. 60–93). Frankfurt. a. M.: Suhrkamp.
Elias, N. and Scotson, J. (2010). *Etablierte und Außenseiter* Frankfurt a. M: Suhrkamp.
El-Mafaalini, A. (2012). *BildungsaufsteigerInnen aus benachteiligten Milieus. Habitustransformation und soziale Mobilität bei Einheimischen und Türkeistämmigen.* Wiesbaden: Springer VS.
Esser, H. (2001). Integration und ethnische Schichtung. https://www.mzes.uni-mannheim.de/publications/wp/wp-40.pdf.
Esser, H. (2003). Ist das Konzept der Assimilation überholt? *Geographische Revue* 2003/2, S. 5–22.
Esser, H. (2006). *Migration, Sprache und Integration.* (AKI-Forschungsbilanz, 4). Berlin: Wissenschaftszentrum Berlin für Sozialforschung gGmbH FSP Zivilgesellschaft, Konflikte und Demokratie Arbeitsstelle Interkulturelle Konflikte und gesellschaftliche Integration -AKI-. https://nbn-resolving.org/urn:nbn:de:0168-ssoar-113493.
Esser, H. (2009). „Der Streit um die Zweisprachigkeit: Was bringt die Bilingualität?" in Gogolin, I. and Neumann, U. *Streitfall Zweisprachigkeit – The Bilingualism Controversy* Wiesbaden: VS Verlag für Sozialwissenschaften. pp. 69–88.
Fourier, K. et al. (2017). Integration von Flüchtlingen an deutschen Hochschulen. Erkenntnisse aus den Hochschulprogrammen für Flüchtlinge. DAAD/DZHW, Hannover. https://www.daad.de/medien/der-daad/studie_hochschulzugang_fluecht-linge.pdf.
Fürstenau, S. & Niedrig, H. (2011). Die kultursoziologische Perspektive Pierre Bourdieus: Schule als sprachlicher Markt. In **Fürstenau,** S. and **Gomolla,** M. (eds.) *Migration und schulischer Wandel: Mehrsprachigkeit* (pp. 69–87). Wiesbaden: VS Verlag für Sozialwissenschaften.
Fürtjes, O. and Arslan, E. (2016). Soziale Herkunft, Habitus und Zukunftsvorstellungen von Studierenden mit Migrationshintergrund: "Kulturelle Adaption" durch Bildungsbeflissenheit. In Arslan, E. and Bozay, K. *Symbolische Ordnung und Bildungsungleichheit in der Einwanderungsgesellschaft.* Wiesbaden: Springer Verlag.

Geis, W. (2017). Arbeitsmarktintegration Von Flüchtlingen Antwort auf den Fachkräftemangel? *APuZ* 27–29/2017, pp. 27–33.

Gohlke, H. & Büchner, P. (2006). Das familiäre Bildungserbe als Produkt gelebter Generationenbeziehungen. In Büchner, Peter & Brake, Anne (Hrsg.) *Bildungsort Familie: Transmission von Bildung und Kultur im Alltag von Mehrgenerationenfamilien*. Wiesbaden: VS Verlag für Sozialwissenschaften.

Grüttner, M., Berg, J., Schröder, S., & Otto, C. (2018). Refugees on their way to German higher education: A capabilities and engagements perspective on aspirations, challenges and support. *Global Education Review* 5(4), 115–135.

Lambert, L., Blumenthal, J. von, & Beigang, S. (2018). *Flucht und Bildung: Hochschulen. State-of-Research Papier 8b des Verbundprojekts 'Flucht: Forschung und Transfer'*, Osnabrück: Institut für Migrationsforschung und Interkulturelle Studien (IMIS) der Universität Osnabrück / Bonn: Internationales Konversionszentrum Bonn (BICC).

Lambert, L. (2018). Studium gestattet? Die symbolische Herrschaft des Aufenthaltsstatus und des Asylverfahrens beim Hochschulzugang von Gefluchteten. In Arslan, E. and Bozay, K. (eds.), *Symbolische Ordnung und Fluchtbewegungen in der Einwanderungsgesellschaft*. Wiesbaden: Springer.

Mannheim, K. (2015, [1929]). *Ideologie und Utopia*. Frankfurt a. M.: Verlag Vittorio Klostermann.

Mecheril, P. et al. (2010). *Migrationspädagogik*. Weinheim und Basel: Beltz.

Nohl, A.-M. (2013). *Interview und dokumentarische Methode*. Wiesbaden: Springer Verlag.

Nohl, A.-M., Schittenhelm, K, Schmidtke, O. (2006). Cultural capital during migration: A multi-level approach for the empirical analysis of the labor market integration of highly skilled migrants. *Forum: Qualitative Social Research* 7(3).

Pries, L. (2008). Die Transnationalisierung der sozialen Welt. Sozialräume jenseits von Nationalgesellschaften. Frankfurt/M.: Suhrkamp.

Pries, L. (2015a). Teilhabe in der Migrationsgesellschaft: Zwischen Assimilation und Abschaffung des Integrationsbegriffs. Imis-Beiträge Heft 47/2015, pp. 7–36.

Pries, L. (2015b). Transnationalisierung. Theorie und Empirie neuer Vergesellschaftung. Wiesbaden: VS Verlag.

Schittenhelm, K. (2012). Qualitative Bildungs- und Arbeitsmarktforschung: Frühere Entwicklungen und aktuelle Zugänge. In Schittenhelm, Karin (Hrsg.) *Qualitative Bildungs- und Arbeitsmarktforschung: Grundlagen, Perspektiven, Methoden*. (pp. 9–30). Wiesbaden: Springer Fachmedien.

Schütze, F. (1983). Biographieforschung und narratives Interview. In: *Neue Praxis* 13 (1983), 3, pp. 283–293. https://nbn-resolving.de/urn:nbn:de:0168-ssoar-53147.

Statistisches Bundesamt (2017). Bevölkerung und Erwerbstätigkeit: Bevölkerung mit Migrationshintergrund – Ergebnisse des Mikrozensus 2016. https://www.destatis.de/DE/Publikationen/Thematisch/Bevoelkerung/MigrationIntegration/Migrationshintergrund2010220167004.pdf?__blob=publicationFile.

Thiersch, S. (2014). Bildungshabitus und Schulwahl: Fallrekonstruktionen zur Aneignung und Weitergabe des familialen 'Erbes'. Wiesbaden: Springer Fachmedien.

van Essen, F. (2013). Soziale Ungleichheit, Bildung und Habitus: Möglichkeitsräume ehemaliger Förderschüler. Wiesbaden: Springer.

Vodafone Stiftung Deutschland. (2011). *Zwischen Ehrgeiz und Überforderung: Bildungsambitionen und Erziehungsziele von Eltern in Deutschland.* Eine Studie des Instituts für Demoskopie Allensbach im Auftrag der Vodafone Stiftung Deutschland.

Wimmer, A., & Glick Schiller, N. (2003). Methodological Nationalism, the Social Sciences, and the Study of Migration: An Essay in Historical Epistemology, *International Migration Review* 37(3), 576–610.

# "But I Am (not) from...": A Qualitative Analysis of Intragroup Self-Differentiation Processes Among International Degree Seeking Students in Germany

Jesús Pineda

## 1 Introduction

The number of students enrolled at higher education institutions outside their home country has risen considerably over the last 30 years from 0.8 million in 1975 to 5.1 million in 2016 (DAAD and DZHW 2019). Several estimates have suggested that this trend will continue, and the number of international students is expected to further increase within the next decades (Luu et al. 2015; OECD 2009; Böhm et al. 2004). Choudaha (2017) proposes a typology of three different waves to understand international student mobility since the end of the 1990s. His classification offers a valuable contextualization of socio-political events that shaped higher education worldwide. He argues that Wave I was defined by terrorist attacks of 2001, Wave II was shaped by the global financial recession and Wave III is currently being influenced by changes in the Chinese economy as well as major political transformations in Europe (Brexit) and the USA (the Trump Era). Through his analysis it becomes clear that even though the numbers show a consistent trend, drivers and rationales for recruiting and retaining international students are constantly evolving. In recent years many countries have declared explicit targets for the number of international students that are supposed to be hosted by a certain period. These specific targets have intensified the competition

---

J. Pineda (✉)
Deutscher Akademischer Austauschdienst, Bonn, Germany
E-Mail: pineda@daad.de

© The Author(s), under exclusive license to Springer Fachmedien Wiesbaden GmbH, part of Springer Nature 2021
J. Berg et al. (eds.), *Refugees in Higher Education*, Higher Education Research and Science Studies, https://doi.org/10.1007/978-3-658-33338-6_7

between countries and institutions to not only reach quantitative targets but to attract and retain certain groups of students.

In the context of internationalization of higher education, it has become imperative to understand the reasons why international students decide to go abroad as well as what influences their choice of location. Different theoretical perspectives have been proposed over the years to explain these dynamics. One well-established model is the pull–push factor, which argues that certain factors in a person's home country would encourage them to look for opportunities abroad whereas others would make certain destinations more attractive than others (see De Wit 2008; Lee and Tan 1984; McMahon 1992; Mazzarol and Soutar 2002). Some authors have used other theoretical approaches such as the human capital model and the migration model to help understand and predict the reasons to study abroad triggered by different personal interests (see Kaushal and Lanati 2019). In essence, Kaushal & Lanati argue that the human capital theory would explain the motivation of students who go abroad to obtain skills and qualifications that are not available in their home countries. This would provide a competitive advantage once the person returns. On the other hand, the neo-classical migration theory would explain that students who go abroad use higher education as an entrance into the labor market of that country.

A recent development in the debate on international students is the integration of individuals with a refugee background[1] into higher education. In recent years the issue of forced migration has attracted a great deal of attention for a variety of reasons. Millions of individuals have been forced to leave their home countries trying to overcome starvation, war, natural catastrophes, religious discrimination and political repression (Taylor et al. 2016; Hatton 2016; Gatrell 2016; Ghaderi and Eppenstein 2017; Schneider 2016). Educational systems of receiving societies have tried to react to these developments to offer chances and improve the integration potential of these individuals. While different reports suggest that approximately 22 to 24% of refugee children and teenagers have managed to enter secondary schools worldwide (UNHCR 2019; Zubairi and Rose 2016), access to higher education still presents a challenge. It is estimated that only about one percent of refugees manage to enroll in higher education (Federal Foreign Office et al. 2019; UNHCR 2015). Some researchers have already addressed the challenges and potentials of higher education for refugees (Goastellec 2018; Earnest et al.

---

[1] The term "refugee" is often used to refer to groups of individuals who might be facing different life circumstances such as asylum seekers who want to file an asylum request, asylum seekers who are waiting for a decision and persons who are entitled to be granted asylum, refugee protection or subsidiary protection (see BAMF 2019).

2010; Crea 2016; de Wit and Altbach 2016; Harris and Marlowe 2011; Lenette 2016; Mangan and Winter 2017; Morrice 2013; Stevenson and Baker 2018).

## 2 Case Study: International Students in Germany

In the field of internationalization of higher education, Germany has positioned itself as one of the worldwide leaders. This position has been confirmed by several recent publications (MPD 2019; DAAD and DZHW 2019). It is important to clarify that statistically speaking,[2] foreign students in Germany consist of two different groups of individuals which are generally grouped together. The first group (Bildungsausländer) is referred to as international students for the purpose of this article. These are students who hold a foreign nationality and acquired their higher education entrance qualification in a foreign country before accessing higher education in Germany. The second group (Bildungsinländer) subsumes all students of foreign/non-German nationalities who obtained their higher education entrance qualification in Germany. There are several regional classifications used to further categorize the international student population in Germany. The Federal Statistical Office distinguishes between Europe (European Union, Rest of Europe), Africa, America, Asia, Australia and Oceania, Stateless, Unresolved and Unspecified (Destatis 2019). Other organizations such as the German Research Foundation (DFG), the Alexander von Humboldt Foundation or the German Academic Exchange Service (DAAD) use different regional classifications. The DAAD for instance combines groups of countries based on so-called cultural areas. Under the DAAD's classification of world regions, the following regions are grouped together for statistical purposes: Western Europe, Middle and South-Eastern Europe, Eastern Europe and Central Asia, North America, Latin America, North Africa and Middle East, Sub-Saharan Africa and Asia and Pacific. The fact that there seems to be a lack of consensus regarding the use of the same categories confronts research on international students with a variety of difficulties. Nevertheless, these categories are relevant, given that belonging to different groups brings along a variety of legal frameworks and institutional labels. Differences in applicants' experiences can be identified in terms of whether a residence permit is required, the conditions concerning health insurance and the access and

---

[2] Given that this is a qualitative analysis, the discussion of statistical classifications is merely intended to offer background information for the argument that this analysis presents. For a more complex and detailed account of the statistical classifications and the classification of the world regions see DAAD 2010, DAAD and DZHW 2019, Destatis 2019.

constraints in the labor market to name a few. Furthermore, there might be differences regarding the requirements to access higher education and whether tuition fees are to be paid.[3]

On August 15th 2019, the Federal Ministry of Education and Research (BMBF) published a press release (Pressemitteilung: 085/2019[4]) to announce the publication of the latest edition of "Wissenschaft Weltoffen".[5] The statement described the current situation of international students in Germany as follows:

> In Winter Semester 2017/18 375,000 foreign students were enrolled in Germany, including 282,000 international students with a university entrance qualification from abroad ("foreign students") who came to Germany for the purpose of studying or for humanitarian reasons. The eight countries with the highest inflows of asylum seekers (Syria, Afghanistan, Iraq, Nigeria, Eritrea, Iran, Pakistan and Somalia) accounted for 24,000 international students at German universities. Most of them are likely to be refugees. The DAAD programmes for refugees funded by the Federal Ministry of Education and Research (BMBF) have made a significant contribution to their integration into higher education institutions. Syrian refugees are now the sixth largest group of foreign origin at German universities (own translation)

The homogenization of the cultural and ethnical diversity of the group of international students with and without a refugee background is clear in the official formulation. Even though I am doing research on international students my analysis rests on the assumption that one cannot regard any individual as a student exclusively, but always as a member of a broader societal discourse. This is because higher education can be regarded as one more stage of an individual's biography. Understanding the discourses surrounding guest workers, highly skilled migrants, international students and refugees in German society is vital to being able to understand the impact of these labels on the students' identities and experiences as members of different groups.

Given demographic dynamics in Germany, migration has historically played a relevant role for German society. In the post-war period, the German government established agreements with other governments to recruit foreign workers

---

[3] Since Winter Semester 2017/2018 a tuition fee of 1500 € per semester has been introduced for non-EU/EEA/Swiss students in the federal state of Baden-Württemberg.

[4] Available at: https://www.bmbf.de/de/deutschland-bei-internationalen-studierenden-beg ehrt-9380.html (retrieved on 18.12.2019).

[5] "Wissenschaft Weltoffen" is a bilingual publication which offers up to date information and relevant data on the international nature of higher education and research in Germany. It is published on yearly basis by the German Academic Exchange Service (DAAD) and the German Centre for Research on Higher Education and Science Studies (DZHW).

in order to combat labor shortages and help rebuild the nation (Richter 2015). In the framework of Germany's knowledge-based economy and with the recent acknowledgement of the shortage of skilled professionals, the need for a qualified workforce demanded a different approach. The Federal Employment Agency has systematically examined the situation of the labor market and compiled priority lists of occupational fields and roles that need to be compensated in certain areas (Bundesagentur für Arbeit 2018). To address this issue, several strategies can be identified to attract high-skilled foreign nationals[6] and to recruit and retain international students.

Since 2015 a change in the discourse can be observed about the accelerated influx of migrants in the framework of what has been titled as the "refugee crisis".[7] The influx of refugees within a short period of time triggered a series of debates. As a reaction, a series of social movements have emerged both in favor of and against the reception of migrants. The discourses around this demographic group have tried to answer questions about the exact number of refugees in Germany, their age, gender, specific origin, costs related to their integration, the integration in the educational system as well as labor market and possible social benefits they receive (see Schammann and Kühn 2016; Weiss et al. 2019; Kiziak et al. 2019; Brücker et al. 2018; Holmes and Castañeda 2016; Kunz and Ottersbach 2017; Kury and Redo 2018). Ever since this development took place, various initiatives have been established to help immigrants and facilitate their integration. Researchers from a variety of disciplines have discussed this issue in detail. As an example, problems with the label "refugee" and its implications have been addressed (see Arslan and Bozay 2019; Schacht 2018, 2019). Several authors have also analyzed the experiences of stigma, online hatred, rejection and violence which refugees have been subjected to (Will et al. 2019; Benček and Strasheim 2016; Funk 2016; Goebel 2017; Jäckle and König 2016; Köhler et al. 2019; Vollmer and Karakayalic 2017). When it comes to the issue of refugee students in higher education, extensive research on the particularities of their experience, case studies and analyses of various initiatives supporting this group can be referred to (Beigang et al. 2018; Bouchara 2019; Berg 2018; Halkic and Arnold 2019; Jungblut et al. 2018; Steinhardt and Eckhardt 2017; Morris-Lange and Brands 2016; Schammann and Böhm 2017; Schammann and Younso 2016; Schneider 2018; Streitwieser et al. 2018; Streitwieser et al. 2017; Streitwieser

---

[6]For instance, a new law on the immigration of skilled workers "Fachkräfteeinwanderungsgesetz" has been passed.

[7]The "refugee crisis in Germany" refers to the entry into Germany of more than one million of individuals seeking protection in the years 2015 and 2016.

and Unangst 2018; Streitwieser and Brück 2018; Maschke and Riehle 2017; Gast 2018; DAAD 2018).[8]

## 3 A Qualitative Approach Embedded in a Mixed-Method Study

This article is derived from a larger longitudinal mixed-method study on "Success and withdrawal of international students in Germany" (SeSaBa). The joint project SeSaBa[9] focuses on the interdisciplinary study of sociological and psychological determinants of academic success and the drop-out of international students in Germany (see Falk et al. 2019). The project started with a preliminary qualitative analysis (see Pineda 2018) prior to the development of the quantitative study, which consists of six surveys over the course of three years. In addition to this, further qualitative methods are carried out throughout the study under the logic of complementarity of mixed methods (Kuckartz 2014).

This article presents preliminary findings of the qualitative component of this mixed-method study. Since the beginning of my qualitative work in the framework of this study, I was confronted with the need to both differentiate and at the same time homogenize the group of international students. Over the course of the preliminary qualitative study I became aware of the fact that international students may face a different treatment based on their specific background. One participant of an expert workshop shares their experience the following way:

> "We currently have the experience that Syrian students no longer say they come from Syria because they then realize that conversations are broken off. I already know that, not quantitatively, but qualitatively, people from Western Europe, South America,

---

[8]For data protection reasons, the residence status of international students is generally not recorded during enrolment. This means that international students become a homogeneous group in practical terms regardless of their educational biography. However, many special programs address the needs and particularities of different groups. From a sociological perspective, it is interesting to explore this paradoxical process between normalization and differentiation. In this paper I address how these differences affect the students' own identity and experiences but not necessarily the institutional structures as such.

[9]The joint project "Success and withdrawal of international students in Germany" (SeSaBa) is being conducted by the German Academic Exchange Service (DAAD), Hagen distance education university (FernUniversität in Hagen) and the Bavarian State Institute for Higher Education Research and Planning (IHF) in Munich. It is funded by the Federal Ministry of Education and Research (BMBF) between 2017 and 2021. Funding code: 01PX16016A-C.

North America, are perceived as interesting by German students, but from Eastern Europe, Africa, etc., not so much." (own translation)[10]

One of the further qualitative methods that I carry out is the explorative analysis of the free-text comments that participants enter at the end of each survey. Once a participant has filled out one of the surveys, the following statement is presented:

> "You made it! In the final section, you have the opportunity to inform us of anything else important if you feel it has not been covered in the questionnaire"

This qualitative analysis allows the research team to identify possible difficulties in understanding and receive the feedback of the participants about the survey. Furthermore, it also offers a rich source of data regarding topics and themes that might be particularly important to the respondents. A literature review during the development of this idea suggested that some authors consider the open comments to complement and enhance the results of quantitative analyses (Gallan et al. 2017; Rich et al. 2013; O'Cathain and Thomas 2004; Thomas et al. 1996; Popping 2015; Chambers and Chiang 2012). I also realized that there is also a growing trend in social media research to analyze online discussions, comments on online newspapers as well as social media. Researchers reconstruct the topics that individuals address to point out thematic trends and attitudes expressed by selected social groups. Some examples are analyses of climate change discussions online (Lörcher and Taddicken 2017), online hatred on YouTube (Ernst et al. 2017), political comments on Facebook (Maier 2016; Hintze 2015) and discussions about pandemics on Twitter (Chew and Eysenbach 2010).

One advantage of my approach is that I do not analyze comments of random individuals but those of a sample of international students who shared a variety of characteristics that were mandatory requirements during the recruitment process of the SeSaBa study.[11] Using a content analysis approach based on Kuckartz (2018) I used a mixed form of category formation to organize the information. Kuckartz (2018) argues that not only the manifest meaning but also

---

[10] The original quote in German language can be found in Pineda (2018, p. 29).

[11] The sample of the study consists of 4751 international students. To participate in the SeSaBa study a registration phase took place between October 2017 and February 2018. The aim of the registration was to ensure that only international students in their first semester who intend to graduate in Germany would participate in the study. The questions of the registration concerned the study status of the potential participants, the institution, the desired degree, the country of acquisition of the high school diploma and the nationality. After these questions had been successfully answered according to the criteria of the target group, the students were asked to provide their contact data (see Falk et. al. 2017).

the latent content must be the object of qualitative content analysis. The first step was a classification of comments using what Kuckartz calls A-priori (deductive) category formation. For that purpose, I used the general challenges that I identified over the course of the preliminary qualitative study (Pineda 2018). Once the material had been classified using those categories and the amount of comments in each category had been registered, a second step was carried out. Further categories were then formed inductively with comments that had not been covered by my categories. During the analysis of the first waves of the survey, it was determined that there were certain themes that had been mentioned more frequently and with a stronger focus such as the issue study financing.[12] Even though the longitudinal study consists of six surveys at the time of writing only the first four surveys had been conducted. The data considered for this article consists of 2423 comments[13] that were analyzed.

## 4 Preliminary Findings

This section discusses what can be regarded as a content-oriented structured qualitative analysis. The aim is to show how the content analysis allowed me to explore the self-differentiation processes among international degree seeking students in Germany that I found in the data.

### 4.1 Self-Differentiation Based on Legal Constraints

After the A-priori (deductive) category formation I realized that the category that had been mentioned most frequently was the issue of "student financing". Interestingly an in-depth analysis of some of the comments allowed me to identify a subcategory that I labeled "experienced inequality in comparison to other student groups". The following quotes present examples of some of the statements[14]:

---

[12] See Pineda et al. (2019) for an example of how this qualitative analysis was used to explore a specific subtopic.

[13] 792 after the first survey, 806 after the second, 461 after the third and 364 after the fourth.

[14] I have tried to preserve the original texts as much as possible. Grammar mistakes have not been corrected. In some cases, the text has been cut to present the information that is relevant for the analysis, given that some quotes are very long and detailed.

"Universities in Baden-Württemberg charge non-EU students 1500 per semester[...] It is difficult for me to afford this semester fee which my classmates from Germany and other EU countries are not paying…"

"I came with the intention of funding my life and studies, as I have been a functioning adult for more than 5 years now. Doing this in Germany, as a non-EU student is apparently quite difficult [... ]So far, I love the education I am receiving, and some future promise to live and work as a foreign resident in the dynamic and exciting EU, but the entire past 5 months have been a big bureaucratic and financial scare for me. I wish this experience upon nobody and I hope the situation can be improved for future self-supported students from outside the EU."

The second quote shows that the issue of not only having to deal with additional financial burdens. It refers to the need to deal with additional paperwork and bureaucracy that some students need to go through depending on their countries of origin. It seems from the way the student expresses themselves that they have had a positive experience despite the differential treatment. In the comments I also found a different angle. Some students seem to have difficulties to comprehend the reason of this differentiation. Accordingly, once can interpret their statements as comments with a certain degree of resentment and frustration about their given status:

"Germany gives everything to refugees and migrants but there is nothing for students from students for example Iran. Refugees get everything paid for and offered to for example apartment and rent, pension fund, health insurance, permanent residence permit immediately and are allowed to study and work and to make money that is not fair. Students are also human like refugees. You are expected to just study and work because you are not a refugee" (Own translation)

In comparison to the first quotes, this student is not addressing the difference between European and non-European students. The comment expresses the clear feeling of experienced inequality due to legal categorizations. Another student complains about the same issue but in a subtler way:

„It was very difficult to see that Germans and refugees obtain financial assistance to study and support and I do not. I have to work during the weekends and at the same time study. It is very difficult" (Own translation)

Nevertheless, these differences are pointed out not only in comparison to groups that are considered different on a legal basis. In the following quote a student expresses their frustration over feeling that individuals even within their own group are still given preferential treatment:

> "I would like to say that I am very frustrated and sad with this new law from the state of Baden-Württemberg, that says that non-EU citizens have to pay 1500 euros per semester. I understand that the government has to obtain resources to cover other things, but I think a little bit unfair that the government don't look at the real situation of the students. There are many students of the selected poor countries that have conditions to pay these due and they don't do it, just because they come from these selected countries, and there are many students that almost have no money to pay, but they have to, simply because their country is not on this list. I agree that students of other countries have to pay more than German students. But you have to agree with me, that we pay the same amount of 10 German students, and that is unfair. If we had to pay the double or triple of what a German student pay, it is completely reasonable. But 10 times, in my opinion, it is too much. I see every day on TV that Germany supports people from all over the world, giving them all things they need, not looking at where they come. But when it comes to education, it seems that Germany wants distance from no-EU citizens."

I would like to focus on the complaint about the rule when it comes to non-EU students from disadvantaged backgrounds. The rules of exemption are more complex than described by the student in question.[15] The interesting matter at this point is the experienced disadvantage expressed since this student cannot comprehend the reasons behind these regulations.

## 4.2 Self-Differentiation Based on Sense of Belonging to Subgroups

As I further explored the material, I noticed that some students were also expressing their desire to differentiate themselves from those who were regarded as disadvantaged. The following quote shows the view of a European student who talks about other international students from outside, as if this individual was a member of a different group:

> "The thing I'm most grateful for, ever since I moved to Germany, is the capacity to study without extra costs. Talks of limiting this education to European students might not stress me personally, as an European citizen, but feels in a way like a loss of the vision that made Europe, and especially Germany, the forefront of social progress in the last two decades. It worries me that if that idea is thrown away and indeed international students lose this possibility, Germany will set the possibility for other,

---

[15] The website of the Ministry of Science, Research and Arts of Baden-Württemberg lists fee exemptions in detail. See https://mwk.baden-wuerttemberg.de/de/startseite/. (retrieved on 18.12.2019).

less idealistic nations to take this step back as an argument for why such a system is not worth pursuing in the first place."

The most interesting aspect of this statement is the fact that the student seems to separate themselves from the group of non-Europeans but at the same time expresses a certain degree of empathy towards those who do not have the same privileges. In contrast, I also was able to identify statements where students tried to differentiate themselves in an even stronger fashion:

> "Sometimes I was a little bit confused about whether or not the questionnaire was thought for me as a EU citizen... As far as I am concerned I am the only foreigner in my study programme. This might have influenced my answers in respect to contact to other people. When it comes to finances I am receiving support from my home country. I mentioned that under miscellaneous." (Own translation)

I started to notice statements similar to this in which students challenge the fact that they were being considered international students because in their opinion they did not share many of the features of being "a foreigner". In some cases, these were made by students who had been living in Germany for a long time before they became students. In other cases, some students did not see themselves as coming from a different place:

> „For students from a German speaking country or from Central Europe some questions are difficult to answer (life style, customs, typical German features) given that the culture in Austria and Switzerland is almost identical." (Own translation)

It has been established that some students from German speaking countries or with German roots commented on the fact that they did not see themselves as belonging to the group of international students. It seems to me that in some other cases some students reflect on the fact that they might be regarded as members of stigmatized groups which was something that they perhaps initially did not expect.

> "There was a recent demonstration against immigrants in the town that I am studying in. At first I did not think much about it. But after hearing in reports and some students that there has been attacks on people that is perceived to be immigrants, I started to feel worried and uneasy walking around in my town. I'm certain that the situation will eventually subside. But at the same time, I would like to express how I feel regarding this situation, which perhaps mirrors the feelings of other student who came from outside of Germany."

This realization of being a part of an undesired group can have serious repercussions for individuals who have to cope with this kind of experience for the first time in their lives. I also observed that students who identified as refugees mentioned this fact explicitly to point out that their experience differs from that of others:

> „It could be that I am not an international student because I have lived in Germany for four years. In other words I am a refugee or have been granted asylum." (Own translation)

> "I would like to thank you that you provide me as well other students the opportunity to express our live facts and so on. but as I am a refugee and I study hier I could not find some question the could define und clear my situation e.g. financing, integrations difficulties and many other things."

These students with a refugee background felt like many questions of the survey could not adequately describe the steps that they had taken on their path through German higher education. Consistent with this observation a similar pattern can be observed among students who wish to differentiate themselves from those who entered the country as refugees.

> "When I first came to Germany, I couldn't get a room in Student dormitory and I had really really hard time finding private accommodation. I was applying to 30 - 40 rooms and was getting no response or negative responses. I wasn't even invited for a potential interview or to have a look of the room. After many such experiences and comparing it to others, I found out that I was being ignored because I was writing in English and maybe because I wasn't German, and assumed a Muslim and/or refugee."

> "I find that German people and authorities are not well informed of the various types of international people living in Germany (refugees, students with clear financial situation, students with unclear financial situation.). This leads to treating everyone the same despite the differences (no discrimination meant). This is particularly seen while looking for accommodation, most landlords think we're refugees without finances, and thus we don't get the apartment or WG. The problem is also present while looking for a job. More information is needed for Germans about international students in Germany."

## 5 Implications and Outlook

The central aim of this article was to contribute to the debate on what higher education institutions can learn from a comprehensive consideration of their international students' diversity. A brief review of the current state of research about international students shows that these are generally considered as an extraordinary group for a variety of reasons. Current developments worldwide show new dynamics, regional transformations as well as the coexistence of a more heterogeneous international student body than ever before. Many higher education systems consider these students all part of the broader category "international students" regardless of the conditions in which they entered the system. In other cases, a variety of categories and subdivisions of smaller groups are used to address different challenges and needs.

Both positions hardly consider how the students react to and perceive these labels which is what my analysis makes evident. As a higher education researcher focusing on the analysis of academic success and reasons of drop-out of this heterogeneous group, I have observed how international students negotiate between statistical, legal categorizations and their own complex biographical trajectories and motivations. As my analysis shows, however, this brings along a series of implications for both research and policy development.

This article explored the dynamics of homogenization and differentiation of a highly heterogeneous group from an individual perspective. It showed a series of intragroup tensions and ambivalences that can be found among international students in Germany. Some of the manifestations in the data analyzed were statements from students who differentiate themselves from others international students, students who might stigmatize certain groups and students who do not feel that they belong to a special group. Nevertheless, there are some methodological challenges and constraints that must be pointed out. First, the analysis cannot be regarded as representative due to the limited sample size. The approach of analyzing the comments is unidirectional and therefore does not allow the researcher to interact with the individuals. Despite a lack of context when evaluating the comments, students who mention certain topics cannot be contacted for further questioning due to data protection measures. The fact that the students are given no constrictions on what they can enter presents a methodological challenge during the analysis as several issues might be mentioned at the same time.

The main implication of this contribution would be the need for institutions and those individuals serving international students to understand the individual perceptions of these students to help them integrate not only with domestic students but among themselves. I argue that higher education institutions should work towards the development of a shared sensitivity to self and external positioning processes when it comes to addressing different groups of students. This approach might be beneficial to determine the pertinence and composition of support programmes and measures to facilitate the educational paths of international students. By doing this, the institutions could play a preventing role in the reproduction of stigmatizing labels as well as in the prevention of potential intergroup conflicts on campus. The preliminary results discussed in this article also suggest that the distinctions between groups at times do not reflect the actual diversity that the institutions have to deal with.

Another important consideration of this analysis would be the acknowledgement of the limits of the institutions to mediate some of these processes. As previously discussed, many of these labels and separation of groups cannot be avoided by the institutions themselves. This is because they are imposed by legal and political forces external to them. Nevertheless, institutions likely have to address self-exclusion processes. This means that some students might not profit from certain offers given that they do not feel as a part of the target group. Until the end of the research project SeSaBa further aspects will be discussed both from qualitative and quantitative perspectives. The research project seeks to provide recommendations for policy development and implementation which can be expected by 2021.

## References

Arslan, E. & Bozay, K. (eds). (2019). *Symbolische Ordnung und Flüchtlingsbewegungen in der Einwanderungsgesellschaft*. Springer VS, Wiesbaden.

BAMF (2019) Ablauf des deutschen Asylverfahrens: Ein Überblick über die einzelnen Verfahrensschritte und rechtlichen Grundlagen. *Bundesamt für Migration und Flüchtlinge*, 02/2019, 2. aktualisierte Fassung.

Beigang, S., von Blumenthal, J. & Lambert, L. (2018). *Studium für Geflüchtete: Aufgaben für Hochschulen und Politik. Policy Brief 8b*. Verbundprojekt ‚Flucht: Forschung und Transfer', Osnabrück: Institut für Migrationsforschung und Interkulturelle Studien (IMIS) der Universität Osnabrück/ Bonn: Internationales Konversionszentrum Bonn (BICC), April 2018.

Benček, D., & Strasheim, J. (2016). Refugees welcome? A dataset on anti-refugee violence in Germany. Research & Politics, October-December 2016, 1–11.

Berg, J. (2018). *A New Aspect of Internationalisation? Specific Challenges and Support Structures for Refugees on Their Way to German Higher Education*. In Curaj, A., Deca, L. & Pricopie, R. (Hrsg.). European Higher Education Area: The Impact of Past and Future Policies (S. 219–235). Cham: Springer.

Böhm, A., Follari, M., Hewett, A., Jones, S., Kemp, N., Meares, D., Pearce, D., & Cauter, K. (2004). *Vision 2020: Forecasting International Student Mobility a UK Perspective*. British Council 2004.

Bouchara, A. (2019). Bildungsbedürfnisse und Hindernisse von Geflüchteten in Deutschland: eine empirische Studie zu sozialen Netzwerken von Geflüchteten an deutschen

Hochschulen. *interculture journal: Online-Zeitschrift für interkulturelle Studien 18*(31), 53–72.

Brücker, H., Rother, N & Schupp, J (2018). *IAB-BAMF-SOEP-Befragung von Geflüchteten 2016: Studiendesign, Feldergebnisse sowie Analysen zu schulischer wie beruflicher Qualifikation, Sprachkenntnissen sowie kognitiven Potenzialen*. IAB-Forschungsbericht 13/2017, Korrigierte Fassung vom 20. März 2018.

Bundesagentur für Arbeit. (2018). *Fachkräfteengpassanalyse*. Berichte: Blickpunkt Arbeitsmarkt. Juni 2018.

Chambers, T. & Chiang, C. (2012). Understanding undergraduate students' experience: a content analysis using NSSE open-ended comments as an example. *Qual Quant 46*, 1113–1123.

Chew, C., & Eysenbach, G. (2010). Pandemics in the age of twitter: Content analysis of tweets during the 2009 h1n1 outbreak. *PLoS ONE 5*(11), e14118.

Choudaha, R. (2017). Three waves of international student mobility (1999–2020). *Studies in Higher Education 42*. 1–8.

Crea, T. (2016). Refugee higher education: Contextual challenges and implications for program design, delivery, and accompaniment. *International Journal of Educational Development 46*, 12–22.

DAAD & DZHW (2019). *Wissenschaft weltoffen kompakt: Daten und Fakten zur Internationalität von Studium und Forschung in Deutschland*. mbv Media.

DAAD (2010). *Internationalität an deutschen Hochschulen- Konzeption und Erhebung von Profildaten*. Deutscher Akademischer Austauschdienst (DAAD, eds.).

DAAD (2018). *Paths to the Future: Successes and Challenges of Refugee Integration in German Higher Education*. DAAD, Bonn.

De Wit, H. (2008). Changing dynamics in international student circulation: Meanings, push and pull factors, trends, and data. In De Wit, H., Agarwal, Said, M. E., Sehoole, M., & Sirozi, M., (eds). *The dynamics of international student circulation in a global context*. Rotterdam/Taipei: Sense publishers, (pp. 15–45)

De Wit, H., & Altbach, P. (2016). The Syrian refugee crisis and higher education. *International Higher Education 84*, 9–10.

Destatis (2019). Bildung und Kultur: Studierende an Hochschulen, Wintersemester 2018/2019. Fachserie 11 Reihe 4.1. Statistisches Bundesamt (Destatis), 2019.

Earnest, J., Joyce, A., de Mori, G., & Silvagni, G. (2010). Are universities responding to the needs of students from refugee backgrounds? *Australian Journal Of Education 54*(2), 155–174.

Ernst, J., Schmitt, J., Rieger, D., Beier, A., Vorderer, P., Bente, G., & Roth, H. (2017). Hate beneath the counter speech? a qualitative content analysis of user comments on youtube related to counter speech videos. *Journal for Deradicalization 10*, 1–49.

Falk, S., Thies, T., Yildirim, H., Zimmermann, J., Kercher, J. & Pineda, J. (2019): *Methodenbericht zur Studie „Studienerfolg und Studienabbruch bei Bildungsausländern in Deutschland im Bachelor- und Masterstudium* (Sesaba). Dokumentation der Welle 0 bis 2. Release 1.

Federal Foreign Office, DAAD, & UNHCR (2019). *The other 1%: Refugees at Institutions for Higher Education Worldwide*. Conference Report, 18th–19th June 2019, Berlin.

Funk, N. (2016). A spectre in Germany. Refugees, a ›welcome culture‹ and an ›integration politics. *Journal of Global Ethics 12*(3), 289–299.

Gallan, A., Girju, M., & Girju, R. (2017). Perfect ratings with negative comments: Learning from contradictory patient survey responses. *Patient Experience Journal 4*(3), 15–28.

GAST Gesellschaft für akademische Studienvorbereitung und Testentwicklung e.v. (Hgr.) (2018) Sprache, Studium, Integration: Die g.a.s.t.-Studie zu Geflüchteten. Online-Befragung unter TestDaF-, TestAS- und onSET-Teilnehmenden. Gesamtbericht.

Gatrell, P. (2016). Refugees—What's wrong with history? *Journal of Refugee Studies 30*(2), 170–189.

Ghaderi, C., & Eppenstein, T. (2017). *Flüchtlinge: Multiperspektivische Zugänge*. Springer Fachmedien Wiesbaden GmbH 2017.

Goastellec, G. (2018). Refugees' access to higher education in Europe: Comparative insights into on a new public issue. In Détourbe, M. (ed.). Inclusion through Access to Higher Education: Exploring the Dynamics between Access to Higher Education, Immigration and Languages. Rotterdam: Sense Publishers, (pp. 21–38).

Goebel, S. (2017). Politische Talkshows über Flucht. Wirklichkeitskonstruktionen und Diskurse. Eine kritische Analyse, Bielefeld: transcript.

Halkic, B., & Arnold, P. (2019). Refugees and online education: student perspectives on need and support in the context of (online) higher education, *Learning, Media and Technology 44*(3), 345–364.

Harris, V., & Marlowe, J. (2011) Hard yards and high hopes: The educational challenges of African refugee university students in Australia. *International Journal of Teaching and Learning in Higher Education 23*(2), 186–196.

Hatton, T. (2016). Refugees, Asylum Seekers, and Policy in OECD Countries. *American Economic Review 106*(5), 441–45.

Hintze, S. (2015) Emotionalitätsmarker in Kommentaren auf der PEGIDA Facebook-Seite, ser. Networx, 2015, vol. 71, mediensprache.net.

Holmes, S., & Castañeda, H. (2016). Representing the "European refugee crisis" in Germany and beyond: Deservingness and difference, life and death. *American Ethnologist 43*(1), 12–24.

Jäckle, S., & König, P. (2017). The dark side of the German 'welcome culture': investigating the causes behind attacks on refugees in 2015. *West European Politics 40*(2), 223–251.

Jungblut, J., Vukasovic, M., & Steinhardt, I. (2020). Higher education policy dynamics in turbulent times – access to higher education for refugees in Europe. *Studies in Higher Education 45*(2), 327–338.

Kaushal, N., & Lanati, M. (2019). *International student mobility: Growth and dispersion*. NBER Working Paper 25921.

Kiziak, T., Sixtus, F., & Klingholz, R.. (2019). *Von individuellen und institutionellen Hürden. Der lange Weg zur Arbeitsmarktintegration Geflüchteter*. Discussion Paper 23. Berlin-Institut für Bevölkerung und Entwicklung.

Köhler, C., Ziegele, M., & Weber, M. (2019). Wie gefährlich ist der Hass im Netz? Wirkungen von Hasskommentaren gegen Geflüchtete auf das prosoziale Verhalten von Rezipierenden. In I. Engelmann, M. Legrand, & H. Marzinkowski (Hrsg.), *Politische Partizipation im Medienwandel* (pp. 299–319).

Kuckartz, U. (2018). *Qualitative Inhaltsanalyse: Methoden, Praxis, Computerunterstützung*. Beltz Juventa.

Kuckartz, U. (2014). *Mixed Methods: Methodologie, Forschungsdesigns und Analyseverfahren*. Springer VS; Auflage: 2014 (11. September 2014).

Kunz, T., & Ottersbach, M. (Hrsg.). (2017).: *Flucht und Asyl als Herausforderung und Chance der Sozialen Arbeit*. Beltz Juventa (Weinheim und Basel) 2017.

Kury, H., & Redo, S. (Hrsg.) (2018). *Refugees and Migrants in Law and Policy: Challenges and Opportunities for global civic education*. Berlin: Springer.

Lee, K., & Tan, J. (1984). 'The international flow of third level less developed country students to developed countries: Determinants and implications'. *Higher Education 13*(6), 687–707.

Lenette, C. (2016). University students from refugee backgrounds: why should we care?. *Higher Education Research & Development 35*(6), 1311–1315.

Lörcher, I., & Taddicken, M. (2017). Discussing climate change online. Topics and perceptions in online climate change communication in different online public arenas. *Journal of Science Communication 16*(2), A03.

Luu, D., Bain, O., & Green, M. (2015). Students on the Move: The Future of International Students in the United States. *International Higher Education* (47), 11–12.

Maier, S. (2016). *Analyse von Facebook-Kommentaren zu politischen Themen: Wie deutsche und französische Jugendliche und junge Erwachsene Nachrichten bewerten und kommentieren*. Angewandte Linguistik aus interdisziplinärer Sicht, Band 47, Hamburg.

Mangan, D., & Winter, L. (2017): (In)validation and (mis)recognition in higher education: the experiences of students from refugee backgrounds, *International Journal of Lifelong Education 36*(4), 486–502.

Maschke, K., & Riehle, K. (2017). Integration von geflüchteten Menschen ins Hochschulstudium: Erfahrungen aus den DAAD-Programmen. In Goth, G. & Severing, E. (Hg.). (2017). *Asylsuchende und Flüchtlinge in Deutschland. Erfassung und Entwicklung von Qualifikationen für die Arbeitsmarktintegration*. Bielefeld 2016.

Mazzarol, T., & Soutar, G. (2002). "Push-pull" factors influencing international student destination choice", *International Journal of Educational Management 16*(2), 82–90.

McMahon, M. (1992). 'Higher education in a world market: A historical look at the global context to international study', *Higher Education 24*(4), 465–482.

Morrice, L. (2013). Refugees in Higher Education: Boundaries of Belonging and Recognition, Stigma, and Exclusion. *International Journal of Lifelong Education 32*(5), 652–668.

Morris-Lange, S., & Brands, F. (2016) German Universities Open Doors to Refugees: Access Barriers Remain, *International Higher Education 84*, 11–12.

MPD. (2019). How do OECD countries compare in their attractiveness for talented migrants? Migration Policy Debates, N°19 May 2019.

O'Cathain A., & Thomas K (2004). "Any other comments?" Open questions on questionnaires – a bane or a bonus to research? *BMC Med Res Meth 4*(1), 1–7.

OECD. (2009). Higher Education to 2030, Volumen 2: Globalisation OECD Publishing, Paris.

Pineda, J., Kercher, J., Falk, S., Thies, T., Yildirim, H. H., & Zimmermann, J. (2019). Studienfinanzierung: eine Hürde für internationale Studierende in Deutschland? *Qualität in der Wissenschaft 13*(3+4), 88–94.

Pineda, J. (2018). *Problemlagen und Herausforderungen internationaler Studierender in Deutschland. Ergebnisse einer qualitativen Vorstudie im Rahmen des SeSaBa Projekts*. DAAD Studien.

Popping, R. (2015). Analyzing Open-ended Questions by Means of Text Analysis Procedures. *Bulletin of Sociological Methodology/Bulletin de Méthodologie Sociologique 128*(1), 23–39.

Rich, J., Chojenta, C., & Loxton, D. (2013). Quality, rigour and usefulness of free-text comments collected by a large population based longitudinal study – ALSWH. *PLoS ONE 8*(7), e68832.

Richter, H. (2015). Die Komplexität von Integration. Arbeitsmigration in die Bundesrepublik Deutschland von den fünfziger bis in die siebziger Jahre. *Zeitgeschichte-online*, November 2015.

Schacht, F. (2018). Zwischen Schwarz und Weiß gibt es viele Farben! Eine kontrapunktische Perspektive auf die Flüchtlingskategorie. In Reese-Schnitker, A., Bertram, D., & Franzmann, M. (eds.). *Migration, Flucht und Vertreibung. Theologische Analyse und religionsunterrichtliche Praxis*. Stuttgart: Kolhammer.

Schacht, F. (2019). „So, we´re civilized" Eine kontrapunktische Perspektive auf die Flüchtlingskategorie. In Böttcher, A., Hill, M., Rotter, A., Schacht, F., Wolf, M., & Yildiz, E. (2019). *Migration bewegt und bildet. Kontrapunktische Betrachtungen*. Innsbruck university press.

Schammann, H., & Böhm, T. (2017) Refugees in higher education: Constraints, challenges and lessons learned from early surveys and practical experiences. *Journal of the European higher education area 7*(4), 13–31.

Schammann, H., & Kühn, B. (2016). *Kommunale Flüchtlingspolitik in Deutschland*. Bonn: Friederich-Ebert-Stiftung.

Schneider, L. (2018). Access and aspirations: Syrian refugees' experiences of entering higher education in Germany. *Research in Comparative and International Education 13*(3), 457–478.

Schneider, P. (2016). Migranten und Flüchtlinge als Herausforderung für Deutschland und Europa. S+F, *Sicherheit und Frieden - Security and Peace 34*(1), 1–19.

Steinhardt, I., & Eckhardt, L. (2017). "We can do it" - Refugees and the German Higher Education System. In: Jungblut, J. & Pietkiewicz, K. (Hrsg.): *Refugees Welcome?* (pp. 25–42).

Stevenson, J., & Baker, S. (2018). *Refugees in Higher Education: Debate, Discourse and Practice*. Emerald Publishing Group Ltd: Sheffield, UK.

Streitwieser, B., & Brück, L. (2018). Competing Motivations in Germany's Higher Education Response to the Syrian Refugee Crisis. *Refuge: Canada's Journal on Refugees 34*(2), 38–51.

Streitwieser, B., & Unangst, L. (2018). Access for Refugees into Higher Education: Paving Pathways to Integration. *International Higher Education* (95), 16–18.

Streitwieser, B., Brueck, L., Moody, R., & Taylor, M. (2017). The Potential and Reality of New Refugees Entering German Higher Education: The Case of Berlin Institutions, *European Education 49*(4), 231–252.

Streitwieser, B., Schmidt, M., Brück, L., & Gläsener, K. (2018). Needs, Barriers, and Support Systems for Refugee Students in Germany. *Global Education Review 5*(4), 136–157.

Taylor, J., Filipski, M., Alloush, M., Gupta, A., Valdes, R., & Gonzalez Estrada, E. (2016). Economic impact of refugees. *Proceedings of the National Academy of Sciences* 113, 7449–7453.

Thomas, L., McColl, E., Priest, J., & Bond, S. (1996). Open-ended questions: do they add anything to a quantitative patient satisfaction scale?. *Social Sciences in Health 2*(1), 23–35.

UNHCR. (2015). Sustainable Development Goal 4 and Refugee Education. Education Brief: SDG4. UNHCR, The UN Refugee Agency.

UNHCR. (2019). Stepping Up: Refugee Education in Crisis. UN High Commissioner for Refugees (UNHCR).

Vollmer, B., & Karakayali, S. (2018). The Volatility of the Discourse on Refugees in Germany, *Journal of Immigrant & Refugee Studies 16*(1-2), 118–139.

Weiss, G., Adam, F., Föbker, S., Imani, D., Pfaffenbach, C., & Wiegandt, C. (2019). Angekommen in postmigrantischen Stadtgesellschaften? Eine Annäherung an subjektive Integrationsvorstellungen von Geflüchteten und beruflich oder ehrenamtlich in der Flüchtlingsbetreuung Tätigen. *Geographica Helvetica 74*, 205–221.

Will, G., Balaban, E., Dröscher, A., Homuth, C., & Welker, J. (2018). Integration von Flüchtlingen: Erste Ergebnisse der ReGES-Studie (LIfBi Working Paper No. 76). Bamberg: Leibniz-Institut für Bildungsverläufe.

Zubairi, A., & Rose, P. (2016). *Supporting primary and secondary education for refugees: the role of international financing.* Cambridge: Research for Equitable Access and Learning (REAL) Centre University of Cambridge.

# Facilitating Access of Syrian Refugees to Higher Education in Turkey as an Instrument for Integration

Armağan Erdoğan and M. Murat Erdoğan

## 1 Introduction

The twenty-first century is a complex period with multi-layered challenges on a global scale. Higher education is one of the key fields to respond actively to these challenges and provide solutions for the current and future problems. Nevertheless, accessing higher education has been relatively recently transformed from being an elite phenomenon to one that is now accessible by the masses. In addition to its intellectual and educational functions of teaching and research, higher education's responsibility to the public needs to be more clearly defined in order to adequately respond to new social challenges, such as migration. Due to social, economic, political, psychological, or other reasons, migration is increasing globally and higher education systems are adapting their policies to the particular needs of the newcomers. Nevertheless, forced migration, which is unintended, unplanned, and in high numbers has increased dramatically in the last decades, is different from the voluntary migration, and must be evaluated as such.

Setting up the basic global facts will be helpful in clarifying the main arguments of this paper. Perhaps the first fact is the magnitude of the numbers which directly influence the plans and implementations of the policies. As of 2019, there are 272 million international migrants and 70.8 million displaced people throughout the globe. Of this group, 25.9 million are refugees (IOM 2020). Another

---

A. Erdoğan (✉)
Beykoz University, Istanbul, Turkey
E-Mail: armagan.erdogan2012@gmail.com

M. M. Erdoğan (✉)
Türk-Alman-University, Istanbul, Turkey
E-Mail: merdogan1103@gmail.com

© The Author(s), under exclusive license to Springer Fachmedien Wiesbaden GmbH, part of Springer Nature 2021
J. Berg et al. (eds.), *Refugees in Higher Education*, Higher Education Research and Science Studies, https://doi.org/10.1007/978-3-658-33338-6_8

alarming fact is that almost half of the refugees are under the age of 18 and in need of education. Nevertheless, their access to every level of education is far behind the global rates. The third fact is that unlike the voluntary migrants, 84% of refugees live in neighboring countries that have their own socioeconomic problems. In the last nine years, one of the largest forced migrations since the second world war happened due to the conflict and ongoing civil war in Syria. More than 6.5 million Syrians have been forced to flee their homes and more than 55% of this Syrian refugee[1] inflow, that is 3 million 576 thousand, lives in Turkey (UNHCR 2020). Additionally, around 368 thousand people from other countries, such as Afghanistan, Iraq, Iran, and Pakistan (IOM 2019), were added to this number with the total number of displaced people under "international protection" sheltered in Turkey reaching almost 4 million (DGMM 2020). The sheer number and the emergency of the situation have triggered immediate action in terms of structure, legislation, and mind-set in response to the many challenges precipitated by the migration flow (Erdogan 2018a).

In the Syrian crisis, Turkey has a special place since not only has it taken the most substantial part of the more than 6.5 million refugees but also because of its policy on their settlement, legal status, and on providing free public services in health, education, and socioeconomic fields. Sharing the longest border (911 km) with Syria and following an "open-door policy" for those coming from Syria, Turkey has faced a massive influx of refugees in emergency conditions and become the country hosting the largest refugee population in the world since 2014. "Refugees" reached 5% of the total population (82 million) in less than nine years from 58,000 refugees (international protection holders and applicants) in 2011 to 4 million in 2019 (DGMM 2020). Turkey's international obligations to refugees andasylum seekers have been identified in the framework of the "1951 Geneva Convention" and "1967 Protocol Relating to the Status of Refugees" (UNHCR 2010). However, Turkey as one of the parties of the Geneva Convention declared that it applies the "geographical limitation" exception to the declaration of 29 August 1961, therefore whoever comes from countries outside of Europe are not be accepted as "refugees". Following this limitation, Syrians were given "temporary protection" instead of refugee status. There is no time limit defined by this "temporary protection" status, and it still creates an approach of temporality towards Syrians even after nine years (Erdogan 2018b). This temporariness has been another unique parameter in planning integration policies in the medium

---

[1] In this paper, refugee is not used in its legislative meaning in Turkey, but as a widely accepted sociological meaning. According to law in Turkey, Syrians are under temporary status.

and long term and this paper attempts to explain the conditions from the higher education perspective.

Syrian refugees started to cross the borders into Turkey in 2011. Since 2013, Turkey has actively accepted Syrian students into its higher education system even though it has had its own pre-existing challenges both in higher education and in its socioeconomic situation (Erdogan et al. 2017). Syrian students accessing higher education in Turkey increase dramatically each year and reached 27,034 in 2018–2019 (MoNE 2019). Despite the large numbers and initiatives taken centrally by the government to facilitate access in a very competitive higher education system, to date, there has been insufficient research on refugees in higher education in Turkey. This paper aims to contribute to the discussions on the integration of Syrian refugees in Turkey through Syrian university students.

It is based on the fieldwork of a research study that was conducted in the context of a Hopes-MADAD project entitled "Elite Dialogue II- Dialogue with Syrian Refugees in Turkey through Syrian Academics and Students". ED II research had three main goals:

1. To explore the conditions, challenges, and expectations of the Syrian university students and academics[2] among the Syrian refugees in Turkey.
2. To analyze the role of Syrian elite groups (students and academics) in the integration process of Syrian refugees.
3. To make policy recommendations based on data for comprehensive and long-term policies.

## 2 Integration, Social Cohesion, Inclusion

Operational and academic needs have searched out for the conceptual framework to define complex and multidimensional notions of migration or to explain the relations between the host and the newcomer individuals and societies more in the last decades (Castles 2003; Castles et al. 2013). Parallel to the complexity of the phenomenon, integration as a concept is not defined clearly. Berry lists the four strategies in acculturation to the host society as assimilation, separation, marginalization, and integration and states that integration as a two-way process can function when the host society is open and inclusive in its approach towards cultural diversity (Berry 1997). The international organization of Migration (IOM) defines integration as "the process of mutual adaptation between the host society

---

[2] Syrian academics in our research are not included in this paper.

and the migrants themselves, both as individuals and as groups" (IOM 2012). Ager and Strang propose conceptual domains of successful integration in different layers and see employment, housing, education, and health as markers of integration. Social connection is defined as social bridges, bonds, and links (2008). Social cohesion, on the other hand, is often identified as 'solidarity' and 'togetherness' (Demireva 2017). Jenson mentions five dimensions of social cohesion as belonging, inclusion, participation, recognition, and legitimacy and defines inclusion of refugees as equal access to housing, health care, education, training, and employment (1998). The integration process involves diverse subjects and a multidisciplinary approach from development to finance, from psychology to political science and this paper attempts to observe Syrian students having a bridging role between their communities and host society in their integration process.

There is however, a clear consensus that voluntary migration and forced migration have different backgrounds, motivations, needs, and experiences. The circumstances and experiences of forced migration have profound effects on refugees' health and integration into the host society. Besides, the status of the newcomers, other parameters affect the social cohesion process. One is the magnitude of the group, the other is population, the socioeconomic conditions, and the administrative structure of the host country. If the social cohesion process is not managed well, it may cause newcomers to close in, ghettoization, and the host community to take a negative attitude towards them (Erdogan 2019). This vicious cycle may create a lessening of public services, job loss, social insecurity, and other social problems. ED research starts at this point to investigate the role of the "elite" groups among the newcomers during the integration process. Considering the lower education level among the Syrian refugees than the average in Turkey, educated groups, such as the university students, may play a crucial role to develop dialogue with the host community, to play a role model for the others, and to start better communication channels. This paper recommends that it be considered as a part of the integration process beyond being a tool for career planning, employment, and empowerment through higher education.

Higher education plays a very crucial role particularly for vulnerable groups, such as displaced people, refugees, and asylum seekers (de Wit and Altbach 2016; Streitwieser et al 2016; Stevenson and Baker 2018). It is a major path for those groups to empower their personal, intellectual, professional and social capacity (UNHCR 2019d). Moreover, as is argued in this paper based on our research, higher education has a significant role for integration, thus having a role to mediate between the host society and the refugees. This role promotes mutual understanding and contributes to living together in peace. (Zeus 2011;

Cremonini 2016; Hynie 2018). Nevertheless, there is a clear and alarming situation that refugees accessing higher education's 3% (1% in 2017) compared with 37% globally (UNHCR 2019a). Higher education for refugees has not been prioritized even in the basic documents and conventions until recently, while access to primary and secondary education was accepted as crucial for the wellbeing, protection, and livelihood of the children (Watenpaugh et al. 2014; UNHCR 2019b). It was relatively recent that higher education started to be seen as a critical tool to enhance the self-reliance of refugees at the individual, social, and economic levels (UNESCO 2019; Steward 2010; Stevenson 2018; UNHCR 2019c). UNHCR's education strategy set higher education as a key priority and listed the benefits for three possible scenarios: returning to the country of origin, integration to the host country, or resettlement into a third country (UNHCR 2019d). International organizations, higher education systems, higher education institutions, and INGOs are working to reduce the barriers that displaced people are facing. New targets such as to achieve 15% are set for 2030 in the Sustainable Development Goals and Global Compact on refugees (UNHCR 2019d). Since the voluntary migration is different from the forced migration, policies to enhance access to higher education need to be compatible with the distinct vulnerabilities of the latter. Nevertheless, reality is far from reaching the targets.

## 3   Syrian University Students in Turkish Universities

One of the most striking points about Syrians in Turkey is their demographic characteristics. In addition to Turkey's own young population, the Syrian population is also quite young, which creates challenges for education policies. 1.7 million Syrians under 18, which is almost 50% of their population. Another demographic point is the gender imbalance as the male population is 54.1%, while the female population is 45.8%. Studies show that return intentions and opportunities are decreasing as their stay in Turkey continues to be extended (Erdogan and Erdogan 2018). In this sense, integration policies come into question. Our research argues that Syrian university students may play a key role in the integration of the Syrian people in Turkey.

Higher education, in particular seems to be one of the key strategic fields for the over 3.6 million Syrian refugees to live in harmony with Turkish society. Syrian "elite" groups are crucially important as "role models", "leaders", and "bridges" for future integration policies. It is important to understand the qualifications, perceptions, and expectations of this group who has the ability to establish a bridge between the Turkish and Syrian communities both for social and economic integration and through positive relations between different groups.

Turkish higher education system started to be massified in the last two decades. The numbers of both national and international students increased dramatically due to the newly established HEIs as well as to the new policies facilitating the access. In Turkey (2018–2019) there are 7.7 million Turkish students in universities, 52.5% are male and 47.4% are female. 2.2 million of the students are associate degree students (28.7%), 4.4 million are undergraduate students (57.1%), 394 thousand MA (5%) and 96 thousand (1.2%) are PhD students. There are in the 2018–2019 academic year 154.505 international students, (100.220 male, 54.285 female) (CoHE 2019). This number corresponds to 2% of the total number of 7.7 million national students. When we consider Syrian stuents (27.034; in Turish universities they make 17.5% of total international students. They are having the highest number among international students in Turkey since 2018 in Turkey (CoHE 2020).

The Turkish government has both facilitated Syrian students who had to postpone their education due to the war in Syria and has also created places for those who attended secondary school in Turkey. The increase in the number of student enrollment confirms these efforts. The majority of students in Turkey are the ones whose education was abandoned due to the war. Turkey has implemented different policies for Syrian students to be able to access higher education since 2013 (CoHE 2017). The responses of Turkish higher education institutions to the Syrian crisis can be classified into three areas: academic, financial, and legislative facilities (Erdogan et al. 2019).

Together with the UNHCR and other international organizations, the Ministry of Education and The Council of Higher Education took on a very active and positive role in including Syrian youth into the higher education system through different mechanisms (Yıldız 2019; Watenpaugh et al. 2014; Hohberger 2018; Yavcan and El-Ghali 2017). According to Directory General of Migration Management (DGMM) and Ministry of Education (MoNE) data, the Syrian population of compulsory school age (5–17) is 1,082,172 as of October 2019, and it comprises 30.2% of the total Syrians in Turkey. 684,000 of this age group have been enrolled in public schools, which is a great success on the one hand but also a big "lost generation" considering the remaining 400,000 children without access to education. This enrollment rate also indicates the potential numbers for higher education in the forthcoming years. Again, according to MoNE data there are 10,077 students in 12th grade that have potential access to higher education in 2020–2021.

To sum up the regulations and policies put forward to facilitate Syrian students' access to higher education in Turkey both the Turkish government and the Council of Higher Education (CoHE) designed flexible and inclusive policies and regulations despite the large numbers of Syrian students and criticism and reactions by the public:

1. September 3rd 2012, (CoHE) made a regulation for the 2012–2013 academic year for Syrian students (and Turkish citizens whose education was interrupted while studying in Syria). According to this, seven state universities identified in the border region were allowed to accept Syrian students as "special students".[3] This gave them the first chance to attend universities without any documents.
2. October 9th, 2013, (CoHE) made a new regulation on "special students" and provided the opportunity to "transfer" to those who had the relevant documents without specifying any academic year or university. Accordingly, CoHE announced in October 2013 that Syrian refugees with proof of previously earned academic qualifications in Syria or elsewhere would be able to apply for all universities across Turkey. Although the quota for Syrian refugees was restricted to ten percent of that of the local students, this allowed many eligible refugees to enroll in universities as degree-seeking students (The Official Gazette 2013). Additionally, those students who did not have the required documents could take courses as "special students" in seven universities, mostly in the border cities.
3. November 9th, 2015, "It is decided that universities (eight universities including Kahramanmaraş Sütçü İmam University) can open programs in Turkish and/or foreign languages with the approval of the Executive Board of Higher Education for students coming from Syria." Thus, it became possible to open programs in Arabic or another language in line with the needs and suitability for Syrian students in these universities. Different from previous regulations, this innovation was regarded as more inclusive in that it enabled the Syrian refugees who did not have an adequate level of proficiency in Turkish to be able to enroll in universities (CoHE 2015)
4. Under the decisions of the Council of Ministers, the tuition fees for Syrian students enrolled as part of the foreigners admission quotas within the framework of their means from the 2012–2013 academic year were paid from the budget of the Foreign Turks and Relative Communities Presidency, which means that

---

[3]These universities are Gaziantep, Kilis 7 Aralık, Harran (Şanlıurfa), Mustafa Kemal (Hatay), Osmaniye Korkut Ata, Çukurova (Adana) and Mersin.

unlike other international students Syrian students are exempt from paying tuition fees. This is an important practice in paving the way for Syrian students to access higher education. Tuition fees to be taken as student contributions to current service costs in higher education institutions are determined by the Council of Ministers every year. In September 2014, the Council of Ministers decided that Syrian students would not be charged the tuition fees paid by other international students in Turkey. Instead, the Presidency of Turks Abroad and Related Communities (YTB) was assigned to pay Syrian students' university tuition fees. In addition to the exemption from tuition fees, Syrian students were provided scholarships by YTB to cover their educational and living costs. International donors, INGOs, and UNHCR supported these national resources and policies, particularly to find funds and facilitate language learning before applying to universities.

For the Syrian students studying at the state or foundation universities in Turkey, international student admission procedures are applied within the framework of both central examinations and the Foreign Student Examination (YÖS). For the students whose education was interrupted in Syria, a more effortless transfer can be provided. Universities are the leading decision-makers in this process. The issue of transfer and recognition of qualifications may vary from university to faculty, even within the same university. It sometimes involves risks, such as different applications, non-comparable recognition, and especially counterfeit documents (Yıldız 2019).

One of the most controversial issues in Turkey for Syrian university students is the scholarship opportunities. Scholarships are also provided for students' living expenses. Removing tuition fees for the Syrian students and free language courses for the prospective students are significant steps to facilitate their access to higher education and lessen the lost generation.

## 4 Elite Dialogue-II Survey: Methodology & Findings

### 4.1 Methodology

This article analyzes Syrian refugees in the Turkish higher education system, using data from the "Elite Dialogue" research project, conducted on Syrian university students and academics in Turkey. However, the scope will focus on students, and leave the academics out. The online survey tool SurveyMonkey was chosen due to its user-friendly design, multiple response options, and easy question skipping logic. Students were invited to participate online by using students' communication groups and the snowball survey method, allowing for the collection of representative data on Syrian students and the observation of trends, which fits the age group and technology use of the young target population.

In the sample selection, quota-based interventions were made considering the real distribution of the participants, according to the cities and universities. Quantitative data was collected through Survey Monkey from 1058 Syrian students in 46 cities. 747 answered more than 70% of the questionnaire and these were taken into account for the analysis of the data. Due to the general limitations of working on vulnerable groups such as refugees and the lack of official data, the research has some limitations. It focuses on a fragile subject, that is, on refugees. There are difficulties and limitations to research on this sensitive mass. This may be reflected in the findings. Therefore, the data obtained are thought to indicate a limited reality. Part of this shortcoming relates to our limited access to female students despite all efforts, while another reason is our finding regarding the lower survey completion rate of female students. Therefore, our evaluations and analysis should be taken into consideration with regard to these limitations. However, the findings provide significant information to fill the gap between the literature and the fieldwork. Additionally, the research was structured according to the following hypothesis and framework with reference to the first phase of the project Elite Dialogue-I (ED-I) conducted in a more limited scope for 497 students out of which 395 responses were evaluated in 2017 (Erdogan et al. 2017). Comparing two phases of the ED Projects allows a limited comparison in terms of statistics and content due to timing, model, participant profile, and other variables.

The research consists of questions about profiling, detecting problems, and adaptation processes. The questionnaire was designed to obtain data regarding the following topics to examine higher education and integration perspectives: Basic Demographics, Educational Background; Immigration Background: Support Network, Diaspora, Duration of Stay, Secondary Education; Satisfaction with Different Aspects of Education in Turkey; Vulnerabilities: Trauma, Housing, Income; Livelihoods: Scholarships/Work; Economic Integration Attitudes/Future Prospects; Social Integration Attitudes: Prejudice, Social Distance, Institutional Trust; and Policy Recommendations.

## 4.2 Elite Dialogue-II Survey Findings and Discussions

The research was designed both to determine the profiles of Syrian students and also to define the potential roles they might play in future integration processes in mediating between their community and Turkish society. In this framework, the main question the research addressed regarded how Syrian university students adapt to the universities and integrate into society in Turkey. 185 students (25%) were female and 562 (75%) were male. With regards to the types of programs that students are enrolled in, about 3% of the Syrian students in our sample are enrolled in associate degree programs, 88% of the students in undergraduate programs, and the remaining 9% are pursuing graduate studies either in MA or PhD programs. According to the official data, the gender distribution of the Syrian students in Turkish higher education was 36.7% female and 63.2% male in the 2018–2019 academic year; and, in terms of education level (degree) 2% are Ph.D., 7% are MA, 82% are BA, and 9% are associate degree students (CoHE 2020). Regarding the distribution of their chosen field of study, the following figure is indicative that about 40% are enrolled in various engineering programs with civil and computer engineering being the most popular departments within this field. About 30% are enrolled in administrative and social sciences, including political science and international relations, chosen by 6% and 18% are health sciences, including medicine, dentistry, and pharmaceutics departments.

The survey findings of the ED II research will be evaluated below through a few tables and figures to support our argument in this paper. The first significant finding from the survey is about their perception of the quality of education in Turkey. The question was asked to compare higher education in Syria vs. Turkey. As illustrated in the table below, 73% of the respondents evaluated the educational conditions in Turkey more favorably (better and a lot better than in Syria) with only approximately 7% arguing that Syrian educational conditions were better. This indicates their bond, motivation, and positive attitude towards the higher education system in Turkey, and it can be regarded as a good sign for their integration process (Table 1).

Another indicator that was deemed important regarding their success in higher education is the students' network of friends and relatives, as they are instrumental

**Table 1** Evaluation of Higher Education Experiences in Turkey as Compared to the One in Syria

| | Number of Respondents | Percentage (%) |
|---|---|---|
| A lot better | 79 | 22.77 |
| Better | 175 | 50.43 |
| Same | 69 | 19.88 |
| Worse | 21 | 6.05 |
| A lot worse | 3 | 0.86 |

Source: ED II questionnaire

# Facilitating Access of Syrian Refugees ...

**Table 2** Are Their Parents or Siblings in Turkey?

|  | Number of Responses | Percentage of Respondents (%) |
|---|---|---|
| No one | 221 | 29.54 |
| Mother | 358 | 47.86 |
| Father | 280 | 37.43 |
| Sibling | 510 | 68.18 |

Source: ED II questionnaire

in coping with hardships, easing the process of social cohesion, and providing economic support when needed. As the extensive diaspora across countries is the norm rather than the exception when it comes to refugees, we were interested in illustrating the frequency of split families and the level of scarcity of this resource for Syrian university students. The following table illustrates remarkable findings and the severity of potential vulnerabilities. In a question where multiple responses were allowed, 30% of the Syrian refugee students interviewed indicated that neither of their parents nor siblings were in Turkey. This finding points to a limited support network that only consists of friends or, if any, distant relatives. 48% stated that their mothers reside in Turkey, and 37% said their fathers were in Turkey. Finally, 68% indicated that their siblings are in Turkey (Table 2).

Moreover, their families are split in different cities or countries. Additionally, regarding the support network, the location of residence and the location of studies tend to differ due to placement at the university. Based on grades and quotas available, many refugee students end up attending college in places other than their residence in Turkey. This was an issue frequently indicated; it is a very common issue among the students that many of them study in different cities than their residence. In addition to the lack of an immediate support network and economic burden manifested in the cost of traveling as well as the higher cost of food and accommodation due to living separately, access to family members becomes even more difficult with the requirements of travel permits.

The type of challenges or particular problems they faced during their studies are asked in our survey and the findings are consistent with the literature. Learning Turkish is the highest rated problem at 38%, followed by grades, the registration process, and course comprehension. All these give insights into their academic success as well as their social adaptation to higher education and the society. Areas where the students faced the least challenges are admin staff, academic faculty members, and fellow students, which demonstrates that students

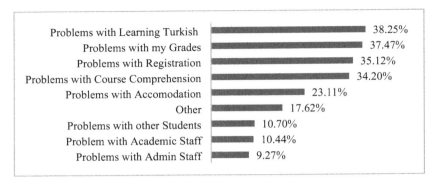

**Fig. 1** Problems Faced During Studies. (Source: ED II questionnaire)

have relatively fewer challenges with their social environment despite the language problem. Even if they seem to have few problems with the local students, academics, and administrative staff, this result is open for further investigation about their relation (Fig. 1).

Following this, another significant data finding is indicated when they are asked how they solve problems if they face any, concerning their studies. About half of the students indicated that they solved their problems on their own, and 33% pointed to the support of their Syrian friends. This dramatic result of almost 85% indicates that Syrian students have a social environment with their Syrian peers and do not have much communication with Turkish students or their Turkish advisors. Only about 9% of the students got help from their Turkish friends, 3% solved their problems with help from their academic advisor, 2% with the assistance of other professors, and another 2% with the support of the admin staff. In the integration process, multiple parameters and actors play a role, therefore in order to clarify this finding, further questions to the students and the actors in the higher education institutions must be asked.

Future expectations of refugees are shown to influence their economic and social attitudes. As important indicators of integration, the following questions on Syrian students' future expectations have been presented to them and the results are as follows:

Financial conditions are one of the major indicators that dramatically dropped after the displacement. Their income levels at four stages (before, just after displacement, current, and future) were asked about in order to compare. As can be expected, sudden changes in income level were experienced by 73% of the students surveyed, which constitutes an important source of vulnerability. The results clearly illustrate a major income level drop in the household income of refugee students following their forced displacement. Their economic wellbeing seems to have slightly improved since their immediate arrival to Turkey. Furthermore, their income expectations in the future in Turkey are slightly higher than their initial levels of income in Syria, indicating their positive future outlook after their graduation in Turkey (Fig. 2).

With regards to their expectations from the future, on a scale from 1 (weak) to 4 (strong), our student sample seems to hold pessimistic attitudes towards the political and economic conditions in Syria with a $M = 2.13$ and $M = 2.37$, respectively. On the other hand, their attitudes towards Turkish politics and the economy rate higher as $M = 3.86$ and $M = 3.53$. More significantly, their expectations for their personal economic conditions are rather high $M = 3.82$, and their life in general receives the highest rate $M = 3.95$ implying a high inclination to continue their lives in Turkey. Future expectations and feeling secure in the host country are important indicators of both integration and host countries'

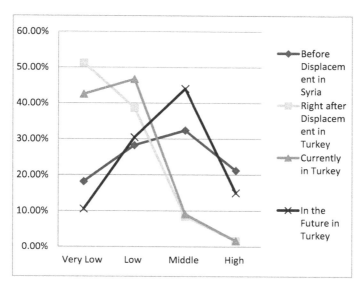

**Fig. 2** Income Levels Before and After Displacement and Future Expectations. (Source: ED II questionnaire)

success in accommodating a population. Therefore, we compared the results of the first wave of Elite Dialogue, conducted in 2017, to this wave as illustrated in the following figure. Significantly, when we compare our findings in two waves, increasing rates in all indicators are seen. It highlights their tendency to live in Turkey with lessening hope for the Syrian politics and economy.

While the two samples are different in terms of size, group, and time, the methodology used for collecting the data was the same, thereby allowing for some meaningful comparisons. Accordingly, there is a meaningful increase in every item, while the future expectations are inquired upon at similar rates. For instance, average expectations regarding their personal employment students increased from $M = 3.47$ to $M = 3.82$. Considering the highest number one can score on this item is '4', this indicates very high expectations regarding employment. Also, students seem to have become slightly more optimistic regarding the situation in their country of origin, Syria, with a visible increase in their expectations regarding its politics and economy (Fig. 3).

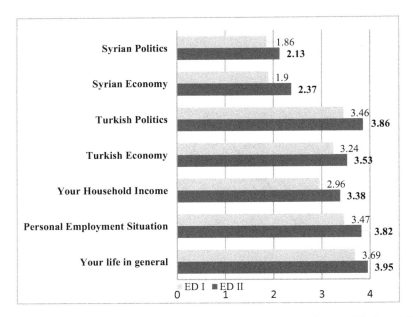

**Fig. 3** Future Expectations ED-I (2017) and ED -II (2019). (Source: ED I and II questionnaires)

When we asked students about their intentions to return to Syria—a much-debated issue both nationally and internationally-34% indicated that they have no intention to return to Syria, whereas 6% indicated high interest in returning even if the war continues. Another 6% is interested in returning even if their desired regime is not established in Syria. Nevertheless, a bulk of the respondents, 55% indicated that they would return only if their desired regime is established, a rather difficult task to meet for every refugee.

In addition to integration and voluntary return, the third option of a refugee response is resettlement. Despite limited numbers of quotas being offered by countries of resettlement, as evidenced by the continuous—albeit much declined—numbers of crossings across the Aegean Sea, living in a third country is a desirable option for many refugees. In order to explore this issue for the case of Syrian university students, we asked a set of questions on prospects of resettlement and hypothetical countries of choice. The results are illustrated in the following tables.

When refugees' interest in settlement is considered, about 45% intend to stay in Turkey, whereas the remainder could consider resettlement. For 13%, resettlement is conditional upon an opportunity, for 10% if they cannot finish their studies, for 5% if they find a relative that can help them, and for an important 27% if they cannot find a job in Turkey. These results constitute important inputs for future policy regarding the young and educated refugees in Turkey. The fact that the number of permits issued to Syrians under temporary protection remained limited, the need for producing more efficient policy tools for employment proves imminent.

It was indicated earlier that this demographic group assumes great importance socially as they are role models to their community and in terms of intergroup relations provides best-case scenarios. Students were asked about their quality of relations with other students. About 40% indicated that they have good relations with other students, while a remarkable 33% identified their relations either as poor or medium. When we compared the two waves of Elite Dialogue in terms of students' assessment of their intergroup contact, we observed that there has been a sharp decrease in the percentage of those students who assess their relations with local students as poor and a shift to better evaluations, such as 'above average' and 'good.' This finding is a good indicator of social cohesion and indicates that there is more and better intergroup contact from the perspective of Syrian students.

When students were asked about their willingness to engage in contact with members of the host society, they elicited a rather low distance overall (the range of the response categories is from 0 to 4) in that for most categories they were rather willing to engage in contact. The kinds of interaction least preferred by

Syrians are being roommates, being in a romantic relationship, or being married to a member of the host society. As part of their ongoing interaction with Turkish students, they showed the lowest distance about being schoolmates, followed by neighbors and coworkers. It is argued that the time spent in the host country may increase the level of contact and hence decrease the levels of social distance. When we compare the two waves of this survey, we find that, indeed, for all indicators of distance, there is a decrease from ED I to ED II at similar rates as illustrated in the following Figure (Fig. 4).

Using the independent variables widely employed in the literature, we hoped to unpack the determinants of social distance attitudes and constructed the following table with a few cross tabular illustrations. This Table aims to compare different groups of students regarding their social distance attitudes to the overall mean value of social distance 8.34. Before starting the comparison, it should be noted that the social distance variable is an additive index created using the separate distance items discussed above following a factor analysis. The variable ranges

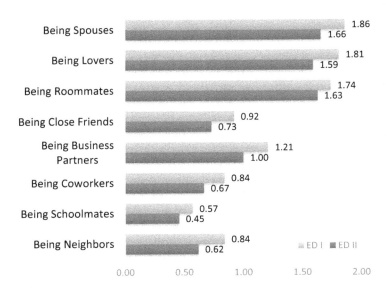

**Fig. 4** "Social Distance" levels of Syrian students to Turkish society. (Source: ED I and II questionnaires)

from 0 to 32, and the overall mean is 8.34 indicating very low social distance. Still, one can compare the different groups to understand what makes refugee students more distant to members of the host society.

## 5 Concluding Remarks and Recommendations

Higher education conveys individual, intellectual, social, and economic benefits (McMahon 2009). Facilitating paths to higher education and removing the barriers help upward mobility. Therefore, higher education systems in this age of challenges have crucial roles and responsibilities. The diversity of the population needs to be represented in higher education both for themselves and for the welfare, peace, and development of societies. In addition to the disadvantaged citizens, newcomers, and displaced people, refugees or asylum seekers are fragile and experience multiple vulnerabilities (EduMAP 2019). Their conditions, needs, and experiences differ from the traditional international students. For this reason, new, flexible, and inclusive policies are required to integrate them both to higher education and to the society in which they will be living. Their empowerment will foster their community, the next generations, and will ease the burden of the host country.

The integration and involvement of Syrian students in the Turkish higher education system is a hot topic both for integration and tension in Turkey. Chronic problems in the higher education system, such as supply and demand balance due to large numbers of students taking the National Selection Exams annually, creates a reaction in the public for new regulations to facilitate the enrollment of Syrian students. The supply-demand imbalance due to demographic factors, shortcomings of the higher education system, and the unemployment rate among university graduates have been some long-term challenges for Turkish higher education (Erdogan 2014; Kavak 2011) On the other hand, loss of economic, social and cultural capital, being in a temporary status, language inadequacy, lack of qualification documents, or other vulnerabilities hinder Syrian refugees' access to higher education. Still, enrollment rates for Syrian students in Turkish higher education have increased from 1785 in 2013–2014 to 27,034 in 2018–2019 (CoHE 2020). This is far above (around 6%) the global rate (3%). Both the Turkish state and people have taken on a burden since the first arrival of the Syrian refugees in 2011, and the case of Turkey can be regarded as a success story, especially considering the magnitude of the population and emergence of the situation. Nevertheless, for a smoother integration and positive future prospects data-based policies are needed. Starting from this picture, this paper aimed to analyze the integration of Syrian university students into Turkish universities and society. ED II research on which the paper is based have limitations in terms of technique and sample; however, it is possible to mention the following findings and recommendations that represent "survey participants" in our research.

Integration (social cohesion) seems to be the best process to live together. Students' being the crucial actors, role models, and bridges between their community and host society is very valuable. However, this situation is not without problems. ED research and other studies indicate that the feeling of "temporariness and uncertainty" is at the top of the problems (Erdogan 2018a). Temporariness has been another unique parameter in planning integration policies in the medium and long term and this paper attempts to explain the conditions from the higher education perspective. At the beginning of the process, both the legal status of Syrians in Turkey and also the overall attitude of the basic actors in Turkey placed them in a temporary status to go back home soon. Nevertheless, after nine years and the war continuing in Syria, it seems unrealistic to expect their return. Our findings in a limited sample also support this tendency. The majority do not prefer to resettle in a third country in our sample (Fig. 5), which is similar to findings in another research with a bigger sample (Erdogan 2019). It would be beneficial to clarify their legal status so that their sense of belonging to the host

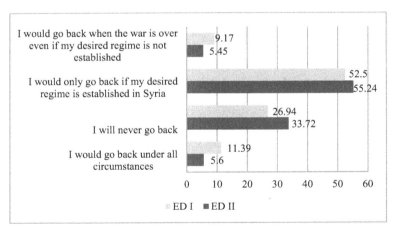

**Fig. 5** Intentions to return to Syria ED-1 (2017) - ED-II (2019). (Source: ED I and II questionnaires)

**Table 3** Support in Problem Solving

| Options | Number of Respondents | Percentage (%) |
|---|---|---|
| All by myself | 317 | 52.05 |
| With the support of Syrian Friends | 199 | 32.68 |
| With the support of Turkish Friends | 53 | 8.70 |
| With the support from Academic Advisor | 17 | 2.79 |
| With the support of another Professor | 12 | 1.97 |
| With the support of Administrative Staff | 11 | 1.81 |
| Total | 609 | |

Source: ED II questionnaire

country may increase and longer-termm policies can be implemented. A comprehensive integration strategy in which higher education will have a specific role is needed for coordination of different institutions and new policies.

The second recommendation, based on our findings, is to set up an active and inclusive multi-layered communication strategy both with refugees and also Turkish citizens. Information channels must be transparent and accessible to different groups in society. Considering the education level of the majority of the refugees in Turkey, university students can play an active mediating role to relay information. Yet, it seems that they have difficulties reaching basic information regarding application procedures, documents, their studies, and institutions. Findings in Table 3 indicate that more dialogue is needed with their student pairs, their professors, and the administrative staff at the university. Moreover, transparent communication will be helpful for the Turkish students and the public to understand the real situation of the Syrian refugees and eliminate the prejudices and wrong assumptions that cause tension. It is also valuable to share success stories and role models with Turkish society. 85% of Syrian students in the table above indicate that they have a social environment with their Syrian peers and do not have much communication with people from Turkey.

In addition to these two macro-level recommendations, further support mechanisms are needed, which can be listed as academic, cultural, and financial. Language learning is both the first step and also a crucial barrier of communication and studies. Although they take language courses before starting their programs, it is the most frequently stated problem they voice. Our argument for their inadequacy in Turkish based on our observations and interviews during our EduMAP and ED I-II research is that they learn everyday language in the courses given by TÖMER but need to improve their academic level of language, and since

**Table 4** Resettlement Intentions

| Options | Number of Respondents | % |
|---|---|---|
| Not at all interested in resettlement | 310 | 44,67 |
| I would go in an instant if I have an opportunity | 89 | 12,82 |
| I would go if I cannot finish my studies in Turkey | 72 | 10,37 |
| I would go if I cannot find a job in Turkey upon graduation | 187 | 26,95 |
| If I have a relative over there who can help me out | 36 | 5,19 |

Source: ED II questionnaire

they have to work to support their families or to earn their living their attendance is irregular. Connection with their peers through some programs and getting mentorship are important to provide more correct and up to date information about Turkish society in order to eliminate incorrect information. Their answers in Fig. 5 provide some clues about their social and cultural distance to their Turkish counterparts. This data needs further study and discussions to apply more inclusive policies. Another support mechanism must be increasing scholarships and other means to improve their financial status. International donors can be more active in providing more resources to students before and during their studies so that they can concentrate on their programs and do not need to work.

In addition to the need to work during their studies, as seen in our survey, it can be foreseen that Syrian graduates will have difficulty finding a job after graduation. In Table 4, 27% of the respondents state that they will go to a third country if they cannot find a job in Turkey. This is an indirect positive outlook on their future regarding employment opportunities in Turkey. Nevertheless, the more than 25% youth unemployment rate will be a big challenge for them as they have to compete with the Turkish graduates. These results constitute important inputs for future policy regarding the young and educated refugees in Turkey. Policies should be developed to motivate Syrian students after graduation to entice them to remain in Turkey as a part of the integration strategy.

There is a big need to produce and share the official data about Syrian students; this will be useful both for the researchers to reach the reliable uptodate information and for the policy makers to design new policies based on detailed data. Hence, the recommendation is to collect and share statistics of foreign students' gender, university, province, education program, faculty, etc. breakdowns just like Turkish students. The gender imbalance is clear. While the average distribution of Turkish students is 52.5% male and 47.5% female, for Syrians 63% are male and 37% are female. Special work should be performed to increase the number of female Syrian students, who are culturally and financially not encouraged to pursue for higher education. Although there are some limitations in terms of field implementation and number of participants in both phases of our research (ED-I and ED-II) which are the data source for this article, it has provided important clues to understand the actual conditions of Syrian higher education students in Turkey. We hope this study contributes both to further and qualitative research and to new policies on a national and international scale in order to ensure peaceful and inclusive societies.

## References

Ager, A., & Strang, A. (2008). Understanding integration: A conceptual framework. *Journal of Refugee Studies*, 21(2), 166–191.

Berry, J. W. (1997). Immigration, Acculturation, and Adaptation. *Applied Psychology: An International review*, 46(1), 5–68.

De Berry, J.P., & Roberts, A. (2018). Social Cohesion and Forced Displacement: A Desk Review to Inform Programming and Project Design. *World Bank Group*. Retrieved from: https://documents.worldbank.org/curated/en/125521531981681035/pdf/128640-WP-P163402-PUBLIC-SocialCohesionandForcedDisplacement.pdf.

Castles, S. (2003) Towards a Sociology of Forced Migration and Social Transformation, *Sociology*, 77(1), 13–34.

Castles, S., Haas, H., & Miller, M.J. (2013). *The Age of Migration: International Population Movements in the Modern World* (5th ed.), Palgrave Macmillan.

CoHE (2015) Executive Board Decision. Retrieved from: https://www.yok.gov.tr/ogrenci/ek-madde-2-uyarinca-misir-ve-suriyeden-yapilabilecek-yatay-gecis-islemlerine-iliskin-esaslar.

CoHE (2017) International Conference of Syrian Students in Turkish Higher Education System. Retrived from: https://www.yok.gov.tr/Documents/Yayinlar/Yayinlarimiz/turk_yuksekogretiminde_suriyeli_ogrenciler_uluslararasi_konferansi_hatay.pdf.

CoHE (2019) International Student Statistics. Retrieved from: https://istatistik.yok.gov.tr/.

CoHE (2020) Higher Education Statistics. Retrived from: https://yok.gov.tr/web/guest/anasayfa.

Cremonini, L. (2016, March 11) Higher education has a key role in integrating refugees. *University World News*. Retrieved from: https://www.universityworldnews.com/article.php?story=20160311205508924.

de Wit, H., & Altbach P. (2016). The Syrian Refugee Crisis and Higher Education. *International Higher Education*, 84, 9–10.

DGMM (Turkish Ministry of Interior, Directorate General of Migration Management) (2020). International Protection Statistics, Retrieved from: https://en.goc.gov.tr/international-protection17.

Demireva, N. (2017). Immigration, Diversity and Social Cohesion. Briefing, The Migration Observatory, University of Oxford.

EduMAP (2019) Adult Education as a means to Active Participatory Citizenship, Project Funded by Horizon 2020. Retrieved from: https://blogs.uta.fi/edumap/about-edumap/

Erdogan A., (2014). Türkiye'de Yükseköğretimin Gündemi için Politika Önerisi (Policy Proposal for Higher Education Agenda in Turkey), *Yükseköğretim ve Bilim Dergisi (Journal of Higher education and Science)* 4(1), 1–17. Retrieved from: https://higheredu-sci.beun.edu.tr/text.php3?id=1629.

Erdogan A., & Erdogan M.M., (2018). *Access, Qualifications and Social Dimension of Syrian Refugee Students in Turkish Higher Education*, In Curaj, A., Deca, L., Pricopie, R. (eds.). The European Higher Education Area: The Impact of Past and Future Policies, Springer VS, Doi: https://doi.org/10.1007/978-3-319-77407-7.

Erdogan, M. M., (2018a). *Türkiye'deki Suriyeliler: Toplumsal Kabul ve Uyum* (Syrians in Turkey: Social Acceptance and Integration) (2nd ed.) İstanbul Bilgi Üniversitesi Yayınevi: Istanbul.

Erdogan, M.M., (2018b). *Suriyeliler Barometresi: Suriyelilerle Uyum içinde Yaşamın Çerçevesi* (Syrian Barometer: A framework for achieving social cohesion with Syrians in Turkey) İstanbul Bilgi Üniversitesi Yayınevi.

Erdogan, M.M. (2019). Türkiye'deki Suriyeliler: 9 Yılın Kısa Muhasebesi, Perspektif. Retrieved from: www.perspektif.online/tr/siyaset/turkiyedeki-suriyeliler-9-yilin-kisa-muhasebesi.html.

Erdogan, M.M., Erdogan A., & Yavçan, B. (2017). Elite Dialogue II- Dialogue with Syrian Refugees in Turkey through Syrian Academics and Students Project Report. Retrieved from: https://www.mmuraterdogan.com/raporlar?pgid=k8ypprcv-c68 1a74f-7da6-11ea-8c85-12879e2400f0&lang=en.

Erdogan, M.M., Erdogan A., Yavçan, B., & Mohamad, T. (2019). *Elite Dialogue II- Dialogue with Syrian Refugees in Turkey through Syrian Academics and Students Project Report*. (unpublished).

Hohberger, W. (2018). *Opportunities in higher education for Syrians in Turkey. The perspective of Syrian university students on the educational conditions, needs and possible solutions for improvement*, Istanbul: Istanbul Policy Center.

Hynie, M. (2018). Refugee integration: Research and policy. *Peace and Conflict: Journal of Peace Psychology, 24*(3), 265–276.

IOM (2012). *IOM and Migrant Integration*. Retrieved from: https://www.iom.int/files/live/sites/iom/files/What-We-Do/docs/IOM-DMM-Factsheet-LHD-Migrant-Integration.pdf.

IOM (2019). *Migrant Presence Monitoring (MPM) Turkey Quarterly Report* (July-August-September 2019). Retrieved from: https://turkey.iom.int/sites/default/files/sitreps/Q3_qua rterly-july-aug-sep-19.pdf.

IOM (2020). *World Migration Report 2020*. Retrieved from: https://publications.iom.int/sys tem/files/pdf/wmr_2020.pdf.

Jenson, J. (1998). Mapping Social Cohesion: The State of Canadian Research. Canadian Policy Research Networks Inc. CPRN Study No F/03.

Jungblut, J., Vukasovic, M., & Steinhardt, I. (2018). Higher education policy dynamics in turbulent times – access to higher education for refugees in Europe. Studies in Higher Education, online first, 45(2), 327–338.

Kavak, Y (2011). Türkiye'de Yükseköğretimin Görünümü ve Geleceğe Bakış, *Yükseköğretim ve Bilim Dergisi (Journal of Higher Education and Science),* 1(2), 55–58.

McMahon, W. (2009). *Higher Learning, Greater Good: The Private and Social Benefits of Higher Education*, John Hopkins University Press: Baltimore.

(MoNE) Ministry of National Education, Statistics, (2019). Retrieved from: https://hbogm.meb.gov.tr/meb_iys_dosyalar/2019_06/26115239_14_HAziran___2019_YNTERNET_SUNUUU_.pdf [20.12.2019].

Official Gazette (2013). *Regulation on Principles of Transfers between Associate and Undergraduate Degree Programs of HEIs...*21 September 2013. Retrieved from: https://www.resmigazete.gov.tr/eskiler/2013/09/20130921-9.html.

Stevenson, J., & Baker, S., (2018). *Refugees in Higher Education: Debate, Discourse and Practice*, Emerald Publishing Limited: London

Streitwieser, B., & Miller-Idriss, C., de Witt, H. (2016). *Higher Education's Response to the European Refugee Crisis: Challenges, Strategies, and Opportunities*, Working Paper, Graduate School of Education & Human Development, The George Washington University. Retrieved from: https://gsehd.gwu.edu/sites/default/files/documents/bernhard_streitwieser_working_paper_10.2016_final.pdf.

UNHCR (2010). Retrieved from: https://www.unhcr.org/1951-refugee-convention.html.

UNHCR (2019a). Figures at a glance. Retrieved from: https://www.unhcr.org/figures-at-a-glance.html.

UNHCR. (2019b). *Stepping up: Refugee education in crisis.* Geneva. Retrieved from: https://www.unhcr.org/steppingup/wp-content/uploads/sites/76/2019/09/Education-Report-2019-Final-web-9.pdf.

UNHCR (2019c). *Tertiary Education.* Retrieved from: https://www.unhcr.org/tertiary-education.html.

UNHCR (2019d). *Global Framework for Refugee Education*, Global Refugee Forum Education Co-Sponsorship Alliance. Retrieved from: https://www.unhcr.org/5dd50ce47.pdf.

UNHCR (2020). Retrieved from: https://data2.unhcr.org/en/situations/syria.

UNESCO (2017). *Migration and Education, Think-piece prepared for the 2019 Global Education Monitoring Report Consultation.* Retreived from: https://es.unesco.org/gem-report/sites/gem-report/files/Think%20piece%20-%20International%20migration%20and%20education%20-%20Tani%20-%20FINAL.pdf.

Watenpaugh, K. D., Fricke, A. L. & King, J. R. (2014). *We will stop here and go no further: Syrian university students and scholars in Turkey*, New York: Institute of International Education. Retrieved from: https://www.scholarrescuefund.org/sites/default/files/pdf-articles/we-will-stop-here-and-go-nofurther-syrian-university-students-and-scholars-in-turkey-002_1.pdf.

Yavcan, B. & El-Ghali, A. (2017). *Higher education and Syrian refugee students: The case of Turkey. Policies, practices and perspectives*, Beirut: Issam Fares Institute for Public Policy and International Affairs.

Yıldız, A. (Ed.) (2019). *Integration of Refugee Students in European Higher Education: Comparative Country Cases.* Izmir: Yasar University Publications.

Zeus, B. (2011). Exploring barriers to higher education in protracted refugee situations: the case of Burmese refugees in Thailand, *Journal of Refugee Studies*, 24(2): 256–276.

# Desk Research

# Admissions Policy and Practice Regarding Refugee Students in U.S. Higher Education: What is Known?

Bryce Loo

## 1 Introduction

In the wake of the enormous worldwide refugee crisis at the end of the 2010s, the higher education sector in the United States of America is well-poised to help integrate refugees that come into the country, albeit with major challenges. As Allan Goodman, president of the Institute of International Education, puts it (2016): "Higher education in the United States has a long tradition of providing support to and sanctuary for the world's students. However, the nature and enormity of human displacement in our era is such that America's universities and colleges are facing a new and unique challenge" (p. 4). Those challenges are not just sociopolitical, but also structural. What are these challenges? And what is being done to address these challenges?

The literature on refugee access to higher education is quite limited. Among countries that resettle a significant number of refugees, there is a particular dearth of literature regarding access in the United States. There is, generally speaking, more research on barriers for refugees in other major predominantly English-speaking industrialized nations that resettle refugees, namely Australia (e.g., Hannah 1999; Earnest et al. 2010; Baker et al. 2018), Canada (e.g., Ferede 2010; Shakya et al. 2010; Bajwa et al. 2017), and the United Kingdom (e.g., Morrice 2013; Gateley 2015). Two prominent reviews of the worldwide literature on refugees in higher education in English feature only a few studies in the U.S. context (Ramsay and Baker 2019) (even though a large number of researchers are based at U.S. institutions) and no U.S.-based studies (Mangan and Winter 2017)

B. Loo (✉)
World Education Services, Bakersfield, USA
E-Mail: bloo@wes.org

© The Author(s), under exclusive license to Springer Fachmedien Wiesbaden GmbH, part of Springer Nature 2021
J. Berg et al. (eds.), *Refugees in Higher Education*, Higher Education Research and Science Studies, https://doi.org/10.1007/978-3-658-33338-6_9

respectively. There are only a few empirical studies in the U.S. (e.g., Kanno and Varghese 2010; Perry and Mallozzi 2011; Felix 2016), while there is a greater preponderance of literature on primary and secondary school (K-12) education for refugees (see McBrien 2005). There is also very little literature on policy issues at the federal, state, and institutional level on addressing these barriers, particularly compared to literature about K-12 education. In many ways, this reflects a worldwide trend of focusing more on basic education than higher education when it comes to refugees (Dryden-Peterson 2010).

This conceptual piece examines policy and practice regarding two known initial barriers to entry for refugees attempting to access higher education in the United States: academic documentation required for admission, and financing. It attempts to describe the current known landscape around these two barriers. In particular, it works to answer the following questions, as best as is known at this time: What are some key factors that likely are preventing institutions from mitigating these barriers for refugee students? What are some ways in which institutions and the higher education sector overall *are* addressing these barriers? What rationales do institutions have for addressing the status quo when it comes to refugee and displaced students? This is while acknowledging that there are many other barriers, including those that occur beyond initial acceptance into an institution and arrival on campus. While not identified in major international, English-language reviews of the literature (Mangan and Winter 2017; Ramsay and Baker 2019), which (as mentioned) include few or no U.S.-based studies, these two challenges are identified in both the scholarly and professional literature in the U.S. (e.g., Perry and Mallozzi 2011; Stanton 2016; Yi and Marquez Kiyama 2018; American Association of Collegiate Registrars and Admissions Officers (AACRAO) 2019).

While not strictly a literature review, I look at both the available scholarly and professional[1] literature from the U.S. available on the topic, providing context as needed. I first take the time to examine with some depth who is a "refugee" in the U.S. context, which is important as discussions of refugees can be lost among broader discussions involving immigrants and international students. I then provide a very brief overview of the structure of U.S. higher education, with a focus on oversight at the state and federal levels and basic governance structures. I then look at the two barriers under discussion, providing a description of the problem, factors contributing to these barriers in the U.S. context particularly

---

[1] I define the latter type of literature as written work from practitioners and scholar-practitioners rooted in experience working with refugee/displaced students and/or explicitly practice-oriented research, which has increased substantially since roughly 2015.

from the policy level, and some efforts underway to address them. I also take a brief look at incentives for the higher education sector to do more for refugees in general within the U.S.

The focus of this chapter is four-year universities and colleges in the U.S., those that grant bachelor's degrees and higher. Community colleges (or junior colleges), which grant mostly two-year associate's degrees and are often open access and relatively inexpensive (Loo 2018), certainly play a crucial role in integrating refugees across the U.S. (Tuliao et al. 2017). However, because of their differing structure, they are not a main focus of this chapter (though many of the same policies and practices will apply to some). Additionally, I focus on students, those wishing to attend academic institutions for the purpose of getting a degree. Scholars and highly-educated professionals are related groups deserving of attention but are not the focus here. This piece is also focused largely on the decade of the 2010s and is not meant to be exhaustive.

## 2 Who is a "refugee" in the U.S. Context?

In the U.S., the term "refugee" is a complex conceptualization, whether in the minds of policymakers, higher education institutions, or the public at large. In the U.S. higher education context, refugees may not seem to some to be any different from other immigrants, though the circumstances of arrival in the U.S. are often very different. Additionally, on many university and college campuses, faculty and staff may view anyone who was educated in another country as an international student, though both legally and experientially, immigrants are distinct from international students.

In fact, the term "refugee" has a specific legal definition in the U.S. found in the Immigration and Nationality Act of 1965, mostly following the international definition as delineated by the 1951 Refugee Convention and succeeding protocols (American Immigration Council 2019). The United States Citizenship and Immigration Service (USCIS) (2020c) summarizes the definition as a person who

- "Is located outside of the United States
- Is of special humanitarian concern to the United States
- Demonstrates that they were persecuted or fear persecution due to race, religion, nationality, political opinion, or membership in a particular social group
- Is not firmly resettled in another country
- Is admissible to the United States"

In the U.S. context, the broad term "refugee" is often applied to someone who has come to the U.S. through the Refugee Resettlement Program. In this program, the government selects officially-designated refugees, usually families, mostly located in refugee camps and usually upon referral from the United Nations Refugee Agency (UNHCR), to be resettled into the U.S. (American Immigration Council 2019). The Office of Refugee Resettlement (ORR) places these refugees in specific communities, usually with lower costs of living, around the country and under the care of one of nine volunteer agencies, or VOLAGs—non-profit, mostly faith-based organizations—that help the refugees settle and become economically self-sufficient as soon as possible. Resettled refugees come in with full legal status; within one year in the U.S., they can apply for permanent residency and begin the path towards citizenship.

The President determines the annual refugee "ceiling"—that is, the maximum number of refugees allowed into the U.S. for resettlement (American Immigration Council 2019). This is done with the consultation of Congress, the Department of State, and the Department of Homeland Security. President Donald Trump consistently lowered the refugee ceiling each year of his presidency, which began in January 2017. In fiscal year (FY)[2] 2018, the ceiling was set an historic low of 45,000, followed by a lowering to 30,000 in FY 2019. However, only 22,415 refugees were admitted to the U.S. in FY 2019.

Another potential pathway for displaced individuals to come to and stay in the U.S. is asylum. By U.S. law, individuals can enter the U.S. through various means, including appearing at a port-of-entry (airport, seaport, or border crossing), and apply for asylum (USCIS 2020a). Asylum-seekers generally must meet the usual definition of a refugee and have a "credible fear" of returning home. By law, asylum-seekers are allowed to remain in the country while their case is processed. However, the Trump Administration sought to work around these laws, by requiring asylum-seekers from predominantly Central America who have come to the southern border to wait in Mexico to process their claims; this was challenged in the federal court system (Liptak 2019). Asylum-seekers cannot work, unless a certain amount of time has elapsed, after which they can apply for employment authorization (USCIS 2020a). They should, however, be allowed access to education at any level. If granted asylum, the asylee (the term typically used for one granted asylum) can eventually apply for permanent residency.

---

[2]The U.S. federal government defines a fiscal year (FY) as running from October of the previous calendar year to the end of September of the current year. For example, FY2018 would run from October 2017 to September 2018.

Beyond resettled refugees and asylees, U.S. law also makes allowance for displaced persons to come in through a variety of other means, which can come with temporary or permanent status. Additionally, in some cases, individuals who could be classified as refugees by international or U.S. legal definitions may actually come as international students (Stanton 2016). That is, they come in on one of several non-immigrant (temporary) student visas (Loo 2018). In some cases, these students may have come to the U.S. before crisis hit their home countries and have essentially become de facto refugees while abroad. However, because of the temporary nature of these visas, students are required to leave the country after either graduating or working at a job through work experience programs tied to their visa status. Or, they must attempt to transition into another status, by claiming asylum, transitioning onto a temporary work visa (notably the H-1B visa), or through some other means. They must comply with the strict regulations imposed on international students while on such a visa, even if now displaced from their home countries.

Much discussion in the U.S. around refugees is also tightly wrapped up in discussions surrounding undocumented immigrants, those who have entered or remained in the country without legal status. There are nearly 12 million undocumented immigrants estimated to be living in the U.S., as of 2018 (Kamarck and Stenglein 2019). The reasons why they come to the U.S. vary widely, but some do come to escape violence, persecution, or instability elsewhere. The current influx of migrants on the U.S.'s southern border with Mexico is largely comprised of migrants from El Salvador, Guatemala, and Honduras fleeing gang-related violence in those countries (Martinez 2018); most wish to claim asylum in the U.S. A large number of undocumented individuals arrived in the U.S. legally, on various visa types or under different statuses, but simply overstayed their visas and now live in the U.S. without legal status (Kamarck and Stenglein 2019).

While legal status has important bearing on students, particularly when it comes to tuition and financial aid options (as will be discussed), I find individual circumstances and experiences to be more important than legal status in terms of who counts as a "refugee." Thus, this chapter will focus on refugees in the broad sense. Throughout this chapter, I will utilize "refugee student" or "displaced student" for any student who, because of circumstances, can be considered a refugee, regardless of legal status in the U.S.

## 3 The Structure of U.S. Higher Education: A Brief Overview

While immigration is the domain of the federal government in the U.S., the states are responsible for education at all levels, including higher education (Loo 2018). Public universities and community colleges are usually overseen by a board of trustees, or a similar body, that is usually answerable to the state legislature or governor. Some of the direct funding of public institutions also comes from the state government, and many students receive state financial aid, such as grants, to help cover tuition. Private universities and colleges are not directly governed by state governments, but they still face state regulation and may accept students funded in part or full by state financial aid.

All of this results in 50 different state higher education systems, as well as those of the District of Columbia (Washington, DC) and the U.S. overseas territories, all with differing laws, regulations, and policies. For public institutions, the state governments can strongly influence everything from admissions policy to financing, which can have varying impacts on refugee students. In practice, however, most institutions are able to formulate their own policy, particularly as impacts day-to-day operations, with only some oversight from the state. Accreditation, however is actually granted to institutions through peer review procedures by several regional, independent (non-governmental) accreditation agencies, as well as by organizations in charge of specific professions (such as medicine and law).

The federal government, however, can have important impacts on higher education. For example, many students attend institutions on federal student aid, particularly loans, administered by the U.S. Department of Education, part of the executive branch of government. This can give the presidential administration some say in higher education matters, as most universities and four-year colleges rely heavily on federal student assistance for income. Another entity with potentially strong impact is the federal court system, with the U.S. Supreme Court as final arbiter. The courts have provided many final decisions on important, and often controversial, policy matters in higher education.

At the institutional level, governance varies. Most institutions—public or private—are governed by a board of directors or trustees, either appointed or elected (in the latter case for public institutions), who set general policy in accordance with state and federal laws. Day-to-day operations are the domain of a president or chancellor. In many of the public university systems, particularly the larger ones such as the University of California system, there may be a chancellor or president for the entire system, with individual universities within the system having an executive leader of their own. Under the president or chancellor of the institution is usually an extensive hierarchy, depending on the size and scope of operations of the institution.

## 4 Academic Documentation Requirements for Admission

Displaced students may have trouble meeting basic admissions requirements in terms of access to important documents, particularly academic credentials or qualifications (Perry and Mallozzi 2011; Fricke 2016; Luo and Craddock 2016). In order to access most institutions and programs aside from those that are open access (such as community colleges), applicants must be able to prove earlier educational qualifications, such as a high school diploma for an undergraduate program, by providing official, verifiable documents such as degree certificates, transcripts, or mark sheets (Loo 2016). Typically, these documents need to be issued directly by the home institution or ministry of education, or they need to be verified directly with these institutions. This practice allows institutions to ensure that these documents are authentic, particularly as there are instances of document fraud worldwide (Altbach 2012). In the case of institutions from warzones or other fragile contexts, this is often not possible (Loo 2016). In other cases, institutions in home countries may have the ability to send or verify documents but refuse to do so for political reasons. Additionally, students may or may not have had the ability to flee with important educational documents, though many have the foresight to do so.

State policy, and to a lesser extent federal policy, can impact admissions practices at public institutions, which may impact the way universities handle admissions of refugees who cannot meet standard requirements. As Blume (2015) argues, public university admissions is a form of public policy. Admissions policy is impacted by both internal actors—university governance and faculty, mainly—and external actors, notably state actors, such as the legislature, governor, or higher education coordinating board, as well as the federal courts and voting citizens. The state government can pass laws in regards to university admissions. For example, according to Blume, the California legislature passed a law in 2010 requiring the California State University system, one of the state's two public university systems, to receive public comment before changing admissions policies. Public universities across the U.S. have faced challenges to their admissions practices, ranging from the percentage of out-of-state residents who are admitted to how much a student's race can be a factor in admissions decisions, through both legislation and litigation. Even private universities, particularly elite ones, can face pressure from outside forces. In 2019, the U.S. Supreme Court heard a suit against Harvard University about its use of race as a consideration in admissions (in this case, to the alleged disadvantage of Asian-American applicants) (Hartocollis 2019). Admissions to colleges and universities, particularly elite institutions (public and private), are often the subject of intense public scrutiny and debates around fairness from both government and the public (Supiano 2017).

While there is no known direct evidence of state and federal policy impacting the treatment of refugees, aside from undocumented students, in university or college admissions, there is some evidence that it is a consideration among university staff. In a recent policy paper from the American Association of Collegiate Registrars and Admissions Officers (AACRAO) (2019), one section written by several university and college admissions officers notes, "Institutions of higher education have standards we must maintain in order to meet federal and state regulations, accreditation standards, and institutional policy. Keeping these in mind, working with displaced students brings about many challenges and concerns, both from the applicant side and the institutional side" (p. 40). These various potential outside pressures may lead to many institutions avoiding creation of a formal policy on providing exemptions for admission for displaced students who cannot meet usual requirements. Or at least it likely results in opacity of any policies or practices instituted. The pressures put onto admissions officers may be implied, rather than explicit.

That said, some U.S. institutions are doing what they can to help refugees through the admissions process. Helping refugee applicants through the admissions process requires some flexibility on the part of institutions, such as in their documentation and testing requirements (Loo 2016; Stanton 2016; AACRAO 2019). Luckily, there are established best practices worldwide in working with students with limited documentation due to circumstances beyond their control (e.g., Loo 2016; Canadian Information Centre for International Credentials (CICIC) 2017; AACRAO 2019), many of which that have been tested in various national and institutional contexts. Stanton (2016) recommends that "universities interested in welcoming displaced and refugee students ... adjust their processes, not lower their standards" (p. 19). In general, these best practices are flexible in their application within various institutional contexts.

In a 2018 survey of 500 admissions officers mostly from across the U.S. from the American Association of Collegiate Registrars and Admissions Officers (AACRAO), nearly half of public institutions reported having admissions practices in place to help displaced students who cannot meet traditional requirements.

Only 41% of private nonprofit institutions reported the same. A majority of institutions, however, said that this was not based on any formal policy. This seems to indicate that institutions are dealing with admissions issues of refugee students on a case-by-case basis. As mentioned previously, there is likely reticence among institutions to create a formal policy, or at least to state it openly, in this regard because of potential scrutiny from state governments or from the public.

Among the numerous U.S. higher education associations, AACRAO, a membership organization of predominantly U.S. universities and colleges, has been active in trying to mitigate admissions barriers for refugee students. The organization has worked to collect and disseminate potential admissions practices for refugee students, particularly those who cannot meet regular documentation requirements. Most recently, AACRAO assembled a working group of academics and practitioners to create a report synthesizing such practices, *Inclusive Admissions Policies for Displaced and Vulnerable Students*, released in 2019. It is not entirely clear what the impact of AACRAO's work has been on the policies of individual institutions, but as described earlier, some institutions do appear to be developing flexible policies and practices in the admissions of refugee students. AACRAO's other main contribution has been to partner with the University of California, Davis and the American University of Beirut in Lebanon to develop the Article 26 Backpack, a cloud-based online platform for students from countries in crisis to store important documents, notably academic credentials, for later usage (El-Ghali 2018).

Some of the many credential evaluation organizations in the U.S. have also attempted to help reduce barriers in terms of academic credentials. Unlike in many European countries and elsewhere, there is no central authority to evaluate and recognize the credentials and qualifications of individuals educated outside of the U.S. (Loo 2019). Individual colleges and universities have ultimate authority in recognizing held qualifications, and many evaluate these documents themselves. However, many institutions chose to outsource the evaluation of international credentials, which includes authenticating documents and determining equivalency with U.S. degrees and coursework, to one or more of currently 27 organizations that exist each under one of two independent quality assurance associations: the National Association of Credential Evaluation Services (NACES) (2019) and the Association of International Credential Evaluators (AICE) (2016).

Several of these credential evaluation organizations have developed initiatives of their own to address the documentation barriers faced by many displaced students. To tackle the issue of the cost of a credential evaluation, one of the larger organizations, Educational Credential Evaluators (ECE), offers fee waivers for their credential evaluation services, which can be substantial in price for many refugees, through fundraising in an initiative known as ECE®Aid (Educational Credential Evaluators (ECE) 2020). Another major credential evaluation organization, World Education Services (WES), which operates in both the U.S. and Canada, has worked to develop an alternative methodology for assessing credentials in the absence of official, verifiable documentation, based on established worldwide best practices (Kalachova 2019). This methodology is applied through an initiative in Canada known as the WES Gateway Program, with plans to bring it to the U.S. relatively soon. These efforts exist despite the fact that credential evaluation organizations face a similar challenge as colleges and universities in that verification of the authenticity of educational credentials is important for the organization to maintain credibility with the institutions they serve, in most cases.

## 5 Financing of an Education

Another tremendous barrier for many refugees is the ability to finance a university education. The U.S. has one of the most expensive higher education systems in the world (Ripley 2018). Private universities have long been very expensive, but public universities nationwide have increased tuition and fees as state funding for higher education has gradually diminished (Tandberg 2009). Refugees typically have fewer personal funds available to them than other immigrant groups (Yi and Marquez Kiyama 2018). Additionally, the federal government expects resettled refugees to become self-sufficient as soon as possible. There was also increasing pressure on immigrants from the Trump Administration to not become a "public charge," that is, to draw on public assistance such as social welfare payments or food stamps (Barnhill 2020). As a result, many refugees need to work, often to support their family.

States can determine which students are eligible for in-state tuition rates at public universities, which can dramatically impact the price of higher education for students (National Conference of State Legislatures (NCSL) 2019). Typically, U.S. citizens or permanent residents who can prove long-term residence within a state are eligible for a substantially reduced cost of attendance at public universities. Students coming from out of state, including international students, must pay a much higher rate. (International students sometimes pay even higher fees.) Whether or not refugee students, depending on immigration status, are eligible for in-state tuition is determined by the state. The state of Colorado, for example, has stated that refugees and certain other immigrants are eligible for in-state tuition, based on specified documentation (Colorado Department of Higher Education 2018). Many states will detail residency requirements and how to prove them, with some exemptions for refugees with certain government documentation. In-state tuition has been much more controversial when it comes to undocumented immigrants. According to the National Council of State Legislatures (NCSL) (2019), only 16 states and Washington, DC, allow for in-state tuition for undocumented immigrants by law, and seven state university systems allow for in-state tuition for the same group.

A large percentage of domestic students attending universities utilize financial aid—loans, grants, and the like. Both the federal government and the state governments offer financial aid (Federal Student Aid 2020c). The federal government offers aid primarily in the form of low-interest loans, as well as a limited number of grants. State aid varies tremendously, with most offering a combination of grants and loans. To access aid at either level, as well as directly from a university or college, students generally need to fill out the Free Application for Federal Student Aid, or FAFSA, form beginning in early January for the following academic year (Federal Student Aid 2020b). Deadlines vary, with the deadline for federal aid occurring usually in late June, but it can be much earlier for some states and individual institutions. The FAFSA form requires a lot of documentation, particularly of the student's income and of the parents' income, if the student is a dependent (National Association of Student Financial Aid Administrators (NASFAA) 2018). Though there are procedures in place for completing the FAFSA under such circumstances, the requirements are often still burdensome, presenting a potential barrier to completing the form and thus accessing needed funds.

Access to financial aid for displaced students varies tremendously by status. Resettled refugees, those granted asylum, and others with permanent legal status are generally eligible for aid at all levels (Federal Student Aid 2020a). Undocumented students and international students (those on nonimmigrant student visas) are not eligible for federal student aid. State policies regarding these groups, however, vary. Oregon, for example, allows its public institutions to offer all forms of financial aid to students regardless of immigration status (NCSL 2019). Many states, however, have no clear laws or policies. Additionally, graduates of U.S. institutions are increasingly taking on a huge amount of student loan debt, totally around $1.6 trillion (Johnson 2019). Taking on such debt may potentially be a major concern for many displaced students, even when they can take out public or private loans.

Individual institutions can offer grants and scholarships to students, with public institutions in some cases more constricted by state policies. Offering scholarships are one of the main ways in which some U.S. institutions have tried to help refugee students. In December 2019, Columbia University announced the Columbia University Scholarship for Displaced Students, which covers the tuition and living costs of as many as 30 students who are refugees or asylum-seekers admitted to any undergraduate or graduate program across the university (Svriuga 2019). It is backed by US$6 million and touted by university leaders as "the first of its kind in the world." It was initially piloted with seven Syrian refugee students.

One U.S. organization working heavily on the funding issues is the Institute of International Education (IIE), one of the largest and oldest organizations dedicated to facilitating educational mobility into and out of the U.S. One of its stated areas of work is helping "thousands of students and scholars affected by conflict or natural disasters each year" (IIE 2019). One such program under this umbrella is the Syria Consortium for Higher Education in Crisis, which was formed in the wake of the Syrian refugee crisis. It has worked to bring universities in the U.S. and internationally to commit to providing scholarships for Syrian refugee students and to share best practices. As of February 2018, 68 U.S. universities and colleges belonged to the consortium, as well as institutions from many countries around the world (IIE 2018). IIE also launched the Platform for Education in Emergencies Response, or PEER, to provide a database of scholarships available to refugee students, starting with Syrians but later broadening to other groups, in the U.S. and around the world.

Considering all of these efforts, however, it is unclear how many of the roughly 4500 U.S. higher education institutions (Loo 2018) overall are offering such aid directly targeted to displaced students.

## 6  Rationales: Why Reduce Structural Barriers?

The two challenges discussed—documentation for admissions and financing—demonstrate just a few of the barriers that the U.S. higher education system can present to displaced students, whether permanently settled or with temporary or otherwise uncertain status. The two previous sections discussed some of systemic factors surrounding those two barriers, which originate in both the overall higher education system in the U.S. and from individual institutions. As discussed earlier, there may be incentives for institutions *not* to help, in the form of explicit barriers and implicit pressures from many directions, including federal and state policies, among others. The challenges presented are difficult for displaced students to overcome as these students usually come with low levels of information and understanding of the system, as well as financial resources.

Individual institutions in the U.S. can and should do more to help refugees access higher education. U.S. institutions can develop a more flexible system to help lower-resourced but eligible and highly capable displaced students enter.

The goal should be to remove barriers that prevent such students from starting or resuming an education. As discussed in the two previous sections, there are efforts among both individual institutions of all kinds and among collaborations and consortiums across the higher education sector.

Considering incentives to maintain the status quo for institutions, what incentives *are* there for institutions to help, particularly in the face of such pressures? As Streitwieser et al. (2019) point out, there may be incentives for U.S. colleges and universities to take concerted efforts to admit refugee students based on the widely-cited four traditional rationales for internationalization of higher education developed by De Wit (2002), building on the earlier work of Knight and De Wit (1995): academic, political, economic, and socio-cultural. For example, as part of the academic rationale, institutions may want to internationalize both the curriculum and the classroom itself, for the benefit of all students in preparing for global careers and citizenship. Refugees can certainly help do that by bringing their unique perspectives. This is well exemplified by Millner (2016) in talking about a chief rationale of his institution, the University of Evansville, a private university in Indiana, in consciously working to bring in Syrian students as part of IIE's Syria Consortium:

> We have tied comprehensive internationalization to our mission, strategic plan and even accreditation. Our mission calls for providing students with life transforming educational experiences that prepare them to engage the world as informed, ethical, and productive citizens. Our strategic plan specifically requires the University to expand and enrich the university's international programs, including the increase in number and diversity of international students. In addition to embedding international/cultural diversity into our general education curriculum, we deliberately selected our Quality Initiative for the Higher Learning Commission reaccreditation to address the intersection of internationalization and social responsibility. This allowed us even greater incentive for the university community to consider taking on the challenge of displaced students. (p. 29)

Streitwieser et al. argue that yet a fifth rational—humanism (or a humanistic rationale)—should be added, particularly as institutions respond to the refugee crises of the 2010s, notably the Syrian crisis and others of the broader Middle East that have captured media and public attention. While the four traditional rationales of internationalization may partly explain some of the actions of institutions like the University of Evansville, this new fifth rationale may complete the explanation. It works in tandem, rather than at odds, with the other four rationales. According to their argument, higher education institutions worldwide are responding to the crisis, in part, for more altruistic purposes, such as the desire to fulfill the role of higher education as a social good. As Millner notes above, "social responsibility" became an important impetus for the University of Evansville to work with refugee students. A sense of mission—the institution as instrumental of positive change in the world—is important, as well as leadership committed to carrying out such a mission.

The analysis of Streitwieser et al. mentions that students and faculty often drive the humanistic rationale. The University of Evansville provides another example of this. Following the university's intake of several displaced Syrians, a large group of individuals from the university and the surrounding community created a new nonprofit called Scholars of Syria (Millner 2016). When started, it was "dedicated to supporting our displaced students and their families, to help the local community understand Syria's rich culture, humanize the civil war and explain the complexities surround [sic] the region's current crisis" (p. 32). The organization is now based at Seton Hall University in New Jersey (Scholars for Syria 2020). These efforts, though anecdotal, show that members of campus communities can provide a push (or further push) to universities and colleges to act even in the face of institutional inertia.

There is also evidence of broader efforts among the U.S. higher education sector to come together and work to mitigate these barriers. Several other sector-based organizations have arisen in response to the current refugee crisis. One prime example, however, is a new organization formed specifically to address refugee access to U.S. higher education: the University Alliance for Refugees and At-Risk Migrants (UARRM), housed at Rutgers University in New Jersey (UARRM 2020). Following initial meetings, UAARM had its "formal launch" in July 2018. It is composed of "researchers, practitioners, and policymakers" working together in six action areas:

- "Offering More Legal Pathways For Study, Research, and Vocational Training
- Overcoming Barriers to Entry into Higher Education Institutions
- Providing On-campus and In-community Assistance and Empowerment
- Advocacy And Awareness
- Research
- Media and Communications"

At this point, it is unclear the impact that this organization will have on the higher education sector, but it is a promising step. What is clear is that while federal and state policies may be unhelpful or mute in many cases when it comes to refugee access, many U.S. institutions and higher education-serving organizations are moving forward to help where they can.

## 7 Towards Greater Inclusion

Admissions requirements and financing are only a few of the major barriers that refugee students may face. I contend that these other barriers should be explored more from both the student perspective and from the policy-practice perspective, both in the U.S. and worldwide. As this chapter demonstrates, there are some efforts underway to remove initial barriers to entry, proving that there are ways forward for U.S. universities and colleges of all types. As Stanton (2016) notes, "Most universities are better prepared to handle displaced and refugee students than administrators, faculty, or staff may initially assume. Any university that already supports international students is already ready to welcome displaced and refugee students with minimal adjustments and with a high probability of success" (p. 18–19).

Ultimately, too, access is just the first step for students when it comes to higher education. Gidley et al. (2010) argue that for full social inclusion in higher education, marginalized groups, including refugees, move from "equitable access" to "engaged participation" to "empowered success" (p. 138), each successive step representing a greater degree of inclusion. Institutions and other providers can provide specific interventions at each step. Removing admissions requirement barriers and helping students finance their education help with the "equitable access" stage, only the first stage toward inclusion. There is certainly a need to examine more efforts to help refugees become full-fledged, participating members of the higher education community. They can then eventually become full contributing members of their host societies or return to rebuild their home countries when the right time comes.

## References

Altbach, P. (2012). Corruption: a key challenge to internationalization. *International Higher Education, 69*, 2–4.

American Association of Collegiate Registrars and Admissions Officers (AACRAO). (2018). *Admissions practice snapshot: results of the AACRAO November 2018 60-second survey.* Washington, DC: AACRAO. Retrieved from https://www.aacrao.org/research-publicati ons/research/admissions-reports/aacrao-60-second-survey-report-admissions-practice---november-2018.

American Association of Collegiate Registrars and Admissions Officers (AACRAO). (2019). *Inclusive Admissions Policies for Displaced and Vulnerable Students.* Washington, DC: AACRAO. Retrieved from https://www.aacrao.org/signature-initiatives/article-26-bac

kpack-project/aacrao-pledge-for-education/inclusive-admissions-policies-for-displaced-and-vulnerable-students-report.

American Immigration Council. (2019, June 18). *An overview of U.S. refugee law and policy*. Retrieved from https://www.americanimmigrationcouncil.org/research/overview-us-refugee-law-and-policy.

Association of International Credential Evaluators (AICE). (2016). Retrieved from https://aice-eval.org.

Bajwa, J. K., Couto, S., Kidd, S., Markoulakis, R., Abai, M., & McKenzie, K. (2017). Refugees, higher education, and informational barriers. *Refuge: Canada's Journal on Refugees, 33*(2), 56–65.

Baker, S., Ramsay, G., Irwin, E., & Miles, L. (2018). 'Hot', 'cold' and 'warm' supports: towards theorising where refugee students go for assistance at university. *Teaching in Higher Education, 23*(1), 1–16.

Barnhill, S. R. (2020, March 6). Factors government will consider under new public charge rule. *The National Law Review*. Retrieved from https://www.natlawreview.com/article/factors-government-will-consider-under-new-public-charge-rule.

Canadian Information Centre for International Credentials (CICIC). (2017). *Assessing the qualifications of refugees: best practices and guidelines*. Toronto: CICIC. Retrieved from https://www.cicic.ca/docs/2017/Best_Practices_and_Guidelines.pdf.

Colorado Department of Higher Education. (2018, November 1). *Memorandum: clarifying Senate Bill 18–087*. Retrieved from https://highered.colorado.gov/Academics/Refugee-Students/SB18-087-Clarification-Memo.pdf.

De Wit, H. (2002). Internationalization of higher education in the United States of America and Europe: a historical, comparative, and conceptual analysis. Westport, CT, USA: Greenwood Publishing Group.

Dryden-Peterson, S. (2010). The politics of higher education for refugees in a global movement for primary education. *Refuge: Canada's Journal on Refugees, 27*(2), 10–18.

Earnest, J., Joyce, A., De Mori, G., & Silvagni, G. (2010). Are universities responding to the needs of students from refugee backgrounds? *Australian Journal of Education, 54*(2), 155–174.

Educational Credential Evaluators (ECE). (2020). ECE®Aid. Retrieved from https://www.ece.org/ECE/ECE-Aid.

El-Ghali, H. A. (2018, February 6). The Article 26 Backpack: a new tool for empowering vulnerable youth. *WENR: World Education News and Reviews*. Retrieved from https://wenr.wes.org/2018/02/the-article-26-backpack-a-new-tool-for-empowering-vulnerable-youth.

Federal Student Aid. (2020a). Eligibility for non-U.S. citizens. Retrieved from https://studentaid.gov/understand-aid/eligibility/requirements/non-us-citizens.

Federal Student Aid. (2020b). FAFSA® deadlines. Retrieved from https://studentaid.gov/apply-for-aid/fafsa/fafsa-deadlines.

Federal Student Aid. (2020c). Types of financial aid. Retrieved from https://studentaid.gov/understand-aid/types#state-aid.

Felix, V. R. (2016). *The experiences of refugee students in United States postsecondary education*. Doctoral dissertation, Bowling Green State University. Retrieved from https://etd.ohiolink.edu/!etd.send_file?accession=bgsu1460127419&disposition=inline.

Ferede, M. K. (2010). Structural factors associated with higher education access for first-generation refugees in Canada: an agenda for research. *Refuge: Canada's Journal on Refugees, 27*(2), 79–88.

Fricke, A. (2016). Regional opportunities and challenges for Syrian students. In *Supporting displaced and refugee students in higher education: principles and best practices* (pp. 10–13). New York: Institute of International Education (IIE). Retrieved from https://www.iie.org/Research-and-Insights/Publications/Supporting-Displaced-and-Refugee-Students-in-Higher-Education.

Gateley, D. E. (2015). A policy of vulnerability or agency? Refugee young people's opportunities in accessing further and higher education in the UK. *Compare: A Journal of Comparative and International Education, 45*(1), 26–46.

Gidley, J. M., Hampson, G. P., Wheeler, L., & Bereded-Samuel, E. (2010). From access to success: an integrated approach to quality higher education informed by social inclusion theory and practice. *Higher Education Policy, 23*(1), 123–147.

Goodman, A. (2016). Foreword. In *Supporting displaced and refugee students in higher education: principles and best practices* (pp. 4–5). New York: Institute of International Education (IIE). Retrieved from https://www.iie.org/Research-and-Insights/Publications/Supporting-Displaced-and-Refugee-Students-in-Higher-Education.

Hannah, J. (1999). Refugee students at college and university: improving access and support. *International Review of Education, 45*(2), 151–164.

Hartocollis, A. (2019, October 2). Harvard won a key affirmative action battle. But the war's not over. *The New York Times*. Retrieved from https://www.nytimes.com/2019/10/02/us/harvard-admissions-lawsuit.html.

Institute of International Education. (2018). Syria consortium member institutions. Retrieved from https://www.iie.org/Programs/Syria-Scholarships/Syria-Consortium-Member-Institutions.

Institute of International Education. (2020). Protect students, scholars, and artists. Retrieved from https://www.iie.org/en/Work-With-Us/Protect-Students-Scholars-and-Artists.

Johnson, D. M. (2019, September 23). What will it take to solve the student loan crisis? *Harvard Business Review*. Retrieved from https://hbr.org/2019/09/what-will-it-take-to-solve-the-student-loan-crisis.

Kalachova, A. (2019, May 20). WES Gateway Program named "promising practice" in settlement, integration in Canada. *World Education Services (WES) Global Talent Bridge Partner Blog*. Retrieved from https://www.wes.org/partners/gtb-blog/canada-gateway-program-named-promising-practice-in-settlement-integration/.

Kamarck, E., & Stenglein C. (2019, November 12). How many undocumented immigrants are in the United States and who are they? *Brookings Institution*. Retrieved from https://www.brookings.edu/policy2020/votervital/how-many-undocumented-immigrants-are-in-the-united-states-and-who-are-they/.

Kanno, Y., & Varghese, M. M. (2010). Immigrant and refugee ESL students' challenges to accessing four-year college education: from language policy to educational policy. *Journal of Language, Identity, and Education, 9*(5), 310–328.

Knight, J., & De Wit, H. (1995). Strategies for internationalization of higher education: historical and conceptual perspectives. In H. De Wit (Ed.), *Strategies for internationalization of higher education: a comparative study of Australia, Canada, Europe and the United States of America* (pp. 5–33). Amsterdam: European Association for International Education (EAIE).

Liptak, A. (2019). Supreme Court says Trump can bar asylum seekers while legal fight continues. *The New York Times*. Retrieved from https://www.nytimes.com/2019/09/11/us/politics/supreme-court-trump-asylum.html.

Loo, B. (2016). *Recognizing refugee qualifications: practical tips for credential assessment*. New York: World Education Services (WES). Retrieved from https://knowledge.wes.org/wes-research-report-recognizing-refugee-credentials.html.

Loo, B. (2018, June 12). Education in the United States of America. *WENR: World Education News and Reviews*. Retrieved from https://wenr.wes.org/2018/06/education-in-the-united-states-of-america.

Loo, B. (2019). North American policy and practice: refugee qualifications and access to higher education. In K. Arar, K. Haj-Yehia, D. B. Ross, & Y. Kondakci (Eds.), *Higher challenges for migrant and refugee students in a global world* (pp. 97–111). New York: Peter Lang.

Luo, N., & Craddock, A. (2016, December 6). The refugee crisis and higher education: Access is one issue. Credentials are another. *WENR: World Education News and Reviews*. Retrieved from https://wenr.wes.org/2016/12/refugee-crisis-higher-education-access-credentials.

Mangan, D., & Winter, L. A. (2017). (In)validation and (mis)recognition in higher education: the experiences of students from refugee backgrounds. *International Journal of Lifelong Education, 36*(4), 486–502.

Martinez, S. (2018, June 26). Today's migrant flow is different. *The Atlantic*. Retrieved from https://www.theatlantic.com/international/archive/2018/06/central-america-border-immigration/563744/.

McBrien, J. L. (2005). Educational needs and barriers for refugee students in the United States: a review of the literature. *Review of Educational Research, 75*(3), 329–364.

Millner, W. (2016). Displaced students enriching the University of Evansville. In *Supporting displaced and refugee students in higher education: principles and best practices* (pp. 28–33). New York: Institute of International Education (IIE). Retrieved from https://www.iie.org/Research-and-Insights/Publications/Supporting-Displaced-and-Refugee-Students-in-Higher-Education.

Morrice, L. (2013). Refugees in higher education: boundaries of belonging and recognition, stigma and exclusion. *International Journal of Lifelong Education, 32*(5), 652–668.

National Association of Credential Evaluation Services (NACES). (2019). Retrieved from https://www.naces.org.

National Association of Student Financial Aid Administrators (NASFAA). (2018). *Tip sheet for refugee and asylee students*. Retrieved from https://www.nasfaa.org/uploads/documents/ Tip_Sheet_Refugee_Asylee_Students.pdf.

National Conference of State Legislatures (NCSL). (2019, September 26). *Tuition benefits for immigrants*. Retrieved from https://www.ncsl.org/research/immigration/tuition-benefits-for-immigrants.aspx.

Perry, K. H., & Mallozzi, C. A. (2011). 'Are you able… to learn?': power and access to higher education for African refugees in the USA. *Power and Education, 3*(3), 249–262.

Ramsay, G., & Baker, S. (2019). Higher education and students from refugee backgrounds: a meta-scoping study. *Refugee Survey Quarterly, 38*, 55–82.

Ripley, A. (2018, September 11). Why is college in America so expensive? *The Atlantic.* Retrieved from https://www.theatlantic.com/education/archive/2018/09/why-is-college-so-expensive-in-america/569884/.

Scholars for Syria. (2020). Our mission. Retrieved from https://www.scholarsforsyria.com/.

Shakya, Y. B., Guruge, S., Hynie, M., Akbari, A., Malik, M., Htoo, S., ... & Alley, S. (2010). Aspirations for higher education among newcomer refugee youth in Toronto: expectations, challenges, and strategies. *Refuge: Canada's Journal on Refugees, 27*(2), 65–78.

Stanton, A. (2016). Best practices: making use of existing university resources to welcome and integrate refugee students. In *Supporting displaced and refugee students in higher education: principles and best practices* (pp. 17–20). New York: Institute of International Education (IIE). Retrieved from https://www.iie.org/Research-and-Insights/Publications/Supporting-Displaced-and-Refugee-Students-in-Higher-Education.

Streitwieser, B., Loo, B., Ohorodnik, M., & Jeong, J. (2019). Access for refugees into higher education: a review of interventions in North America and Europe. *Journal of Studies in International Education, 23*(4), 473–496.

Supiano, B. (2017, August 2). How colleges can prepare for scrutiny of their admissions policies. *The Chronicle of Higher Education.* Retrieved from https://www.chronicle.com/article/How-Colleges-Can-Prepare-for/240835.

Svriuga, S. (2019, December 4). Columbia will give full scholarships to refugees and other displaced students. *The Washington Post.* Retrieved from https://www.washingtonpost.com/education/2019/12/04/columbia-will-give-full-scholarships-refugees-other-displaced-students/.

Tandberg, D. A. (2010). Politics, interest groups and state funding of public higher education. *Research in Higher Education, 51*(5), 416–450.

Tuliao, M. D., Hatch, D. K., & Torraco, R. J. (2017). Refugee students in community colleges: how colleges can respond to an emerging demographic challenge. *Journal of Applied Research in the Community College, 24*(1), 15–26.

United States Citizenship and Immigration Service (USCIS). (2020a). Asylum. Retrieved from https://www.uscis.gov/humanitarian/refugees-asylum/asylum.

United States Citizenship and Immigration Service (USCIS). (2020b). Humanitarian. Retrieved from https://www.uscis.gov/humanitarian.

United States Citizenship and Immigration Service (USCIS). (2020c). Refugees. Retrieved from https://www.uscis.gov/humanitarian/refugees-asylum/refugees.

University Alliance for Refugees and At-Risk Migrants. (2020). Retrieved from https://www.uarrm.org.

Yi, V., & Marquez Kiyama, J. (2018). *Failed educational justice: refugee students' postsecondary realities in restrictive times* (ASHE-NITE Paper Series). Las Vegas: Association for the Study of Higher Education (ASHE). Retrieved from https://cece.sitehost.iu.edu/wordpress/wp-content/uploads/2017/02/Failed-Educational-Justice-FINAL-2.pdf.

# The Politics of Restricted Meritocracy: Refugees in Higher Education in Germany

Christin Younso and Hannes Schammann

## 1 Introduction

Following the "long summer of migration" (Hess et al. 2016) of 2015 many German universities established programs for refugees[1] with an academic background and/or academic aspirations. In order to provide the impressively committed volunteers and university staff members with empirically-derived recommendations, between December 2015 and February 2016, we carried out an explorative study in nine universities and published our findings open access (Schammann and Younso 2016). We conducted 39 interviews with 49 experts encompassing university vice-presidents, staff of different departments, students with and without a refugee background, volunteers and external cooperation partners. We triangulated the interview data with document analysis. In order to validate the findings and come up with recommendations, we organized a focus group discussion. Some of the recommendations were addressed to policymakers, most of them to Higher Education Institutions (HEI) and their cooperation partners. As researchers of public policy and migration studies, we also wondered how those new

---

[1] In the following article we use the term "refugee" for persons, who fled from their country of nationality or former habitual residence. Where relevant, we distinguish on the basis of a person's residence status.

---

C. Younso (✉) · H. Schammann
Institut für Sozialwissenschaften, Universität Hildesheim, Hildesheim, Deutschland
E-Mail: younso@uni-hildesheim.de

H. Schammann
E-Mail: hannes.schammann@uni-hildesheim.de

© The Author(s), under exclusive license to Springer Fachmedien Wiesbaden GmbH, part of Springer Nature 2021
J. Berg et al. (eds.), *Refugees in Higher Education*, Higher Education Research and Science Studies, https://doi.org/10.1007/978-3-658-33338-6_10

programs related to broader tendencies in the politics of forced migration in Germany. The concluding remarks of our study suggested that the developments in higher education could rather adapt and somehow even reinforce the dominant political discourse in German refugee protection than constitute an independent contribution (Schammann and Younso 2016, p. 54/55).

Over the course of the next four years, university programs for refugees and the body of academic literature surrounding the field have evolved significantly. Several larger research projects examine the access and challenges for refugees in the German higher education system and have published status reports, policy recommendations and refereed journal articles, some also confirming and complementing our findings (e.g. Blumenthal et al. 2017; Berg et al. 2018; Grüttner et al. 2018; Halkic and Arnold 2019; Jungblut et al. 2018; Schneider 2018; Streitwieser and Brück 2018; Streitwieser et al. 2018; Reinhardt et al. 2018; Unangst and Streitwieser 2018; Zlatkin-Troitschanskaia 2018).

When it comes to policy developments in the field, most notably the Federal Ministry of Education and Research (BMBF), has extended two major packages of measures. The first one supports access to education and training, the second funds German universities with approximately 100 million € (BMBF (n.y.)). The universities themselves have left the 'crisis mode': enrollments of refugees to full academic studies seem to run quite smoothly within the framework of established enrolment processes, 'special study programs' for refugees who do not want or are not able to enroll in a regular program are managed by Uni-Assist.[2] It is still impossible, though, to quantify the number of refugee students as universities do not register refugees by their legal status. Instead, they refer to the country of origin and to their own estimates or surveys that are hardly comparable between universities or even verifiable (HRK 2019). This also goes for the numbers of refugee students mentioned in obligatory reports within state-funded programs like the 'Integra' program and the 'Welcome' program (DAAD 2018, p. 5).

Against the backdrop of the impressive efforts undertaken in research and practice alike, we feel obliged to take another critical look at our own findings. In 2016, we assumed *"that numerous fundamental challenges will remain on the agenda in the medium term"*[3] (Schammann and Younso 2016, p. 54). Yet, do we really still find similar challenges? Are there not significant changes in the new programs to be taken into account? Which of the emerging tendencies of 2015/16

---

[2] The free examination procedure for refugees was closed on 31.12.2019 (https://www.uni-assist.de/bewerben/vorab-informieren/informationen-fuer-gefluechtete/. Last access 26.01.2020).

[3] Translation by the authors.

have prevailed, which have vanished? And last but certainly not least, how do the current programs for refugees in higher education relate to the constantly evolving political context of migration and asylum in Germany?

In this contribution, we will try to shed light on these questions by contrasting some core findings and recommendations from our 2016-study against the backdrop of ongoing developments in the fields of HEI and migration politics. For the purpose of this article, we have relied on desk research background discussions with experts in the field and participant observation in various committees on the matter such as project or selection committees. We will concentrate on the remaining challenges in two fields: the field of migration and asylum and the field of higher education. The analysis in both fields comprises challenges generated by the legal framework and administrative discretion, governance issues within the universities, and strategic questions like the framing of refugee programs as part of local internationalization strategies. Moreover, we will analyze the interplay of changing refugee policies and the university programs. We will argue that, in German higher education programs for refugees, meritocratic and restrictive elements, i.e. specific access restrictions, converge, reinforcing an overall tendency in German refugee policies.

## 2 How far have German Universities Come? Progress and Remaining Challenges

### 2.1 Challenges in the Field of Migration and Asylum

With regard to the legal framework on migration and asylum, there is an enduring impact of federal residence regulations or even loose guidelines on local praxis. For instance, though not necessarily required by asylum law, in 2016, we found some evidence that a long-term perspective to stay ('gute Bleibeperspektive') facilitated access to preparatory classes (cf. Schammann and Younso 2016, p. 26 ff; see also R Student et al 2017; Schroeder and Seukwa 2017, p. 62). In our recent background interviews, we found the legally rather soft criteria of the 'Bleibeperspektive' to still play an important role, especially when several applicants competed for one place. In this case, university staff, acting as "street-level bureaucrats" (Lipsky 1980), made use of their discretionary spaces and selected those with a more promising residence perspective. In the same vein, Lambert (2019) shows with her qualitative analysis from expert- and prospective students with refugee background interviews from one HEI, that a limited and uncertain residence permit still has a significant impact on the judgements of university officials. To make matters worse, not only the staff, but also refugees doubt whether their requests to enter a program are justified: "*Both* [interviewed refugees] *picture a regular study as being beyond imagination*"[4] (Lambert 2019, p. 353). Due to a "*lack of planning reliablility*" (Lambert 2019, p. 354), persons with a temporary suspension of deportation ('Duldung') or those who still are in the asylum application process with an uncertain outcome, are rarely encompassed in the preferred target group of official university programs. Many university officials continue to perceive German migration law as rather restrictive and of high complexity. At the same time, they picture it as being of higher priority than law on higher education (cf. Lambert 2019). Thus, individual case decisions continue to dominate the everyday praxis (Schammann and Younso 2016, p. 50; see also Blumenthal et al. 2017). Overall, in order to mitigate their own uncertainties, officials hardly make use of their room to maneuver and thus perform rather restrictive administrative acts.

Apart from access to university programs, legal restrictions also shape the everyday life of refugee students. One of the fundamental challenges is the type of housing which they are legally allowed to use, i.e. being obliged to live in state accommodation with no privacy. Moreover, building on the literature on labor market integration (e.g. Brücker et al. 2020), one might assume that the path to higher education has been made more difficult by the (regionally divergent) residence requirements which are backed by a federal law of 2016 ('Wohnsitzauflage'). In 2016, we assumed that the federal government would probably abolish the law after testing it for some time. Instead, it was somehow (i.e. without revealing any criteria) evaluated as being helpful for integration purposes. We also wrongly speculated that the universities would probably try to circumvent restrictive regulations. Yet, four years later, we did not find any responses or strategies the universities might have used to deal with the restrictions. As a consequence, residence requirements are likely to continue complicating the refugees' access to and their performance in academic studies (Berg et al. 2018, p. 77).

Over the last couple of years, a number of fine studies have argued that the toughest challenges for refugee students to enter a regular degree program in Germany do not stem from the refugee's residence status but from general requirements to access higher education (Berg et al. 2018; Morris-Lange 2017). Although this is perfectly true, for refugees to fill in possible knowledge gaps, it would be necessary that they are not legally banned from attending preparation courses. For instance, the obligation to reside in a certain municipality can initiate a vicious

---

[4] Translation by the authors.

circle: without the possibility to make contact with a university, refugees might not know about preparation programs and, once they know about a program in another town, they might not be able to persuade local authorities to lift the residency requirement 'only' to attend a preparation program.

## 2.2 Challenges in the Field of Higher Education

As mentioned above, the requirements to enter full academic studies in Germany are diminishing academic aspirations of refugees. The question whether someone is formally capable to study in Germany is usually answered by evaluating the university entrance qualification ('Hochschulzugangsberechtigung'), starting by considering existing certificates (Angelstein 2017, p. 342 ff.). If these certificates cannot be formally verified or acknowledged, under certain circumstances, applicants can prove their ability to study by passing special tests in order to compensate disadvantages due to forced migration. In 2016, we found, that respective test instruments were rarely used by the higher education institutions (Schammann and Younso 2016, p. 50). In the meantime, based on an agreement between the Federal and State Ministries of Education, some universities have developed formal instructions on how to implement a three-step examination procedure. However, this instrument hardly seems to have found its way into practical use (Berg 2018, p. 225; Sinemillioğlu 2017, p. 10/11).[5] In addition to little progress on alternative ways to assess qualifications, existing hurdles remain, such as the language level C1 in German or challenges of financing the life as student (Schammann and Younso 2016, p. 39, 45).

In our 2016-study, we recommended that programs for refugees were to be clearly structured and communicated, the target groups to be reflected upon and the internal distribution of tasks and competences to be made transparent (Schammann and Younso 2016, p. 48 ff.). Four years later, we can find a lot of universities which did indeed develop a clear vision of where they wanted to go with their programs and which model of governance would suit them best. Many seem to have come to the conclusion that the Central Student Administration Offices or,

---

[5] Another instrument is the aptitude test for international students (Test AS) which was used in one program we analysed in 2016, regardless of whether documents were available. Even though the program did not allow access to full academic studies, Test AS served as a test for entering the program. Thus, it constituted a measure to ensure that the best applicants were selected – particularly those who formally already met the criteria of being admitted as regular student (apart from language requirements).

even more so, the International Offices are the best departments to be in charge. In all models, refugees are still counted among the group of international students. The design and 'culture' of the respective program determines until when refugee students are understood as 'refugees' and when they become 'migrants'. Some programs have developed very specific (and varying) requirements regarding the length of stay or a maximum period of stay in Germany, others have not. Until being naturalized, refugees are never just 'students' in the higher education system.

As a consequence, universities—as they did in 2015 (Schammann and Younso 2016, p. 32)—use the programs for international students to reach out to refugees. Yet, the framing of refugees as 'international students' constitutes a significant barrier to full academic studies. As 'international students' refugees continue to compete with non-EU students in terms of admission rates and grades (cf. Berg et al. 2018, p. 81). There might thus still be need to question the equation of people who are living in Germany and those who apply for a student visa from abroad. This would require to challenge the dominant objective of internationalization, though, which has been experiencing a growing awareness in universities for some years. The findings from the 'German Higher Education Index 2017' show that 'international education' is the fastest developing field of action in universities. In comparison, the area 'equal opportunities in education' is lagging far behind: *"The German higher education system could not keep up with the claim to offer fair access regardless of social or cultural background"* (Stifterverband 2019, p. 52; see also Salmi 2018; Angelstein 2017). 'Diversity at universities', which had also been formulated as a target dimension, is developing at a slower pace and has not achieved its goals for 2017 (Stifterverband 2019, p. 50).

When it comes to networking and exchange among HEI, recent research projects recommended the creation of exchange platforms for universities (e.g. Unangst and Streitwieser 2018, p. 290) or highlighted: *"Networks between HEIs are very important but also contacts with different stakeholders and sharing information. Such networks and contacts help to create a safety net for students/scholars at risk"* (GREET 2019, p. 3). According to our observations, the implementation of networks and exchange fora—e.g. within the Integra and Welcome-programs—might be one of the successful endeavors in the last couple of years. It is, however, uncertain whether these networks are built sustainable enough as soon as funding for the federal programs runs dry.

## 3 Higher Education Programs for Refugees: Echo-chambers of German Asylum Policies?

Looking back at the post-2015 changes in German asylum policies, one might easily come to the conclusion that it was all about tightening up the system and preventing refugees from coming to Germany. This is certainly not entirely wrong. However, concentrating on policy-making on the social inclusion of refugees who already are in Germany, a different picture emerges. Traditionally, building on the lessons of the NSDAP-regime, the German asylum system focused on the vulnerabilities of its applicants only, i.e. the individual need for protection was—at least on paper—all that mattered when deciding on residence permits in the field of forced migration. In contrast to labor migration, the individual's potential for the labor market was willfully ignored. If an asylum seeker had found a job in Germany and, therefore, wanted to leave the asylum procedure, this was legally not possible. He/she would have to leave the country and apply for a work visa. This has been changing gradually since 2015. For instance, the Integration Act of 2016 stated that refugees could contribute to mitigate the skilled labor shortage. Amongst other regulations, it established the possibility for refugees to switch from an insecure status ('Duldung') to a secure residence permit of up to five-years if the person had signed an apprenticeship-contract (cf. Will 2019, p. 117ff). If an asylum seeker thus proofs to be valuable on the labor market, he/she can virtually earn his/her stay. This "meritocratic turn" (Schammann 2017) also implies that being in need for protection does not guarantee a permanent residence permit, any more. Until then, people who had been recognized as refugees under the Geneva Convention often granted permanent residence permits after the first three years of recognition. Since 2016, even recognized refugees have to meet certain requirements to receive a 'Niederlassungserlaubnis' (permanent residence status). If they cannot prove to have a regular job and an apartment, amongst other things, they are only granted a one-year permit—with the unsettling possibility of not getting the next permit. These are just two out of many examples (for more cf. Schammann 2017) which illustrate that meritocratic or even utilitarian elements were gradually induced into a policy field that had previously shied away from economic arguments. In an international comparison, this meant that Germany followed the path of most liberal western immigration countries, like the USA or Australia.

At the same time, the meritocratic turn, however, is considerably mitigated: asylum seekers from so-called 'safe countries of origin' and those with a 'bad' perspective to stay, do not get the opportunity to prove that they deserve their stay. The logics of meritocracy do not apply to them as they are sorted out by regulatory and discursive filters. To put it polemically: The German asylum system characterizes applicants from certain countries and certain backgrounds as irrelevant for the German labor market.

Discussing the findings from the research on higher education programs for refugees against the backdrop of German post-2015 asylum policies, there is reason to believe that HEI aligned with the broader tendencies in asylum politics. Their programs addressing refugees can be characterized as echo-chambers of the political discourse, producing and reinforcing the politics of restricted meritocracy that constitute of two ingredients: firstly, the meritocratic and ultimately utilitarian perspective on the individual performance of refugees; secondly, a collectivist pre-selection mechanism that rejects people due to their group affiliation.

Regarding the meritocratic ingredient, it might be true that university programs for refugees started as 'third mission'[6] efforts with the goal to shoulder the humanitarian task of receiving refugees (cf. Schammann and Younso 2016, p. 23). Shaped by the logics of internationalization and the administrative desire to concentrate on the core business of teaching and research, they have quickly picked up their habit to select the most promising candidates for successful degree programs (see also Blumenthal et al. 2017, p. 234). Back in 2016, a joint publication by various (state) actors pictured preparatory programs as step towards the university entrance qualification (BAMF et al. 2016, p. 22). Four years later the order has somehow reversed: refugees must often already have a university entrance qualification for the preparatory programs (i.e. Goethe University Frankfurt am Main (n.y.); Ruhr-University Bochum (n.y.)). As a consequence, the universities' scouting for talent amongst refugees resembles, reiterates and reinforces the meritocratic turn in German asylum policies.

When it comes to the factors that slow down the meritocratic turn, Higher Education Institutions again adapt to the overarching discourse. By mostly concentrating on recognized refugees or at least on asylum seekers with a long-term residence perspective, universities do not question and are even reproducing the social construction of two groups of refugees. The first group comprises individuals who are allowed to individually prove their value for society. The second group is perceived as irrelevant for labor market purposes and is thus excluded from the benefits of meritocracy.

---

[6]Higher Education Institutions are built on three Cullum's: research, teaching and third mission. The Third Mission are higher education activities in the field of further training, research and knowledge transfer and social engagement (cf. Henke and Schmid 2016, p. 63).

## 4 Conclusion

Balancing the findings from our 2016-study with the status-quo four years later, we found that many of the pressing challenges still exist. This is especially true for the complex interplay of asylum law and higher education law. Moreover, there are some tendencies that had already emerged back then and grew stronger over time. Most notably, this implies narrowing down the target group of higher education programs for refugees to high performing individuals with a good perspective to stay. Not questioning and probably not even reflecting policy developments on the federal level and the evolution of societal discourses, higher education institutions have joined others in producing and reinforcing the politics of restricted meritocracy that have become visible in a number of policies over the course of the last couple of years.

As a result, HEI seem to have continued to rely on the capability of refugee students to master legal and other challenges on their way to full academic studies. Refugees who have made it into higher education have often not only matched the general expectations towards students in the German higher education system but have overcome legal and practical adversities of different kinds. Following their dream of a successful academic study in Germany, many try to resemble an imaginary 'perfect student' and thus meet the explicit and probably also the implicitly felt requirements of university programs. Whereas universities value and reward these unilateral assimilation efforts, they fall short in developing innovative learning methods to inclusively address a diverse student body (cf. Hochschul-Bildungs-Report 2019).

Moreover, many remaining challenges in the field are not accessible via unilateral assimilation or even by re-designing university programs. Instead, tackling the toughest challenges would require structural changes to the higher education system, such as alternative ways to a university entrance certificate, as well as hurdles within the asylum system. Regarding the latter, residency requirements and the uncertainty of procedures and status continue to pose obstacles for refugees to successfully entering and completing higher education.

In this contribution, we have tried to sketch why university programs for refugees should not be analyzed independently from asylum politics. HEI, however, are not necessarily carved out to function as *"actors in the border regime who regulate the access of migrants to societies internally via their own institutional logics in connection with the right of residence"* (Lambert et al. 2018, p.14). Instead, they also could—within the legal framework—strive for a more inclusive society by offering (educational) participation independent of residence status. To do so, universities should remember that most of the activities for refugees at HEI started out in order to foster social inclusion and social cohesion. Though this approach might not always be compatible with implementing successful programs to prepare refugees for a regular study, the spirit of a 'third mission' could be useful as a moral compass for advancing the programs.

# References

Angelstein, R. (2017). Recht und Hochschulbegriff. Das juristische Feld und soziale Ungleichheiten im Prozess des Hochschulzugangs. Wiesbaden, Springer VS.

BAMF – Bundesamt für Migration und Flüchtlinge (2016). Hochschulzugang und Studium von Flüchtlingen. Eine Handreichung für Hochschulen und Studentenwerke. Retrieved from: https://www.bamf.de/SharedDocs/Anlagen/DE/Broschueren/handreichung-hochschulzugang-gefluechtete.html?nn=282388.

Berg, J. (2018). A New Aspect of Internationalisation? Specific Challenges and Support Structures for Refugees on Their Way to German Higher Education. In: Curaj, Adrian, Deca, Ligia, Pricopie, Remus (eds.): European Higher Education Area: The Impact of Past and Future Policies, Springer International Publishing, pp. 219–235.

Berg, J.; Grüttner, M. & Schröder, S. (2018). Zwischen Befähigung und Stigmatisierung? Die Situation von Geflüchteten beim Hochschulzugang und im Studium. Ein internationaler Forschungsüberblick. Zeitschrift für Flüchtlingsforschung, 2(1), 57–90.

Blumenthal, J. von, Beigang, S., Wegmann, K. & Feneberg, V. (2017). Institutionelle Anpassungsfähigkeit von Hochschulen. In: Berliner Institut für empirische Integrations- und Migrationsforschung (eds.): Forschungsbericht. Forschungs-Interventions-Cluster „Solidarität im Wandel?". Berlin: Humboldt-Universität, pp. 225–248. Retrieved from: https://www.integrationsbeauftragte.de/resource/blob/72490/316492/4752a527c9d904ff4ee5834e75867014/forschung-bim-solidaritaet-data.pdf.

BMBF – Bundesministerium für Bildung und Forschung (no date). Flüchtlinge durch Bildung integrieren. Bildung ist der Schlüssel zur Integration von Flüchtlingen. Abgerufen von: https://www.bmbf.de/de/fluechtlinge-durch-bildung-integrieren.html

Brücker, H., Hauptmann, A. & Jaschke, P. (2020): Beschränkungen der Wohnortwahl für anerkannte Geflüchtete: Wohnsitzauflagen reduzieren die Chancen auf Arbeitsmarktintegration. (IAB-Kurzbericht, 03/2020), Nürnberg. Retrieved from: https://doku.iab.de/kurzber/2020/kb0320.pdf.

DAAD – Deutsch Akademischer Austauschdienst (2018). Integration von Flüchtlingen an deutschen Hochschulen Erkenntnisse aus den Hochschulprogrammen für Flüchtlinge. Retrieved from: https://www2.daad.de/medien/der-daad/da_gefluechtete_rz_web.pdf.

Goethe-University Frankfurt am Main (no date). Teilnahmevoraussetzungen. Retrieved July 01,2020 from: https://www.uni-frankfurt.de/58243270/Teilnahmevoraussetzungen.

GREET – Guiding Refugees via European Exchange and Training (2019). Higher Education Values in Practice Integration of highly skilled refugees and at -risk academics in Europe. GREET Stakeholder forum - Summary Report. Retrieved January, 30, 2020 from: https://www.aca-secretariat.be/fileadmin/aca_docs/event_presentations/GREET_event_summary_report_public.pdf

Grüttner, M., Schröder, S.; Berg, J. & Otto, C. (2018). Refugees on Their Way to German Higher Education: A Capabilities and Engagements Perspective on Aspirations, Challenges and Support. Global Education Review, 5(4), 115–135.

Halkic, B. & Arnold, P. (2019). Refugees and online education: student perspectives on need and support in the context of (online) higher education. *Learning, Media and Technology*, 44(3), 345–364.

Henke, J. & Schmidt, S. (2016). Perspektiven der Third Mission in der Hochschulkommunikation. Ergebnisse aus Fallstudien. *Die Hochschule: Journal für Wissenschaft und Bildung* 25 (2016) 1, pp. 62–75.

Hess, S., Kasparek, B., Kron, S., Rodatz, M., Schwertl, M. & Sontowski, S. (2016). Der lange Sommer der Migration. Grenzregime III. Assoziation A.

HRK – Hochschulrektorenkonferenz (2019). Studieninteressierte und Studierende mit Fluchthintergrund an deutschen Hochschulen März 2019. Befragung der HRK-Mitgliedshochschulen (Wintersemester 2018/19). Retrieved January 30, 2020 from: https://www.hrk.de/fileadmin/redaktion/hrk/02-Dokumente/02-07-Internationales/HRK-Umfrage_Gefluechtete_WS2018-19_Erste_Ergebnisse_Veroeffentlichung_Website.pdf.

Jungblut, J., Vukasovic, M. & Steinhardt, I. (2020). Higher education policy dynamics in turbulent times – access to higher education for refugees in Europe. *Studies in Higher Education*, 45(2), 327–338.

Lambert, L. (2019). Studium gestattet? Die symbolische Herrschaft des Aufenthaltsstatus und des Asylverfahrens beim Hochschulzugang von Geflüchteten. In Arslan, E., & Bozay, K. (Hrsg.): Symbolische Ordnung und Flüchtlingsbewegungen in der Einwanderungsgesellschaft. Wiesbaden, Springer VS.

Lambert, L., von Blumenthal, J. & Beigang, S. (2018). Flucht und Bildung: Hochschulen. Research Papier 8b Verbundprojekt ‚Flucht: Forschung und Transfer'. Osnabrück; Bonn: IMIS; BICC.

Morris-Lange, S. (2017). Allein durch den Hochschuldschungel. Hürden zum Studienerfolg für internationale Studierende und Studierende mit Migrationshintergrund. Sachverständigenrat deutscher Stiftungen für Integration und Migration, SVR-Forschungsbereich 2017-2. Retrieved from: https://www.svr-migration.de/wp-content/uploads/2017/05/SVR_FB_Hochschuldschungel.pdf.

R Student, Kendall, K. & Day, L. (2017). Being a Refugee University Student: A Collaborative Auto-ethnography, *Journal of Refugee Studies*, 30 (4), pp. 580–604.

Reinhardt, F., Zlatkin-Troitschanskaia, O., Deribo, T., Happ, R. & Nell-Müller, S. (2018). Integrating refugees into higher education – the impact of a new online education program for policies and practices. *Policy Reviews in Higher Education*, 2:2, pp. 198–226.

Ruhr-University Bochum (no date). Services for Refugees. Internationalportal. Abgerufen am 1. Juli 2020 von: https://www.international.rub.de/refugees/deutschkurse/integra12.html.de.

Salmi, J. (2018). Social Dimension Within a Quality Oriented Higher Education System. In: Curaj, Adrian, Deca, Ligia, Pricopie, Remus (Hrsg.): European Higher Education Area: The Impact of Past and Future Policies, Springer International Publishing, pp. 141–154.

Schammann, H.(2017). Eine meritokratischen Wende? Arbeit und Leistung als neue Strukturprinzipien der deutschen Flüchtlingspolitik. *Sozialer Fortschritt* 66, pp. 741–757.

Schammann, H., & Younso, C. (2017). Endlich Licht in einer dunklen Ecke? Hürden und Angebote für Geflüchtete im tertiären Bildungsbereich. *Zeitschrift für internationale Bildungsforschung und Entwicklungspädagogik* 40 (1) 2017, pp. 10–15.

Schammann, H. & Younso, C. (2016). Studium nach der Flucht? Angebote deutscher Hochschulen für Studieninteressierte mit Fluchterfahrung. Empirische Befunde und Handlungsempfehlungen. Hildesheim, Universitätsverlag Hildesheim.

Schneider, L. (2018). Access and aspirations: Syrian refugees' experiences of entering higher education in Germany. Research in Comparative and International Education, online first, 1–22. https://doi.org/https://doi.org/10.1177/1745499918784764.

Schroeder, J. & Seukwa, L. H. (2017). Access to Education in Germany. In: Korntheue, Annette; Pritchard Paul; Maehler Débora B. (Hrsg.): Structural Context of Refugee Integration in Canada and Germany. GESIS – Leibniz Institute for the Social Science, p. 55–65.

Sinemillioğlu, N. (2017). Ohne Dokumente ins Studium – eine Recherche unter uni-assist Mitgliedshochschulen. In: *Flucht und Studium*. Das Magazin rund um das kostenfreie uni-assist Prüfverfahren für geflüchtete Menschen (2), pp. 10–11.

Stifterverband (2019). Hochschul-Bildungs-Report 2020. Für Morgen Befähigen. Jahresbericht 2019.BAMF – Bundesamt für Migration und Flüchtlinge; KMK – Kultusministerkonferenz; DAAD - Deutscher Akademischer Austauschdienst; DSW - Deutsches Studentenwerk; HRK – Hochschulrektorenkonferenz (2016). Hochschulzugang und Studium von Flüchtlingen. Eine Handreichung für Hochschulen und Studentenwerke. Retrieved from: https://static.daad.de/media/daad_de/pdfs_nicht_barrierefrei/infos-ser vices-fuer-hochschulen/expertise-zu-themen-laendern-regionen/fluechtlinge-an-hochsc hulen/handreichung_hochschulzugang_und_studium_von_fl%C3%BCchtlingen.pdf.

Streitwieser, B., Brück, L. (2018). Competing Motivations in Germany's Higher Education Response to the "Refugee Crisis". Refuge, 34 (2), 38–51.

Streitweiser, B., Schmidt, M. A., Gläsener, K. M., & Brück, L. (2018). Needs, barriers and support systems for refugee students in Germany. *Global Education Review*, 5(4), 136–157.

Unangst, L. & Streitwieser, B. (2018). Inclusive Practices in Response to the German Refugee Influx: Support Structures and Rationales Described by University Administrators. In: Curaj, Adrian, Deca, Ligia, Pricopie, Remus (Hrsg.): European Higher Education Area: The Impact of Past and Future Policies, Springer International Publishing, pp. 277–292.

Will, A.-K. (2019). Die „Guten" in den Arbeitsmarkt, die „Schlechten" ins Abschiebezentrum. Selektionsgrundlagen der neuen symbolischen Ordnung der (Nicht)Aufnahme von Geflüchteten. In: Arslan, Emre; Bozay, Kemal (Hrsg.), Symbolische Ordnung und Flüchtlingsbewegungen in der Einwanderungsgesellschaft. Wiesbaden, Springer VS.

Zlatkin-Troitschanskaia, O., Happ, R., Nell-Müller, S., Deribo, T., Reinhardt, F. & Toepper, M. (2018). Successful integration of refugee students in higher education: Insights from entry diagnostics in an online study program. *Global Education Review*, 5(4), 158c181.

# Beyond "Integration"—Why There is More at Stake

## Katrin Sontag

> This chapter addresses initiatives, university actors, and researchers and points to questions of concepts and contexts.

## 1 Introduction

"Please, tell me: when will I actually be integrated?" After discussing the concept of integration in class for 2 hours, one of the students, looking puzzled, raised his hand and put this question to his fellow students. He had come to Europe as a refugee, spoke fluent German and was now fully enrolled at the university.

This question and the debate that followed highlight quite a few issues around the concept of integration. They illustrate that there is no easy formula for integration, not even enrolling at university. They also show that it is difficult to grasp what this concept actually means. Moreover, I interpret the question as an expression of an additional, yet unclear, demand or even pressure that individuals can feel imposed on themselves.

Higher education is, of course, important for better integration—understood in a narrow sense—into the educational system or the job market and can increase individual career opportunities and social networks. Yet, I will argue in this chapter that the more general framing of and argument for university enrollment of refugees as "integration", as it can be observed in policy and advocacy, is also

---

K. Sontag (✉)
Kulturwissenschaft und Europäische Ethnologie, Universität Basel, Basel, Schweiz
E-Mail: katrin.sontag@unibas.ch

problematic: first of all, because the concept of integration itself is fuzzy and controversial (some of its critique will be recalled in the second section of this chapter) and secondly, because there are a number of concrete structural, institutional issues that could be overlooked when focusing on integration. In fact, these do not only concern students with refugee backgrounds, but point to larger topics and include structural inconsistencies between the migration and education systems, problems of access, processes of economization, internationalization and development of universities, issues which will be discussed in the third section, drawing from our research project. Thirdly, the frame of integration is problematic, if the focus lies on those who should integrate and does not take general diversity at universities and the changing nature of systems or even the change of systems because of newcomers into account, which will be the topic of Sect. 4. In Sect. 5, possible alternative ways of addressing the nexus of refugees and higher education will be laid out.

## 2 Integration: A Problematic Concept

The term integration has been defined and used in different ways. It appeared in the twentieth century in the struggle of migrants for more inclusive rights and participation (Hess and Moser 2009), or as a two way exchange (Korteweg 2017). However, it has also been used as demand on migrants, prescription or assimilation, and an increasing tendency towards these meanings in policy and scholarship has been observed (Korteweg 2017; Hess and Moser 2009).

Integration has, from this perspective, been critically discussed in many respects, especially in critical migration studies (Hess et al. 2009; Goel 2009; Mecheril 2011; Hess 2014; Wieviorka 2014; Favell 2013, 2014). Korteweg, in fact, sees "(...) discourses on immigrant integration as fundamentally a denial of immigrants' already belonging to the nation-state context (...)" (2017, p. 431). In the following, bearing some of this critique in mind, I will point to five issues that are interconnected and that seem most relevant here.

The five points reveal underlying assumptions around social life, such as, first of all, an imagined **homogenous or cohesive national society** into which someone should be integrated. This assumption can be traced to ideologies of nationalism, colonialism, the origins of the modern liberal state (Leach 1965), and traditional functionalist sociology that claim the importance of cohesion of a society (Favell 2014). The vast individual heterogeneity that exists in every social context—in local contexts as well as amongst newcomers is overlooked (Wieviorka 2014). Classic ideas of cohesion and homogeneity also refer to an outdated understanding of individual identity as a static concept, whereas, in current cultural anthropology, it is understood and analyzed as changing and fragmented. In fact, more specific notions of structural integration refer to the participation of migrants in distinct fields such as education or work and show that migrants can be integrated to different degrees in different fields all at the same time (Wichman and D'Amato 2010). Moreover, the importance of the boundaries of nation states seem outdated in times of mobility, transnational lives and spaces such as the EU, in which all citizens are supposed to have their "homeland" (Favell 2013, p. 10).

Secondly, the concept of integration assumes a certain **settledness** or immobilization (Hess 2014, p. 211) as the outcome of migration. Migration research, however, has shown that not all migration trajectories lead to settledness and that migration is not always a one-time move. This understanding of settledness as the norm can rather be seen as part of the same narrative of nation state building, nationalism, and upcoming capitalism—when workers needed to be reliably available in a certain spot (Karakayali 2009). The widespread criticism of methodological nationalism has shown how the national, and thus the perception of migration as "the other", has been produced as the (often invisible) norm (Wimmer and Glick Schiller 2002). In fact, migration may take place in different forms, and people can live transnational, multilocal, or mobile lives. The question then arises as to how integration is imagined if someone lives at more than one place at the same time or is frequently moving. The paradox in the context of higher education is that academia, but also certain sectors of the job market, actually demand mobility and international experience.

A third major issue is the increasing focus of integration on the **performance of the individual** (Hess 2014; Prodolliet 2006). Moreover, it concentrates on the deficits of this performance: "The integration discourse is based on negative narratives" as Mecheril puts it (2011, p. 27). Yet, being a migrant or refugee is not a personal trait or characteristic. Rather, it is determined by structures, policies, and logics of migration systems that ascribe legal categories and that also determine possibilities of access (e.g. to the job market or educational system). Especially in the case of refugees, possibilities are very much structured and limited by policies.

Fourthly, integration debates and demands do not target all migrants in the same way. **Constructions of differences of ethnicities or nationalities** play a role and integration requirements thus strengthen the logics of othering (Goel 2009). In fact, in the past, when social scientists feared the disintegration of society in times of industrialization, this kind of "othering" and similar integration demands were targeted at the working class (Wieviorka 2014; Karakayali 2009). And today, too, differences of class, gender, and other factors play a role in determining how "different" "the others" are. The importance of constructed markers of difference, and the ways in which they are constructed, such as class, gender, ethnicity, nationality, language, culture or—as we see today again—religion change over time and in different contexts (Karakayali 2009).

Fifthly, there is the issue of **economic utility and employability**. In fact, the above-mentioned discussion in the seminar continued with students pointing out the importance of self-sufficiency and work in order to be integrated and that even a person with no migration history can feel like an outsider when he or she does not work. This economic justification of migration has shaped migration policies in various countries for a long time, as can be seen in the different policies for guest workers with their recruitment in the 1950s and 60s and the recruitment stop during the economic crisis in the 1970s in Germany and Switzerland, as well as in today's regulations for immigration of highly skilled migrants. Refugees are often not perceived as highly skilled migrants. In fact, in public debate as well as in academic studies, the topic of migration of the highly skilled is seldom connected with the topic of forced migration. And I would argue that this also affects the way in which refugee students are perceived.

These 5 aspects point to power dynamics and the question as to who is in a position to define the norms of integration, settledness, performance, difference, or employability and for whom.

## 3 What Else is at Stake: Systemic Issues

Conceptualizing access to university as "integration" brings with it the controversial issues laid out in the last section. Moreover, it may, by focusing on individual performances and responsibilities, draw attention away from necessary changes of systems. This section will focus on four such structural aspects.

Firstly, as mentioned before, there is a gap in the perception of refugees on the one hand and migrants who came through other migration channels (Sandoz 2018), such as employment, family reunion or EU/EFTA internal mobility on the other. This gap not only exists in public debate, but also in academic research (Mozetič 2018). Refugees are not perceived as "highly skilled" mobile professionals, because they came through the migration channel of asylum.

In 2017 and 2018, we carried out a qualitative study on the situation of refugee students at three universities in Germany, France, and Switzerland to learn about different preparatory programs, roles of stakeholders, and the ways in which national asylum policies interact with the educational systems. We conducted participant observation and interviews in a systemic approach with the different stakeholders involved: 3–4 refugee students at each university, 1–2 student volunteers, and individual representatives of the universities and cities. We also analyzed educational and asylum policies in the three countries. We showed in the 4-Area-Model of the personal biographical situation, the migration/asylum policies, the educational policies, and funding (Sontag 2019) that the access to universities is often difficult because refugee students are simultaneously subject to asylum policies, policies in the educational system, and regulations regarding financial support/the job market and that these policies and their demands are not well coordinated and are difficult to navigate (Sontag and Harder 2018; Sontag 2018). It is more difficult for refugee students to enter the educational system or the job market than for other migrants, such as international students who come through other channels.

Focusing on the access to universities shows that not only the ability of individuals to integrate is important, but the **accessibility of structures**. It reveals where structural inequalities hamper individuals' possibilities. In our study we found a number of such problems. They concern for example the issue that asylum policies e.g. in Germany or Switzerland do not allow asylum seekers to leave the region they have been assigned to, even when there is no university or preparatory college there. Moreover, there were and still are some gaps in funding possibilities for refugee students in France and Switzerland, even though this issue has been improved. In Switzerland, some foreign diplomas, such as the Syrian high school diploma, are only recognized with an additional test (ECUS—Examen Complémentaire des Hautes Écoles Suisses) that is very expensive. Also language courses at university level can be very expensive (as in Switzerland). Such factors are not in the hands of individuals and their personal ability to integrate.

The refugee students we talked to in the study often reported stress and pressure. They were experiencing family separation or new family responsibility, e.g. when only a part of the family had escaped. They had experienced sometimes years of hazardous circumstances, and there were still a lot of insecurities with regard to their future. New social positions as newcomers in a different context, when families had lost all their property, different positions in the educational system, different gender roles, all made them experience changes in positionalities (Anthias 2008). At the same time there was always a big wish to move on, and to do something that makes sense or contributes to society. As one interviewee expressed it: "I'm 21 years old, I have many dreams, I want to study and I don't want to lose this energy." Anxieties and frustration that other students have as well, that they are not fast enough or that they might not get into the careers they wish for, seemed enlarged for the refugee students because they had the feeling that they had already lost years and were now in a complicated bureaucratic situation.

The Swiss Student Union (VSS) argues for "Bildungsgerechtigkeit"—educational justice and refers to the complex debate as to whether and how education could be considered a public or private good (VSS 2017a; Giesinger 2011). This kind of just access to higher education does not only play a role for refugees but also for other groups. In our study, the student run preparation project at the University of Freiburg, "Uni für alle", stressed that higher education should be accessible to more people and refugees were just one group amongst others.

Secondly, some of the arguments around accessibility play out within the logic of **economic utility** mentioned in the last section. These arguments are also present in the broader sector of higher education, when its economic value is discussed in the context of neoliberal policies and developments. This can lead for example to political discussions as to which disciplines are worth funding and which are not. Refugee students are affected by arguments of economization in both systems: They are supposed to be integrated into the job market as soon as possible as part of integration strategies, such as the current Swiss integration agenda that focuses mostly on pathways for language learning, vocational training, or direct integration in the job market—to avoid being dependent on social welfare (SEM 2019). And they are supposed to study for job market integration within the education system. The classic Humboldt ideals of "Bildung" as self- formation and time for reflection do not have much space in this. Also the VSS in their vision and basic demands postulates that "the aim of education is geared towards the development of a person and enabling a person to a politically mature, active participation in society and not in the first place to the production of economic productivity." (VSS 2017a, p. 11).

In fact, when we interviewed refugee students in our study, enrolment and completion of their studies and thus starting or continuing their careers was important, but they also mentioned that they were happy to be at the university and to be part of preparatory programs in order to connect with other students and the topics they were interested in. A facilitator also argued that it was problematic to evaluate preparatory programs only on the basis of the students' success in their studies. She said that this was important, but providing networks and orientation also helped the students—even if the results were that students decided to drop out, do something else, or move somewhere else. In a larger context, this topic is thus also a chance to question how far economic demands should influence the process of education.

Thirdly, there is a gap between the ways the educational system deals with newly arriving refugee students and scholars on the one hand and the great importance of **internationalization strategies** in academia on the other. In research, internationalization is a pressing demand and national funding agencies such as the Swiss National Science Foundation (SNSF) or the German Research Foundation (DFG) see their support of internationalization as one of their main tasks. The DFG states "internationality is inherent to research funding" and "internationality does not in principle need any specific justification" (DFG 2012, p. 8 my translation). Universities, too, work on international networks and international visibility, e.g. with offices in other continents, as for example the Freie Universität Berlin. Also, students are strongly encouraged to be mobile and gain international experiences, as the mobility webpage of the University of Basel says: "The importance and meaningfulness of student mobility are undisputed in today's world" (Uni Basel). Master programs are developed in English to cater for international students.

Yet, refugee students are often rather seen as those that need to settle down, catch up and fit in. Their international capital is seldom referred to as an important asset in the general discussions, but rather as some kind of deficit. It does not smoothly fit in with the prevalent logic of international orientation. Arslan (2016) describes how a project at the University of Bielefeld addressed this issue by turning the logic around and recognizing the cultural capital of migrants and e.g. offered courses in Turkish, which were not continued for lacking support. A colonial heritage still persists, and universities in the UK, US, or France are more attractive in an academic CV in Europe than universities in Kabul, Asmara, or Damascus. And fluent English or French is more important than fluent Arabic or Farsi (see also Arslan 2016).

This topic was addressed in one of our interviews with a university representative. The interviewee described their university's preparatory program for refugees, which included training for local volunteers who support the refugee students, tutoring, and a cultural program as "internationalization at home". They fully saw the benefits and advantages not only for the refugee students but for the whole university and city. This is an interesting perspective to open up a space for reflections of prevalent narratives and imaginaries of "internationalization".

Fourthly, not only in this respect, but also with regard to global developments and challenges such as sustainability, climate change, or globalization, universities have to ensure that they are "**learning organizations**" (Senge 1990), organizations that think systemically and incorporate dialogue and learning on all levels. And unlike for many other organizations, this is not only important for their own development, but it is central to their role as centers of knowledge production and research to provide knowledge, analyses, questions, and support to the larger society, political and economic actors (Marcu 2018). As Marcu argues for the situation in Spain, universities should be better connected with other organizations that deal with refugees, and "Spanish universities can act as an engine to strengthen the work of city councils and NGOs; raise awareness about the reality of refugees to the host society and to the actors who will intervene in one way or another in their reception and integration (companies, unions, associations, and education centers)" (2018, p. 17).

## 4 "Reverse Integration"

Students have become **more diverse** in general. This has to do with migration, but it also has to do with different requirements of the job market and e.g. continuing education for various age groups. This demand is partly addressed with advanced studies courses for students who are already working in a professional career.

Increasing diversity is also due to the fact that more students of more diverse backgrounds go to universities. It is not only refugee students, but also students of e.g. working class backgrounds or other age groups who encounter classism or other barriers and limits in the current system. Integration here could be thought of as something that connects these different people and developments, allowing space for difference, and thus "renews or refreshes" (as in the Latin root "integrare") the culture at European universities.

Reverse integration could also mean taking the **knowledge and experience of refugee students** seriously. This has many facets. One of them—which was of course a sensitive issue—were the political discussions that we had with refugee students who knew what it meant to struggle for democracy or human rights. We talked to students who had experienced the development of political conflict, or persecution, or who had had to acquire a range of new skills that were suddenly needed in times of war. These kinds of topics are important in order to reflect on one's own positions, to understand current politics and global connections. They are also a chance to continue working on local histories. There was for example a presentation in the German city Freiburg, in which refugee students presented Syria and showed pictures of destroyed cities in Syria and then connected this to a picture from the largely destroyed city of Freiburg after the Second World War—a moment that moved the audience and opened a space of encounter and reflection. There is a big field for learning, discussing, connecting the past, present, and visions for the future, but also for addressing vulnerabilities and experiences of pain. Such conversations are not just important encounters and exchanges, but there is also a danger for political consciousness if this kind of knowledge is not valued or even forgotten.

## 5   Alternative Concepts

The necessary paradigmatic shift is to take refugee migration as well as migration in general as a fact that is here to last, and not as a short-term situation as is often implied in the popular framing of "migration crisis". Moreover, topics such as access, economization, internationality, organizational learning, or diversity play a role, as discussed in Sects. 3 and 4.

Concepts such as participation or inclusion have been used as alternatives to integration. Schröer (2013) proposes that inclusion and belonging are an obligation to be fulfilled by society instead of the duty of the individual. "Inclusion", he argues, includes multiple dimensions of diversity (not only migration-related), as well as trans- or multinational perspectives and could prevent "we/they" dichotomies.

A number of epistemological perspectives have been put forward to overcome the national context, the othering and groupism often involved in demands of integration and to address structures instead of individuals. These include "migration mainstreaming" (Hess and Moser 2009), the "mainstreaming of integration-political issues" (Prodolliet 2006) or "power critical diversity mainstreaming" (Goel 2009). Ongoing discussions of "postmigrant" approaches (Yildiz 2015; Römhild 2015) that look at migration as a fact that has happened and employ a critical reflective perspective or the call for "demigrantising migration research" and "migrantising social science research" (Römhild 2014, p. 7, my translation) are helpful in this context. Korteweg argues for a way back to focussing on intersecting inequalities, discrimination and ways of exclusion instead of integration (Korteweg 2017).

Similarly, critical lenses could be applied to education. Mecheril (2011, p. 28, my translation) refers to the conflict between "societal usability" and "self-development" as goals of education, and argues that societal usability is the more important factor when integration is the goal. As educators, the question thus can be asked as to whether demands of social cohesion and integration are in conflict with educational ideals such as critical reflection, individual self-development, two-way learning, diversity, as well as contradiction and dissent.

The discussions of access to universities for refugees that have been going on during the last few years are a chance and a reminder to rethink how paradigms that determine views on migration, on refugees, on cohesion as well as on higher education can be questioned, and how different views of development of and access to the educational system (e.g. beyond methodological nationalism, Western-centrism, and classism) could look.

**Acknowledgements** This research was supported by the National Center of Competence in Research nccr—on the move funded by the Swiss National Science Foundation. I would like to thank the organizing team of the symposium "Studium gleich Integration?" and editors of the book, as well as Tim Harder, Silva Lässer, and Sarah Wipfli for their support in the preparation, and Hannes Schammann for his helpful feedback.

## References

Anthias, F. (2008). Thinking through the lens of translocational positionality: An intersectionality frame for understanding identity and belonging. *Translocations: Migration and Social Change: An Inter-Disciplinary Open Access E-Journal, 4*(1), 5–20. Retrieved January 15, 2016, from https://hdl.handle.net/10552/3331

Arslan, E. (2016). Reflektionen eines Projektes zur Mehrsprachigkeit in der universitären symbolischen Ordnung. In E. Arslan & K. Borzay (Eds.), *Symbolische Ordnung und Bildungsungleichheit in der Migrationsgesellschaft*, Interkulturelle Studien (pp. 501–522). Wiesbaden: Springer.

DFG (2012). Die Internationalisierungsstrategie der DFG. Bonn: DFG.

Favell, A. (2013). The Changing Face of "Integration" in a Mobile Europe. https://www.adrianfavell.com/CESweb.pdf

Favell, A. (2014). Immigration, Integration and Mobility: New Agendas in Migration Studies. Essays 1998–2014. Colchester: ECPR Press.

Giesinger, J. (2011). Bildung als öffentliches Gut und das Problem der Gerechtigkeit. *Zeitschrift für Pädagogik, 57*(3), 421–437.

Goel, U. (2009). Für eine nachhaltige Migrations- und Integrationspolitik in Deutschland. *FES Gesprächskreis Migration,* 99–113.

Hess, S. & Moser, J. (2009). Jenseits der Integration. Kulturwissenschaftliche Betrachtungen einer Debatte. In: Hess, Sabine, Jana Binder und Johannes Moser (Eds.): *No integration?! Kulturwissenschaftliche Beiträge zur Integrationsdebatte in Europa* (pp. 11–25). Bielefeld: Transcript.

Hess, S. (2014). Von der Integrationskritik zur Kritik des migrationswissenschaftlichen Kulturalismus. In S. Kostner (Ed.) *Migration und Integration: Akzeptanz und Widerstand im transnationalen Nationalstaat. Deutsche und internationale Perspektiven.* Berlin/Münster: LIT-Verlag.

Hess, S., Binder, J. & Moser, J. (Eds.). (2009): No integration?! Kulturwissenschaftliche Beiträge zur Integrationsdebatte in Europa. Bielefeld: Transcript.

Karakayali, S. (2009). Paranoic Integrationism. Die Integrationsformel als unmöglicher (Klassen-) Kompromiss. In S. Hess, J. Binder, & J. Moser (Eds.), *No integration?! Kulturwissenschaftliche Beiträge zur Integrationsdebatte in Europa* (pp. 95–104). Bielefeld: Transcript.

Korteweg, A. (2017). The failures of 'immigrant integration': The gendered racialized production of non-belonging. *Migration Studies, 5*(3), 428–444. https://doi.org/10.1093/mig ration/mnx025

Leach, E. R. (1965). Culture and Social Cohesion: An Anthropologist's View. *Daedalus, 94*(1), 24–38.

Marcu, S. (2018). Refugee students in Spain: The role of universities as sustainable actors in institutional integration. *Sustainability, 10*(6), 2082.

Mecheril, P. (2011). "Wirklichkeit schaffen: Integration als Dispositiv - Ein Essay." In *Interkulturelle Schulentwicklung an Schulen in Nds, Fortbildungsmodul 1/ Oktober 2014*. Niedersächsisches Landesinstitut für schulische Qualitätsentwicklung.

Mozetič, K. (2018). Being Highly Skilled and a Refugee: Self-Perceptions of Non-European Physicians in Sweden. *Refugee Survey Quarterly, online first*, 1–21. doi:https://doi.org/10.1093/rsq/hdy001.

Prodolliet, S. (2006). "Integration" als Zauberformel. *Widerspruch: Beiträge zu sozialistischer Politik, 51*(26), 85–94.

Römhild, R. (2014). Zur Vorgeschichte: Wie dieser Band entstanden ist. In Labor Migration (Ed.), *Vom Rand ins Zentrum: Perspektiven einer kritischen Migrationsforschung* (pp. 7–9). Berlin: Panama.

Römhild. R. (2015). Jenseits ethnischer Grenzen. Für eine postmigrantische Kultur- und Gesellschaftsforschung. In E. Yildiz & M. Hill (Eds.), *Nach der Migration. Postmigrantische Perspektiven jenseits der Parallelgesellschaft*. (pp. 49–64). Bielefeld: transcript.

Sandoz, L. (2018). Understanding access to the labour market through migration channels. *Journal of Ethnic and Migration Studies*. doi:https://doi.org/10.1080/1369183X.2018.150 2657.

Schröer, H. (2013). Inklusion versus Integration - Zauberformel oder neues Paradigma? *Migration und soziale Arbeit, 35*, 249–255.

SEM (2019). Integrationsagenda. Retrieved January 3, 2020 from https://www.sem.admin.ch/sem/de/home/themen/integration/integrationsagenda.html

Senge, P.M. (1990). The Fifth Discipline: The Art and Practice of The Learning Organization. London: Random House.

Sontag, K. (2018). Highly Skilled Asylum Seekers: Case studies of refugee students at a Swiss university. *Migration Letters, 15*(4), 533–544.

Sontag, K. (2019). Refugee students' access to three European Universities – an ethnographic study. *Social Inclusion, 7*(1), 71–79.

Sontag, K., & Harder, T. (2018). What Are the Barriers for Asylum Seekers and Refugees Who Want to Enroll at a Swiss University? NCCR - On the Move, Policy Brief. Neuchatel: National Center of Competence in Research - the Migration Mobility Nexus. Uni Basel. *Mobility*. Retrieved January 3, 2020 from https://www.unibas.ch/en/Studies/Mob ility.html.

VSS (2017a). Positionspapier Hochschulzugang für studentische Geflüchtete. Bern: Verband der Schweizer Studierendenschaften (VSS).

Wichmann, N. & D'Amato, G. (2010). *Migration und Integration in Basel-Stadt: Ein „Pionierkanton" unter der Lupe*. Neuchâtel: Swiss Forum for Migratiosn and Population Studies SFM University of Neuchâtel.

Wieviorka, M. (2014). A critique of integration. *Identities, 21*(6), 633–641. https://doi.org/https://doi.org/10.1080/1070289X.2013.828615

Wimmer, A., & Glick Schiller, N. (2002). Methodological nationalism and the study of migration. *Archives of European Sociology, 43*(2), 217–240.

Yildiz, E. (2015). Postmigrantische Perspektiven. Aufbruch in eine neue Geschichtlichkeit. In E. Yildiz & M. Hill (Eds.), *Nach der Migration. Postmigrantische Perspektiven jenseits der Parallelgesellschaft.* (pp. 19–36). Bielefeld: transcript.

CPSIA information can be obtained
at www.ICGtesting.com
Printed in the USA
LVHW022339230721
693495LV00021B/1835